Principles of Macroeconomics

Harvey Cutler
Colorado State University

KENDALL/HUNT PUBLISHING COMPANY
4050 Westmark Drive   Dubuque, Iowa   52002

Contents

List of Figures

List of Tables

$ Chapter 1

1.1. Introduction

Most textbooks in economics look the same. They are written for the specific purpose of teaching economics in a very serious manner. Economics is a relatively difficult introductory course since it is a mathematically based discipline. Even though there is a minimal amount of math at this level, the material presented has heavy mathematical undertones. Due to this challenge, I have searched for an easier way to teach this class. I have tried card tricks, juggling and standup comedy. I have come to the realization that learning has to be fun. Occasionally, I can be funny but the books I have used in the past were not. I have searched high and low for a book, which was consistent with my strategy of teaching but I have been unable to find an acceptable text. There are very few if any amusing stories added to these textbooks, which could possibly aid in the process of learning the material. Therefore, I have decided to write my own simplified textbook that will be used in this class. Our class will be based on four characters: Arthur, Maria, Robert and Rachel. They come from different regions of the U.S. and it is through their experiences that we will learn economics. I hope we can all have fun in the class as we learn about economics.

1.2. Characters

1.2.1. Arthur (African American)

Arthur was born in 1950 in Los Angeles, California. His parents are John who is an auto mechanic and his mother Cathy is a manager of a physician's office. Both of Arthur's parents graduated high school but did not attend college. They stressed to Arthur and his two younger sisters that earning at least a bachelors degree from college was necessary to become successful in life. Arthur had two passions in life during his days in high school. The first was playing basketball for his high school team and the second was playing the guitar. Even though Arthur was a bright individual, he never really applied himself to his studies in high school. This provided a great deal of frustration for his parents.

1.2.2. Maria (Mexican American)

Maria was born in 1950 in Las Cruces, New Mexico. Her parents are Carlos and Juanita who both own and operate a small family farm. Both of her parents graduated high school but have encouraged Maria that attending college is very important. Maria demonstrated at a very early age that she was very goal oriented. She became involved in many business ventures during high school and college, which helped finance her graduate education at Harvard.

1.2.3. Robert (Fourth Generation American)

Robert was born in 1950 outside of Sterling, Colorado. His father Charles and mother Susan own a large profitable farm. Robert's parents profess a very strong work ethic and required that Robert spend all his spare time working on the farm. However, Robert grew to strongly dislike the rural setting and yearned to live in a large city where there was little memory of grass and trees.

1.2.4. Rachel (European American)

Rachel was born in 1950 in Fairfield, Connecticut. Her father Ken is an orthopedic surgeon and her mother Nancy is a corporate attorney. Rachel was raised in a world of luxury with little financial constraints. Rachel's parents expected great things from their daughter but the path chosen by Rachel took some serious departures from her parent's expectations.

1.3. The Meaning of Economics

1.3.1. The Definition of Economics

From an early age, it was obvious that Maria was very goal oriented and desired to have many possessions. As a ten-year-old, Maria dreamed of owning a yacht, a private airplane, a home on the Riviera, a penthouse in New York and a row of automobiles. She realized that she wanted to purchase a large number of things but her ability to pay for them was limited. Maria was always contemplating different ways that she could make millions of dollars in order to pay for her dreams. What Maria did not realize at ten years old was that she faced the same problem that societies all around the world faced.

ECONOMIC PRINCIPLE

Economics is concerned with how societies attempt to satisfy unlimited wants for goods and services with a limited amount of resources to produce these goods and services.

The above idea reflects one of the major historical problems that have faced all countries around the world. Consider the following two examples.

The U.S. government had to make some hard choices in the early 1980s as to whether they would fund additional military research or increase expenditures for a variety of domestic programs. The government did not have enough money to fund both programs adequately. The wants of the government exceeded what they could pay for. President Reagan became very aggressive in funneling funds toward a buildup of military capabilities at the expense of a number of domestic programs. There was considerable controversy in the country as to this course of action. In the 1980s, there were two movements with regards to a military buildup.

One group wanted to reduce the reliance on the military since they maintained that the need for a strong military was not as great as it was in the 1950–80 period. The opposing group maintained that the world was still a very complex place and that there will always be a need for a strong military. The group supporting a buildup of military capabilities won out and the military expanded at the cost of reduced domestic programs.

The Soviet Union attempted to keep pace with the U.S. military buildup by reallocating their resources away from domestic programs and toward the military. At that time, the Soviet Union did not have the flexibility of the U.S. since the diversion of resources toward the military caused a significant decrease in the standard of living in the Soviet Union. This did not occur in the U.S. Some people maintain that this race for military superiority hastened the fall of the Soviet Union. It is indeed an interesting hypothesis.

In 1962, Robert's parents had a very unprofitable year operating their farm. During one of the harvest seasons, both their farm truck and tractor broke down and they did not have enough money to repair both pieces of equipment. Robert's dad had to choose between the truck and the tractor. Robert wanted to fix the tractor because a farm without a tractor meant that Robert would be spending much more time in the fields with a pick ax and a shovel doing manual labor. Again, we can see that the wants of Robert's parents exceeded their ability to pay for them.

A Brief Outline of the Semester

We need to develop tools, which can help us analyze a variety of economic issues that we will encounter over the semester. The course is divided into two parts. The first part of the course is referred to as **microeconomics**. Microeconomics examines how consumers (demand) make decisions on how much they will purchase at a given price. Firms decide how much to produce (supply) in order to sell in the market place. We are interested in how the interaction of supply and demand determines the level of production in a market as well as the price that good.

The second part of the class is concerned with **macroeconomics**. Macroeconomics is concerned with studying the performance of the entire economy. We will explore why the economy experiences upturns and downturns in overall economic activity. We will also examine the causes and impacts of inflation as well as study the role of the federal government and the Federal Reserve in economic growth.

Microeconomics

1. Theory of the Consumer

All of us are continually faced with decisions on how much to buy and what prices are affordable and unaffordable. Economists believe that there are basic rules that govern the behavior of consumers when they make decisions regarding the choice of goods and services to be purchased. Economists attempt to understand how the price of the good as well as consumer's income impacts consumption decisions. We will summarize all of these ideas in something called a **demand curve**.

2. Theory of the Firm

The role of the firm is to produce the goods and services that are consumed in the economy. The production process requires the successful completion of several different stages. The firm must purchase the appropriate inputs (land, labor and capital), which is the foundation of the production process. The second aspect is to coordinate all these inputs so that they can effectively produce the output. All of these ideas can be summarized in something called a **supply curve**.

After we have developed an understanding of buyers and sellers in our economy, we will merge both of these concepts together and construct the supply and demand curve model. We will use this model to investigate how resources are allocated in our economy to satisfy the desires of the population. The mechanism that we will study is called the **market**. The market is the place where demanders and suppliers of goods and services meet and exchange goods and money.

Macroeconomics

The second and primary objective of this class is to investigate **macroeconomic** issues concerning our economy. Macroeconomics examines the behavior of the overall economy. In a sense we add up all consumers and firms in the economy and analyze their behavior from an aggregate perspective. The issues that we will examine are business cycles, the causes and impacts of inflation and the role of the federal government and Federal Reserve in helping maintain economic stability.

1. Business Cycles

As one views the history of our economy it is observed that the production of goods and services (economic activity) has enjoyed periods of prosperity where the growth in economic activity has been high. During these periods it is relatively easy to find a job so the level of employment is high. At other times in our history, the growth in economic activity has been slow or even been negative. During these times, the unemployment rate has increased, as it is more difficult to find employment. Downturns in economic activity are referred to as recessions or depressions.

Figure 1.1 presents the level of economic activity from 1959–03. Economic activity is represented by the concept called gross domestic product (GDP). GDP represents the total sum of all goods and services produced in the economy for a specified period of time. As Figure 1.1 indicates, there is an upward trend in GDP over time. This growth is due to

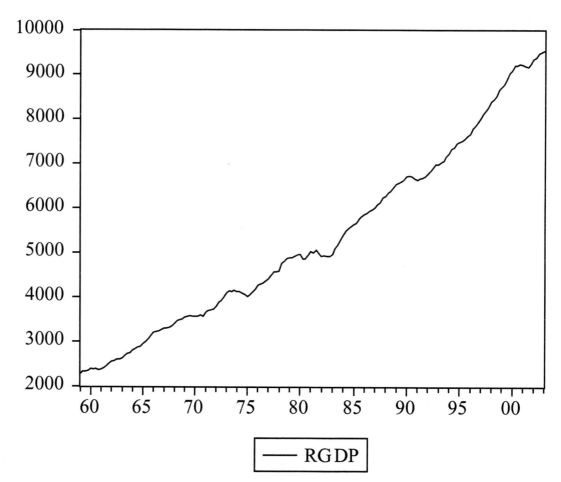

Figure 1.1   Real Domestic Product for U.S.

increases in population, capital and technology. We will spend considerable time this semester understanding the role that these factors play in economic growth.

We can also observe from Figure 1.1 that GDP appears to depart from the upward trend.

As an example, during the 1973–75 period, we experienced a downturn in economic activity. The actual production of goods and services fell during this period. In addition, the level of employment fell or the unemployment rate increased. This period of time is referred to as a recession. Figure 1.1 also indicates that the U.S. economy experienced recessions in 1979, 1981–82 and 1990–91. It is our objective to develop a framework which can be used to understand why these recessions occur and determine whether the federal government and the Federal Reserve can do anything to prevent these downturns from occurring. The Federal Reserve is responsible for determining how much money will circulate in the economy. As we will the see the Fed is one of the more influential institutions in our country.

The second primary macroeconomic objective is to study the causes and impacts of inflation. Inflation is defined as the growth rate in the overall price level in the economy. It has been the case in our economy that high inflation rates can lead to problems in economic growth. Suppose the inflation rate is 5% for a given year but your income has only gone up by 3%. This implies that your wages are able to purchase a smaller set of goods compared to before the changes in the inflation rate and income. From the standpoint of an economist, the standard of living for that person would have declined. It is important to understand what causes changes in the inflation rate. Figure 1.2 displays the inflation rate for the U.S.

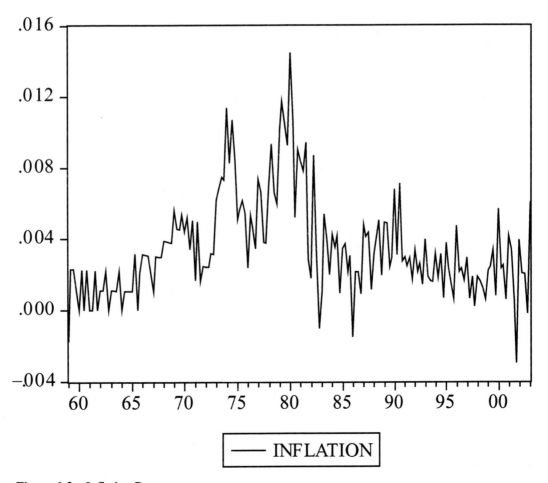

Figure 1.2 Inflation Rates

The vertical axis reports the inflation rate or the percentage change in the price level. As an example, the inflation rate reached a high rate of approximately 12% in the early 1980s.

1.4. The Meaning of Scarcity

During her time in high school Maria was constantly trying fit in all her activities. She was a very dedicated student, which required a great deal of time to be allocated to studying. In addition, she was always involved in two or three business ventures that also required a great deal of time (Maria realized later in life that sleeping was a waste of time). With a limited amount of hours in a day, Maria was constantly juggling her schoolwork with her business ventures. She realized that to buy that first airplane, it was going to be expensive. Maria was always pondering how she could allocate her time in a more efficient manner so that she could make as much money as possible. However, she was never willing to sacrifice her performance in school since she felt that an excellent education was the key to success. Later in life, Maria would realize that you can control your luck in the following sense. Over one's lifetime, there will be many opportunities that could be taken advantage of. Some opportunities will work out and others will not. The better trained you are, the more people you will meet, which will translate into more opportunities. If she can get admitted to Harvard and graduate, there will be plenty of opportunities to seize.

ECONOMIC PRINCIPLE

The idea of scarcity is one of the fundamental issues in economics. All societies are limited as to what they can produce in a given period of time. It is never the case that an unlimited amount of goods and services can be produced in the economy. Each society must decide how it is going to allocate its scarce resources. A resource is a general term to describe the inputs necessary to produce goods and services that people desire to consume. Another term to describe these resources is **factors of production**. All societies expend a great deal of time in deciding how to allocate the factors of production to meet the desires of the individuals that make up that society.

1.5. Factors of Production

During the summer after her sophomore year in high school, Maria decided to go start her own mobile retail store. She remodeled an old wagon her parents had in the barn so that she could use it as a mobile store. Maria also purchased an old horse named Ben who would pull the wagon to different points in town so Maria could sell her wares. As Maria sat at one of her more popular selling points, she was appraising all the aspects of this business venture. She had a fair amount of money invested in remodeling the wagon as well as purchasing Ben. But she realized that the wagon and Ben were very important inputs in her production process. In addition, her own labor was important as well as the inventory of arts and crafts, rugs and everything else she sold from her wagon.

ECONOMIC PRINCIPLE

*The **factors of production** are the inputs required to produce the goods and services that our economy produces. The factors of production are divided into the following groups.*

- **Labor** represents the number of workers that are employed by firms. From the perspective of the entire economy, it is the total number of people that have jobs. In Maria's case, she is the sole worker in her enterprise so she is considered the labor.
- **Capital** refers to fixed investments like machinery, computers, factories or the size of the building that houses a retail outlet. In Maria's case, the wagon represents the capital input in her production process. Since we are attempting to keep our analysis simple, Ben the horse can also be considered capital.
- **Technology** is the ability to coordinate the factors of production to more effectively produce goods and services. An example would be a faster computer, new management techniques implemented by your boss, which allows you to be able to produce more output in a shorter period of time.

There are many other factors of production such as telephones, desks, energy, clothes, etc. In addition, every firm requires some amount of land to locate their firm on. Land is considered a factor of production as it contributes to the production process. There is no need to create an exhaustive list of these inputs since the general idea is that firms require a wide range of inputs in order to produce output. For our purposes, when we refer to the factors of production, they are labor (L), capital (K) and technology (T).

To summarize these concepts, we introduce a relationship referred to as a production function:

$$Y = F (L, K, T),$$

Where Y refers to the output produced by a firm or the entire economy. An increase in L, K or T will result in an increase in the amount of output produced. We will expand on this concept latter in the semester.

To summarize these points, Maria is the labor and Ben and the wagon represent capital. The level of technology used by Maria at this stage of her business activities is much more subtle. As an example, a month after she was operating the portable retail store, Maria was trying to quickly get to one of her better selling locations. Ben was huffing and puffing as the wagon was moving at the top end speed. As she was going down the street, all of sudden she heard a loud noise and the front end of the wagon hit the ground. Maria watched the left front wheel of her wagon role down the street, hit the curb, veer toward a house, hit a large rock, vault into the air and go right through the front window of that house. Maria quickly went to the house and fortunately no one was hurt. Maria assured the owner of the house that she would pay for all repair costs to the house.

Maria had her wagon transported to a mechanic's shop and was informed that the joint that held the wagon wheel to the axel was old and very poorly designed. In fact, the mechanic said that all the wheel joints were in bad shape. The mechanic explained that more modern joints used on automobiles would be a vast improvement on the design for the wagon. This improvement is an example of a **technological** advancement. This was Maria's first exposure to how changes in technology could improve the performance of her business. Maria decided that she could fix the wagon herself. She had the wagon transported back to her parent's barn and it took her a month to replace all the wheel joints with improved parts. It was expensive but a wheel would never again fall of that wagon.

Since the factors of production are scarce, there is a limit as to what can be produced. Each society has to develop a means for allocating these factors so that the goods and services desired by the people are in fact produced. The market is the mechanism that our economy uses to allocate these resources.

1.6. Economic Models

A model is an abstraction from the real world that simplifies our view of the world so that a limited amount of important factors can be examined.

If we wanted to travel from Fort Collins to Aspen we would look at a road map. From the map we could learn what routes exist between the two destinations. However, we could not learn about the population of the areas, sociological conditions or air pollution levels of Fort Collins and Aspen. The road map is an abstraction from reality—a simplification, which in this case, contains the information we need so that we can travel from Fort Collins to Aspen. The map ignores many important issues like living conditions in the towns between Ft. Collins and Aspen but these issues are irrelevant with respect to traveling from Fort Collins to Aspen.

An economic model will be structured in such a way as to allow the analysis of a particular issue; however the model will ignore many other important issues. At the present time we are concerned with the limitations that an economy faces when deciding how much of alternative goods to produce. Since our economy can produce millions of different types of goods, it could be difficult to describe all these options. Instead we will simplify the problem by assuming that the economy produces only two kinds of goods. After understanding all the issues related to two kinds of goods, we could generalize the arguments to many types of goods. But in terms of our analysis, we will only examine two kinds of goods.

The other objective at this point is to familiarize the students with the use of graphical tools, which is one of the primary tools of economists. Consider that we have two goods, apples and oranges. Consider Figure 1.3 that describes the different amounts of the two goods that are available.

The horizontal axis describes the quantity of oranges. The distance OA represents a certain amount of oranges. The distance OB represents a greater amount of oranges. Therefore, the further right you move along the horizontal axis, the larger the number of oranges there are. The vertical axis measures the quantity of apples. The further up you move along the vertical axis, the more apples there are.

To summarize these ideas consider the following:

- Point OA represents a quantity of oranges
- Point OB represents a greater quantity of oranges
- Point OC represents a quantity of apples
- Point OD represents a greater quantity of apples

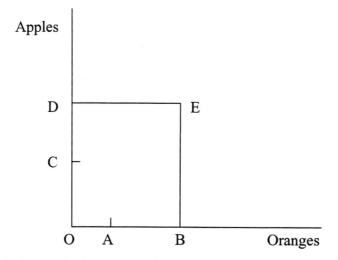

Figure 1.3 An Economic Graph

The point E represents a combination of both apples and oranges. At point E, there is OD amount of apples and OB amount of oranges.

Maria had experimented with many different locations for her retail store and had found over time that the closest city intersection to the interstate had the most automobile traffic. One day in the summer of 1963, she was having a slow day at this spot when a car stopped at her store. Maria always kept a record of the license plates of the cars that stopped by to purchase from her. Of primary interest were the different states that her customers came from. This car was from Connecticut and as she recalled, she never had a customer from this state before.

A man and woman got out of the car and started to look at Maria's merchandise. Maria noticed that there was a girl in the car who was approximately her age and reading a book. The woman approached Maria and said that she was very impressed with the store and found it a good idea that the store was mobile as she eyed Ben. Maria told her that she sold things all over town, but this was her most profitable location. It was the case that this location received the most out of town cars, which had turned out to be her better clients. The woman asked her how long she was in the retail business and Maria replied that she fixed up the wagon about a year ago. The woman and Maria talked for a while as the man went back to the car to talk to his daughter. Maria started to describe to the woman a recent business problem that she was having. Since school was out, she could spend much more time at her store but her income was not increasing very fast and this troubled Maria. The woman said that she was a corporate attorney and many of the large firms that she represented also had the same complaints. Maria smiled and thought it funny that large companies had the same problem.

Maria's problem can be described by Figure 1.4. Let the horizontal axis represent the amount of time that she spends operating her store. We will refer to this as her labor input and call it L. The vertical axis represents her sales or output. We will refer to this variable as Y. The relationship between output and labor input has been briefly discussed above where it has been stated that when more labor is used, then a firm's level of output should increase. We need to delve into this idea in greater depth.

The curved line in Figure 1.4 describes the specific relationship between labor and output. This curved line represents the production function as it is referred to as

$$Y = F(L, K^*, T^*).$$

In this case, we are allowing L to vary but we are holding constant capital and technology. That is why we put a * after these two variables. When Maria expends a work effort of $0L_0$,

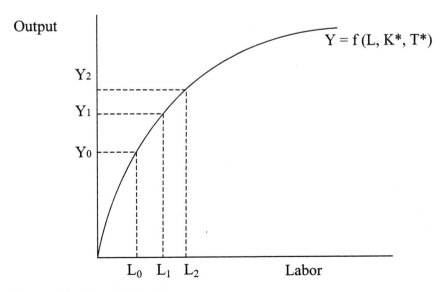

Figure 1.4   A Production Function

she can sell an amount of output $0Y_0$. If she increases the amount of time or work effort to $0L_1$, the amount of her sales increases to $0Y_1$. This describes the idea that when a firm hires more workers, then the amount of output for that firm should increase.

Now consider a further increase in Maria's work effort to $0L_2$ and the increase in output is $0Y_2$. As the graph indicates, the increase in output is smaller for similar size increases in the amount of labor used. The increase in labor from L_0 to L_1 is equal to the increase in labor from L_1 to L_2. If labor used increases from L_1 to L_2, then output increases from Y_1 to Y_2. We can see that the distance Y_0Y_1 is greater than Y_1Y_2. We are seeing that for equal increase in labor, output increases but at a decreasing rate. This idea is called the law of diminishing marginal returns.

1.7. Definition of the Law

As more of a variable input (labor) is increased, given a fixed workspace, output increases but at a decreasing rate".

This is why Maria has been experiencing a slowdown in sales as she has spent more and more of her time with her retail store. In addition, this is the same reason that the woman who Maria was talking to said that the firms that she represents also complain of the same problem.

As Maria and the woman continued to talk, the woman introduced herself as Susan and Maria introduced herself. Susan said that one way of increasing her sales was to purchase a larger wagon and increase the variety of goods that could be sold. A greater variety of goods may hold greater interest for the average shopper. What Susan is referring to is called a shift of the production function. Suppose Maria did purchase a larger wagon and more goods to sell, then the production function shifts from Y to Y' in Figure 1.5.

In our example, a larger wagon implies that the capital stock has increased and is represented as an increase from K^* to $K^{*'}$. With a larger store, the work effort of $0L_0$ can now produce a level of output $0Y_1$, whereas, originally only $0Y_0$ could be produced. To summarize, the production function shifts upward due to an increase in the capital stock (in Maria's case, it was a large wagon). An increase in technology will also shift the production function upward.

Susan asked Maria what she wanted to do when she grew up and Maria was quick to respond that she wanted to go to college and become a millionaire. Susan smiled and said that she had to get going but before she did, she purchased over $100 worth of goods from Maria.

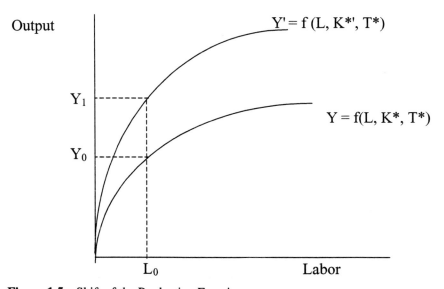

Figure 1.5 Shift of the Production Function

A $100 is what Maria averaged for a month during the summer. As Susan drove off with her husband and daughter, she thought that she would love to know how Maria turns out later in life.

1.7.1. Allocation of Resources

Generally speaking, there have two basic mechanisms that countries have used to allocate resources. The Soviet Union and many of the eastern European nations have used a centralized approach to determine the types and amounts of goods and services produced. Production decisions for the entire country were made by a relatively small group of individuals. The problem with this approach is that a small group of individuals have a great deal of difficulty identifying the desires of the entire population. Therefore, any production decisions may be in conflict with the majority of the population. The only way to find out is to survey a significant percentage of the population and that is typically not done. To ascertain the success of this centralized approach to decision making, all one has to do today is witness the collapse of the economic systems of the Soviet Union and the other eastern European countries.

The United States uses a market economy, which centers on the interactions of millions of sellers and buyers. Buyers indicate to the sellers the products that are desired and the sellers pass on that information to the manufacturers of the specific products. In this manner we find that the wishes of the buyers are communicated to the sellers in our economy. Almost all of the production decisions for our economy are made in separate locales all over the country. In this manner, the desires of the population are more efficiently conveyed to the producers. However, this approach is not perfect since a great many inequities still occur but the free market approach is still the best system available.

1.8. Accounting Costs

Maria has had a slow day at her general store. While sitting behind her mostly empty cash box, she begins to tally in her head the cost of her store. First on her list are the building materials she needed to construct the general store and all the repairs she had to make. Second is Ben the horse. Third are the items she bought to stock the shelves. The money she has spent on all these items are referred to as accounting costs.

ECONOMIC PRINCIPLE

Accounting costs *refer to the costs of building or acquiring a particular activity or possession.*

1.9. Opportunity Costs

As Maria tallies her accounting costs, another building crane goes by. Her mind wonders to the construction site downtown. Suddenly Maria is distraught! She realizes that there is a lot of money to be made by selling freshly baked chocolate chip cookies to the construction workers but here she sits at the side of the street with her general store and Ben. Instead of a general store, Maria could be running a chocolate chip cookie shop. So there is one more cost to Maria's general store, the potential revenue that she could be making by selling cookies to the construction workers.

ECONOMIC PRINCIPLE

Opportunity cost *is the highest valued alternative choice of a foregone opportunity*. In Maria's situation, it is the potential lost profits of not selling chocolate chip cookies (of course you need to sell milk with the cookies).

Rachel is also learning about opportunity costs. Her parents want to give her a special spring break during her junior year in high school. They tell her that she may either spend a week in the Bahamas snorkeling, scuba diving, and sailing or a week in Aspen skiing. For Rachel the Bahamas means warm weather, fresh seafood, and a good tan; Aspen means a new ski outfit (look good, ski well!) and improving her skiing. It's a hard choice to make!

Rachel is only concerned with the opportunity cost of the two choices. Her thoughts revolve around missing out on a good tan if she goes to Aspen; but going to the Bahamas means no new ski outfit. The opportunity costs of these choices are severe. The accounting costs of the two vacations (plane fare and condo) aren't of concern to her. Rachel chooses Aspen, as there is that unique attraction to skiing.

1.10. Marginal Analysis

It is February of 1962 and Arthur is in the 7th grade. His basketball coach invites him to play in a competitive league that will be playing against other teams throughout the state of California over spring break. If Arthur joined the team, he would travel to Santa Barbara, San Jose, Santa Cruz, Stockton, and Sacramento. There is, however, an enrollment fee of $125.00. Arthur excitedly explains the coach's offer to his parents and asks them for the money. Arthur's dad tells him to sit down in the living room and he will be there in a second. His dad comes in also sits down, puts his legs up on the coffee table and rolls his eyes as he looks up at the ceiling. He gives the following speech:

> "You have had a pretty good life so far. You have been blessed with excellent athletic skills, which have allowed you to become a very good basketball player. You also have a great mind, which you have never used. It appears that you do just enough work to get B's but beyond that, you are wasting your intellectual skills."

As Arthur listens to this soliloquy, he starts to wonder where there is going. Whenever his dad sits him down like this, it never works out well. I better start listening again.

> "So Arthur, the free ride is over because you never seem to take school seriously enough. If you want to join the traveling basketball team, then you better GET A JOB".

Arthur is now a bit less excited. These discussions can be exhausting. He goes for a walk downtown to think about whether the chance to play on the traveling team is worth working for it. On the one hand, he'd have to give up all his free time in order to earn enough money to pay for the week of basketball. But he would get to play against kids that he did not know which was always exciting.

As he continued his odyssey around the neighborhood, he passed Vito Coreleone's pawn-shop and saw a guitar in the window for $125.00. A decision has been made! Arthur was always intrigued with learning how to play the guitar and this was the opportunity to do so. He had to buy that guitar. He went home and informed his parents that he was ready to get a job. His parents were pleased that he was willing to earn the money to play basketball. When he informed them that he wanted to buy a guitar instead of going on the basketball trip, his parents just shook their heads. His parents looked at him and realized that there was no way to anticipate what this kid was going to do. The very next day, Arthur begins working at a retirement home.

The important issue in the above story is that Arthur was willing to get a job to purchase a guitar but he was not willing to work in order the finance his week long basketball trip. Obviously, Arthur's decision implies that he places a greater value in terms of benefits derived from owning the guitar than paying for a week long basketball trip.

ECONOMIC PRINCIPLE

Marginal Analysis is a technique used in economics by which the benefits of a particular activity are compared to the costs of that activity. When the benefits exceed the costs, the person will partake in the activity. However, when the costs exceed the benefit, then the activity will not be undertaken.

Unknown to Arthur, he was using a technique known as marginal analysis. For Arthur, the perceived benefits of playing on the basketball team were not great enough compared to the costs of playing on the competitive team (having to work to finance the trip), so he opted not to play. However, the benefits of purchasing the guitar are greater than the costs of acquiring the instrument so he opted to get a job in order to buy the guitar.

1.10.1. Rationality

The year is 1969 and Rachel, a freshman at Dartmouth, is sitting in a philosophy class. Her professor starts discussing the concept of rationality. The professor writes on the board the dictionary definition of "rationality."

Rationality—reason and experience, rather than the non-rational, are the fundamental criteria in the solution of problems.

The professor wants to know if the average individual makes decisions that are rational. The professor asks the class the following: "Does the average individual make decisions that improve his or her welfare?" Before answering the question, the class wants the professor to define "rationality" in everyday English. The professor responds with the following:

Rationality implies pursuing a line of behavior that attempts to correct mistakes. In other words, an individual will not continue to make the same error over again when that error has substantial costs to the welfare of the individual.

The class agrees that the average individual is rational. However, Rachel wants to know if the Viet Nam war is rational. She maintains that to send U.S. soldiers over to Viet Nam to fight a war for reasons that are unclear is irrational (50,000 American soldiers died in the war). Therefore, Rachel concludes that government is irrational and since we elected these officials, we must all be irrational. The professor stares long and hard at Rachel and realizes that this discussion could become complicated and get the class off track. The professor tells her and the class that we are moving on to another subject. Rachel thinks to herself, what a week.

The concept of rationality is very important in economic analysis. As we study the behavior of firms and consumers, it is required that we have some understanding of how these economic agents make decisions. We assume that firms will make production decisions that attempt to maximize profits. Consumers will purchase goods and services that maximize their welfare.

ECONOMIC PRINCIPLE

Rationality assumes that people make decisions that maximize their welfare. All economic analysis rests on the concept of rationality.

When Rachel went on that ski trip to Aspen, she had an interesting experience at one of the local restaurants. Her parents would typically order a chicken dish while Rachel would order soup and salad. It was rare for her to order meat. On this particular evening, Rachel ordered a T-bone steak, which was out of character. She consumed the steak but several hours later she developed some intestinal issues that resulted in a quick trip to the emergency room and the loss of two days of skiing. She never ate meat again. Is this an example of rational behavior?

Marginal analysis and rationality are interrelated concepts. First, marginal analysis is used to assess the costs and benefits. Then rationality dictates that if the costs outweigh the benefits, the activity will not be pursued and vice versa.

Maria is contemplating temporarily closing down her retail store and will concentrate on selling milk and cookies at the construction sight. Maria made the following chart to help determine the course of action she will take.

Milk and Cookie Business	
Benefits	*Costs*
High profits	Noisy environment
	Obnoxious customers
Retail Store	
Benefits	*Costs*
Relatively quiet	Low profits

Maria weighed the costs and benefits of each enterprise. The key to this exercise is for Maria to place value on each of the costs and benefits. It is straightforward to compare low and high profits but assigning value to a serene work environment (retail store) or the noisy construction site is more difficult. Regardless, the key is to compute the difference between the benefits and costs for each activity. The endeavor that has the benefits exceed the costs by the largest amount would be the most attractive choice. Since Maria's primary objective is to make as much money as possible, she put Ben out to pasture and sold milk and cookies.

At 16 years of age, Arthur found himself making a similar kind of list to that of Maria's. His basketball coach told Arthur he was a "hot" player with great potential but like with everything else, he needed to practice. Perhaps, the coach suggested, Arthur should consider using the time he had set aside to play the guitar for basketball. As Arthur left practice that day to get to his guitar lesson, he started to become agitated. The thought of giving up the guitar was stressful. During his music lesson, his instructor told Arthur that he had tremendous potential as a guitar player but like with everything else, he needed to practice. Perhaps, the teacher suggested, Arthur should consider using the time he had set aside to play basketball for the guitar.

Arthur went home that day and was confused. He sat down and discussed his dilemma with his parents. They talked about what it would be like to play basketball in college and the possibilities of playing professional basketball. They wrote down the following table.

Basketball

Benefits	Costs
High likelihood of Scholarship	Risk of injury
Chance of becoming a professional basketball player	Time demands that could hurt school grades

Guitar

Benefits	Costs
Safe—low risk of injury	Low likelihood of scholarship
Would become skilled musician	Little chance for high paying job

Arthur studied his lists carefully but still could not decide what to do. The problem was one of probability. What were his chances of getting an athletic scholarship or becoming professional basketball player? What is the likelihood of getting injured playing basketball or becoming a skilled musician with a recording contract? The costs and benefits were not crystal clear.

1.11. Opinion Verses Fact

    A. Positive vs. Normative Statements

        1. Positive—a statement that can be proved by examining the facts

            a. It is raining outside. This statement can be supported or rejected by simply looking outside

        2. Normative—a statement of opinion or belief. A normative statement cannot be proved or disproved but it can be debated

            a. Abortion should remain legal. This statement could be debated for years and no consensus could be reached.

    B. Positive Economics

        1. Asks what are the impacts or consequences of a specific economic policy

        Example: What are the consequences of raising the income tax? Positive economic analysis is not concerned with the issue of whether the consequences are desirable or undesirable.

    C. Normative Economics

        1. Asks whether the impact of a specific economic policy is desirable.

        Example: Should the income tax be raised?

Economists attempt to address positive issues. They can examine the consequences of various economic policies but commonly it is politicians who make the final decision as to which consequence is more desirable. We will elaborate on this idea later on in the semester.

1.12. Production Possibility Frontier

As Arthur continues to allocate his time between playing basketball and the guitar, he finds that the choice of which to do is becoming more difficult. As he spends more time practicing basketball, his ability to play the game will improve. In addition, as he practices the guitar more, he will also play music at a higher level. Consider Figure 1.6.

Figure 1.6 describes the combinations of ability that Arthur can achieve playing basketball and the guitar. The horizontal axis describes Arthur's ability to play basketball. As you move further to the right along the horizontal axis, it implies that Arthur is achieving a higher level of basketball performance. As you move further along the horizontal axis it implies that Arthur is spending more time playing basketball and therefore the level of his performance is increasing. Since the distance OB_2 is greater than OB_1, it suggests that Arthur has allocated more time to playing basketball and less time playing the guitar. The vertical axis describes the skill level of playing the guitar. As you move higher up on the vertical axis, the graph describes a higher skill level of playing the guitar. As you move up the vertical axis, it implies that Arthur is spending more time practicing the guitar and less time playing basketball.

This model assumes that there is a limited amount of time that Arthur can spend either practicing the guitar or basketball. As Arthur spends more time playing the guitar it implies that he will spend less time playing basketball. This choice suggests that his skill level playing the guitar will increase and his skill level playing basketball will decrease. If Arthur decides to spend all his time is practicing basketball, then he can reach the distance 0B, which is the best that Arthur can be at playing basketball. On the other hand, if Arthur chooses to spend all his time practicing the guitar, then he can reach the distance 0S, which is the best he can be at playing the guitar.

The curved line from point S to point B is the **production possibility frontier**. It describes the different combinations of skill levels that Arthur can achieve by allocating his time differently between the two activities. Point C represents a combination of skill levels that could be achieved. Point C represents a combined skill level of OS_1 for playing the guitar and the skill level of OB_1 for playing basketball. This implies a certain amount of practice time for each endeavor. Suppose Arthur chooses to improve his performance on the basketball court by allocating more time to practicing basketball and less time practicing the guitar. This would

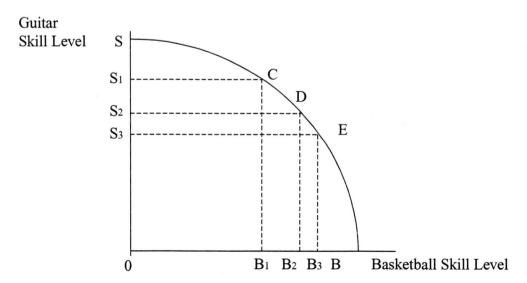

Figure 1.6   Production Possibilities Frontier

imply a movement from point C and point D with the basketball skill level increasing to OB_2 and a reduction in guitar level to OS_2.

There is another important concept implied by Figure 1.6. It has to do with the movement from point C, to point D, and to point E. We see that the giving up his time to play the guitar will result in smaller improvements in playing basketball. Why is that the case? We will explain this concept in the following example.

A classic example of the production possibility frontier is to consider the following two assumptions.

1. There are only two products that exist in the economy—national defense and domestic production
2. The factors of production (land, labor and capital) are fixed.

Figure 1.7 describes the potential level of production for the entire economy in terms of national defense expenditures (stealth bombers, submarines, etc.) and domestic production (cars, clothes, etc.). If the economy chooses to allocate all its land, labor and capital to the production of domestic goods, the amount OP can be produced. On the other hand, if the economy chooses to allocate all their factors of production to the production of national defense goods, then the amount ON can be produced. Obviously, these two extreme points will not be chosen but some combination of the two goods, which lies on the curved line NP. Line NP is the production possibility frontier.

- Point N—all resources or factors of production are allocated to the production of national defense and none for domestic production
- Point P—all resources or factors of production are allocated to the production of domestic production and none for national defense
- Point C—ON_1 of defense goods are produced and OP_1 of domestic production occurs simultaneously
- Point E—ON_3 of defense goods are produced and OP_3 of domestic production occurs which means that greater resources are allocated to domestic production than were at point C

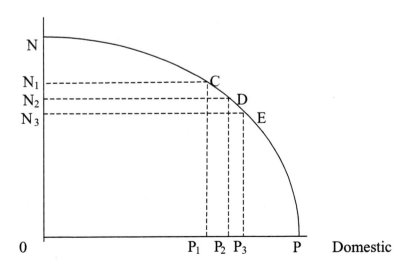

Figure 1.7   Illustrations of PPF

ECONOMIC PRINCIPLE

A simple graphical device called the PPF illustrates the principles of constrained choice, opportunity cost and scarcity. PPF shows all the combinations of goods and services that can be produced if all of society's resources are used efficiently.

In the figure above moving from point C to D a person gain more domestic production (from P1 to P3), and loose (N1–N2) amounts of national defense. The important issue is why the PPF is shaped in the above manner. The following economic principle will explain the shape.

ECONOMIC PRINCIPLE

Law of increasing cost—as scarcer resources are used to produce additional units of a good, production of that good increase but at a decreasing rate. This is because the first resources used are the most suited for that good. As we use additional resources to produce more of the good, they are less suited for the production of that good. Therefore output will increase but at a decreasing rate since less productive inputs are used second.

The Law of Increasing cost: The negative slope of the PPF indicates the trade off that a society faces between the two goods. The opportunity cost of producing more domestic goods is producing less national defense.

Let's explore the idea of increasing cost using Figure 1.7. Point C represents a combination of national defense and domestic output. At point C, ON_1 amount of national defense is being produced and OP_1 amount of domestic goods are being produced. This combination implies that a certain amount of our land, labor and capital are being used to produce national defense goods and the remaining amounts of these inputs are being used to produce domestic goods.

Suppose the economy chooses to move to point D. Some of the factors of production will have to be shifted out of the production of national defense goods and into the production of domestic goods. Therefore, the production of national defense goods will fall from ON_1 to ON_2 and the production of domestic goods will increase from OP_1 to OP_2. From an efficiency idea, the inputs that will be shifted out of the national defense sector and into domestic sector will be the most suitable inputs to produce the domestic goods.

Suppose the economy decides to further increase the production of domestic goods. Let the economy reduce national defense production by an equal amount compared to the reduction from N_1 to N_2. Let the distance N_1N_2 equal N_2N_3. The economy moves from point D to point E. National defense output falls to ON_3 and the production of domestic goods increases from OP_2 to OP_3. However, the increase in domestic production is smaller this round compared to the movement from point C to point D. The distance $P_1 P_2$ is greater than the distance $P_2 P_3$. The reason why this occurs is that the inputs that have to be transferred out of national defense production and into the domestic sector (point D to point E) are less suitable to produce domestic goods as compared to the inputs that were transferred to the domestic sector when we moved from point C to point D. As we further reduce national defense expenditure and transfer those resources into domestic production, those resources are less suited to produce domestic goods. Therefore, the increases in domestic production will become smaller and smaller.

To summarize, the production possibility frontier is shaped in the above manner to reflect the idea of the law of increasing costs. As the economy moves toward producing more domestic goods and less national defense goods, inputs have to be transferred from the national defense sector to the domestic sector. The movement from point C to point D transfers the most suitable inputs to produce domestic goods. The movement from point D to point E uses the second most suitable group of resources. With less suitable resources transferred to domestic production, domestic production increases at a decreasing rate. The PPF illustrates that the

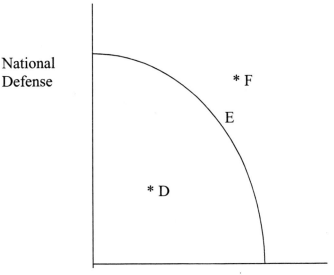

Figure 1.8   Choice between National Defense and Domestic Production

opportunity cost of domestic production increases as resources are shifted from national defense to domestic production.

Points that lie on the PPF represent the points of the full resource utilization and production efficiency. Because a society's choice are constrained by available resources and existing technology, when resources are fully and efficiently employed, it can produce more domestic production only by reducing production of national defense. The opportunity cost of the additional domestic production is the forgone product of national defense and vice versa.

It is also possible that the economy is operating at a point inside the PPF as demonstrated by point D in Figure 1.8. Point D implies that there is land, labor and capital that are currently lying idle or used inefficiently. In this case, it is possible to increase the production of both goods by employing the unused factors in both sectors, and the economy will move from point D (point of inefficiency) to point E (point of efficiency). When resources are not all being used, it is called a recession.

Point F is outside the production possibility frontier. It is unattainable due to the limited availability of resources. In order to obtain F, there would have to be an increase in land, labor, capital, or technology.

With respect to Arthur, point D represents a situation where time is being spent on some other activity (watching TV) instead of practicing basketball or the guitar. Point F would be unattainable in the sense that Arthur is not good enough at either basketball or the guitar to reach such a high level of competence in both activities.

Referring back to the national defense and domestic production model, suppose there was an increase in technology such that the current amount of land, labor and capital could produce larger amounts of both goods simultaneously. The production possibility frontier would shift out in the following manner:

It is now the case that point F can now be achieved as the production possibility frontier has shifted out from PPF to PPF'. The increase in technology has caused the production possibility frontier to shift outward.

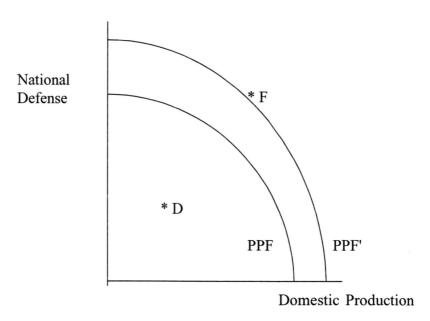

Figure 1.9   Movements of the PPF

1.13. Gains from Trade

During his high school days, Robert's father insisted that Robert become knowledgeable about plumbing, electrical, carpentry, heating systems and of course, concrete work. After school, it was common for Robert to be knee deep in sewage trying to flush out the septic system for his house. In a typical week, Robert would have to fix an electrical or plumbing problem, repair the tractor or do some concrete work. Robert always thought that he was destined to live in a large city and be far away from the drudgeries of working on a farm. One day during the summer before his senior year in high school, Robert decided that he was going to college out of state and as far away from the farm as possible. He needed to go to a college in a large city that had a minimal amount of grass and trees. Robert worked fairly hard in high school and was admitted to Boston University in Boston, Massachusetts. His parents had mixed feelings about Robert going so far away from home but they agreed to support him financially for four years.

The year is 1969 and Robert is a freshman in college at Boston University, majoring in economics. Robert chose economics as his major because the illusionary aspect of money reminds him of his true love: magic. In class one afternoon, Robert's professor is explaining why people trade. "Typically," he says, "people exchange money for goods. In any voluntary trade, it is implied that the good has more value than the money." A light bulb goes off inside of Robert's head. As a child, Robert carefully ignored all the stories his Dad used to tell about the "old days." However, there was one story that oddly remained with Robert over the years. It was a story about his great grandfather, Jeremiah.

Jeremiah started the farm that Robert grew up on in the early 1800s. He came over from Poland with only enough money for a small plot of land and some true grit. There are many aspects about Jeremiah's wild times that we cannot include in this book but you can imagine. Within several years Jeremiah's farm was producing profitable amounts of corn and beef.

The following are the possible combinations of corn and beef that Jeremiah could produce in one year:

Table 1.1 should be interpreted in the following manner. Jeremiah could produce different combinations of corn and beef. He could allocate his time and resources in such a combination

Table 1.1 Possible Combinations of Corn and Beef

Corn (bushels)	Beef (pounds)
10	100
9	120
8	140
7	160

that he could produce 9 bushels of corn and 120 pounds of beef simultaneously. He could alter his time and resources and instead produce more corn, say 10 bushels but he then could produce 100 pounds of beef. The movement from producing 9 bushels of corn to 10 bushels implies that more time is spent raising corn and less time producing beef. Jeremiah could choose to produce any of the above combinations or any fraction in between the above amounts.

Jeremiah's neighbor, Buck, had the farm next to his. Although Buck had the same amount of land, as did Jeremiah, he was not as successful. Jeremiah thought of Buck as a loser. Jeremiah learned later, that Buck had some severe emotional issues that could be traced back to coming to the U.S. by himself when he was fourteen years old.

Buck could produce the following combinations of corn and beef in one year, presented in Table 1.2.

Jeremiah has the **absolute advantage** in producing corn and beef as compared to Buck. In other words, Jeremiah can produce more of both goods than Buck. However, Jeremiah asks himself what is his cost in producing one more bushel of corn.

Cost of 1 bushel of corn = 20 lbs of beef

Cost of 1 lb of beef = 1/20 a bushel of corn

The above results can be obtained in the following manner. Suppose Jeremiah is currently producing 10 bushels of corn and 100 pounds of beef. If Jeremiah desires to produce 120 pounds of beef, he can only produce 9 bushels of corn. Therefore, to produce an extra 20 pounds of beef, Jeremiah has to give up 1 bushel of corn. In terms of the price of beef, the cost of producing 20 extra pounds of beef is 1 bushel of corn and the cost of producing one extra pound of beef is 1/20 a bushel of corn. On the other hand the cost of producing one extra bushel of corn is 20 pounds of beef.

Jeremiah then asks the same question about Buck. Jeremiah wants to know what Buck's cost of producing beef and corn is. After quizzing Buck for several days, Jeremiah determines the following in conjunction with Table 2.

Cost of 1 bushel of corn = 5 lbs of beef

Cost of 1 lb of beef = 1/5 a bushel of corn

Jeremiah determines that Buck is the low cost producer of corn per bushel. The cost to Buck of producing an additional bushel of corn is only 5 pounds of beef. The cost to Jeremiah of producing an additional bushel of corn is 20 pounds of beef. Buck has to give up less beef than does Jeremiah in order to produce one more bushel of corn. However, Jeremiah is the low cost producer of beef. To produce an additional pound of beef, Jeremiah has to give up 1/20 of a bushel of corn while Buck has to give up 1/5 of a bushel of corn. Jeremiah has the **comparative advantage** in producing beef and Buck has the **comparative advantage** in producing corn.

So Jeremiah suggests to Buck that they trade corn for beef. Since Jeremiah is the low cost producer of beef, he will trade beef to Buck and Buck will respond by giving up corn. They

Table 1.2   Buck's Combinations of Corn and Beef

Corn (bushels)	Beef (pounds)
5	50
4	55
3	60
3	65

need to arrive at a price of corn for beef. Jeremiah offers the price of one bushel of corn for twelve pounds of beef. Buck agrees to the price.

Before the trade Jeremiah decides to produce 9 bushels of corn and 120 pounds of beef and Buck decides to produce 4 bushels of corn and 55 pounds of beef. Buck trades one bushel of corn and receives from Jeremiah 12 pounds of beef. Now Buck and Jeremiah have the following combinations:

We can see that both Buck and Jeremiah would not have been able to produce the above combinations by themselves. Both of them are better off by the trade.

	corn (bushels)	beef (pounds)
Buck	3	67
Jeremiah	10	108

The price we chose of one bushel of corn for twelve pounds of beef is one of many prices that could have been chosen. In the next chapter we will examine how prices are arrived at but for now we chose the price arbitrarily. Can you determine the range of prices that are acceptable to both parties so that they benefit from the trade?

Robert finishes thinking about his great grandfather and looks up on the board and sees that his professor has written down a very similar story on the blackboard. Instead of corn and beef, Robert observes that the Federation and Klingons are trading tribbles and dylithium crystals but the message is identical in terms of the benefits of trade. For the first time in his life, Robert sees some value in his Dad's stories. Robert ponders that maybe he should have paid more attention to his Dad's stories as he grew up.

Chapter 2

2.1. The Market

The basis of any well-functioning economy is how effectively consumers and producers (firms) interact. For the purposes of this class, we want to understand how the interaction between firms and consumers helps determine which products are produced and the prices those products are sold at. The structure in which consumers and producers interact is called the **market**. Previously, we discussed how consumers and firms are the major actors in the market place. We will now begin to understand the mechanism that operates in the market—a mechanism that allocates resources in our economy. If money is exchanged in the market place for goods and services in a voluntary manner, both the consumer and firm benefit.

Recalling the example with Robert's great grandfather, Jeremiah, we demonstrated that Jeremiah benefited by trading with his neighbor Buck, who also profited. After the exchange, both neighbors had more beef and corn than they could have had producing each product on their own. Through this example, it is clear that in the case of all voluntary trades, both parties are better off.

2.2. Consumer Demand Theory

Maria eventually decided to close down her general store and concentrate on selling chocolate chip cookies at the construction site in downtown Las Cruces. Like Pavlov's dogs, Maria knew that the construction workers wouldn't be able to resist her highly acclaimed chocolate chip cookies. With the advent of Maria's product, we can learn about a primary issue: price. Since Maria is always profit-conscience, she decided to experiment by charging various amounts per cookie for the largest profit. On the Monday of her first week of selling cookies, Maria charged 10 cents per cookie. She sold 50. This can be seen in Table 2.1.

On Tuesday, Maria raised the price to 15 cents per cookie and the number of cookies sold fell to 45. She continued to experiment with varying prices throughout the week and found

Table 2.1   Maria's Market for Cookie

Day	Price	Quantity Sold
Monday	10 cents	50
Tuesday	15 cents	45
Wednesday	20 cents	40
Thursday	25 cents	35
Friday	30 cents	30

that when she raised the price of cookies, the demanded for cookies fell. Maria has discovered the most basic law in economics: the law of demand.

ECONOMIC PRINCIPLE

The First Law of Demand: *as the price of a good rises (falls) the quantity demanded for the good falls (rises).*

Graphing the above numbers makes the following demand schedule. Notice, when Maria charged 30 cents per cookie, she was able to sell 30 cookies. This is represented by point A in Figure 2.1. When Maria lowered the price to 25 cents per cookie, the quantity demanded increased to 35 cookies, which is represented at point B. This graph is called a *demand schedule*: it describes the relationship between the price of a good and the quantity demanded for that good at each price. The demand curve is downward sloping, which illustrates how the quantity demanded for cookies is inversely related to the price of the cookies. As the price of cookies falls, the quantity demanded rises. *All goods and services have a downward sloping demand schedule.*

With her newfound knowledge, Maria was able to determine the amount of cookies to bake as well as the price she should charge. The concept of profits will be reintroduced when we examine the cost of producing the cookies.

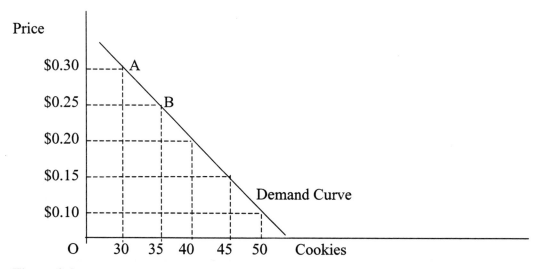

Figure 2.1   Demand Schedule Facing Maria

2.2.1. Factor Causes Shifts in Demand

- *Changes in income*

After Maria had been selling cookies for several weeks, she overheard a conversation between two construction workers. One particularly loud and somewhat boastful, middle-aged man said that everybody on the site had received a raise. All the workers were making five percent more in wages! The following day, Maria observed that the demand for cookies had risen. The new relationship between price and quantity demanded is displayed in Table 2.2.

Table 2.2 Income Increase and Demand Changes

Day	Price	Original Amount Sold	Quantity Sold after the Increase in Income
Monday	10 Cents	50	60
Tuesday	15 Cents	45	55
Wednesday	20 cents	40	50
Thursday	25 cents	35	45
Friday	30 cents	30	40

At every price, the demand for cookies increases. Table 2.2 reproduces the information from Table 2.1 in the third column of the table; the fourth column displays the quantity demanded after the increase in income. The demand schedule in Figure 2.1 illustrates the demand for cookies at 10 cents each; 50 cookies were sold. However, after the wage increase, the construction workers demanded 60 cookies at 10 cents each. As Table 2.2 reveals, the quantity demanded at every price has increased relative to column three. This is graphed as the following:

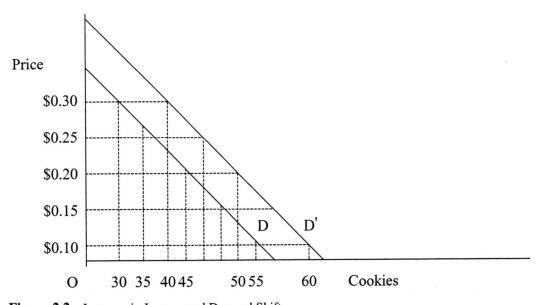

Figure 2.2 Increase in Income and Demand Shift

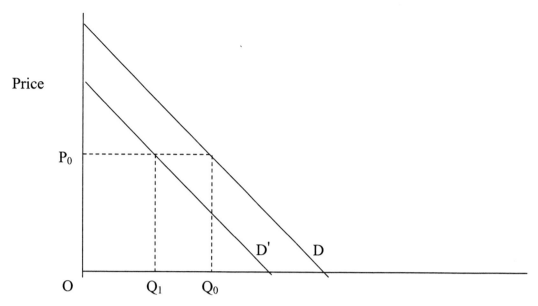

Figure 2.3   Effect of Changes in the Price of a Substitute on Demand

Where D represents the original demand curve and D′ is the new demand curve. As Figure 2.2 indicates, at a price of 10 cents per cookie, Maria can now sell 60 cookies per day whereas before, she could only sell 50. Maria had discovered that there are factors that can cause the demand curve for a given product to shift. In this case, an increase in wages or income caused the demand schedule to shift outward.

There are many factors that can cause the demand curve either inward or outward. Consider some additional examples.

Advertisement   Suppose the Surgeon General reported that eating chocolate chip cookies would increase the quality of life; that the gooey and delectable chocolate chips actually helps you maintain your health and live longer (don't we wish?) This announcement would most likely cause the demand schedule to shift outward.

Price of a Substitute   Besides my wishful thinking, there are many other factors that can shift the demand schedule. A decrease in the price of a substitute, such as candy bars, could affect Maria's cookie sales. As the price of candy bars fell, the construction workers would purchase more candy bars and fewer cookies. In this case, the demand curve for cookies would shift inward from D to D′. This is shown in Figure 2.3 above.

Before the drop in candy bar prices, when Maria charged a price of P_0 for cookies and could sell OQ_0 amount. However, after the fall in candy bar prices, the demand curve for cookies shifted inward from D to D′, and the amount sold fell to OQ_1.

2.2.2. The Relationship of the Demand Schedule to Buyers

Economists maintain that all goods and services have downward sloping demand curves. While we economists are not maintaining that all consumers have specific knowledge about the first law of demand, we are stating that everybody *acts* as if they do. For example, when you shop at the supermarket and observe that apples are selling for 50 cents a pound instead of the usual 90 cents a pound, you will typically purchase a larger amount of apples. When a shopper responds to a sale price by buying more of the good, it reflects the first law of demand. Even though most consumers are not aware of this law, strangely enough, they act as if they understand it perfectly.

ECONOMIC PRINCIPLE

An increase in income causes an outward shift in the demand schedule if the good is a **normal good**. A normal good is defined as a one that we will purchase more of if our income rises. Contrastingly, we also have inferior goods. An **inferior good** is a good that we buy less of as our income rises. In other words, the demand curve shifts inward. Examples of inferior goods could be potatoes, ground beef or bologna. For this class, we will assume that all goods are normal.

We have now drawn a theoretical demand schedule and established that it can shift for a variety of reasons: changes in income or in the price of a related good and also advertisement. Can you think of five more reasons for a shift in the demand curve?

Summary

We have now pointed out two features of the demand curve. The first one describes the downward sloping nature of the demand curve; as the price of a good rises (falls), the quantity demanded falls (rises). The second is concerned with shifts in the curve. A number of factors that can shift the demand curve such as changes in income, tastes, prices of related goods and advertising (just to name a few). We will be exploring some of these factors later in the chapter.

2.3. Theory of the Firm: Supply

Each night, Maria baked the cookies to sell to the construction workers the next day. It was, therefore, her responsibility to determine how many cookies to bake and that amount, she hoped, would coincide with the demand for cookies.

One of the primary decisions Maria had to make was the given price of cookies; how many cookies could she afford to bake? Maria had to be confident about two issues. The first was how the level of production would be influenced by the price she would charge the construction workers. The second was how her profits were related to the price of the cookies as well as the cost of baking the cookies.

Maria realized early on in the cookie business that the cost per unit of cookies increased with the more cookies she baked. To figure out why this, let's consider the following graph.

Figure 2.4 presents a supply curve, which describes how the quantity produced by a firm responds to the price that the firm can charge in the market place. We notice that it is upward sloping, which indicates that as the price a firm charges for goods in the market place increases, the firm, in turn, increases its level of production. For example, at price P_1, the firm is willing to supply OQ_1 amount of the good. If the price rises to P_2, then the firm is willing to supply the increased amount, OQ_2.

2.3.1. Upward Sloping of a Supply Curve

Firms purchase factors of production (inputs) which are used to produce goods and services (output) that are eventually sold. The firm's objective is to maximize profits. Therefore, firms are always searching for the most suitable inputs to purchase. First they will choose the best input to produce the first set of units. Then, as production increases, the firm will purchase the second most suitable set of inputs needed to produce additional output.

Coming back to Maria, consider the cost of producing her famous cookies, which consists of the money expended to purchase the flour, sugar, butter (margarine was not commonly used in the early 1960s), chocolate chips and the electricity needed to operate the oven. The cost of

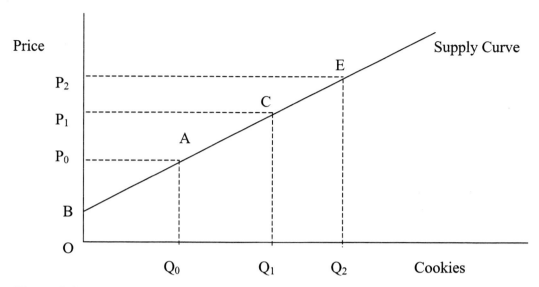

Figure 2.4   The Supply Curve

producing the first unit (designated Q_0) is the area Q_0ABO in Figure 2.4. The area under the supply schedule represents the costs of producing different amounts of cookies. The cost of producing the second groups of cookies is Q_0Q_1CA. The cost of producing the third group is Q_1Q_2EC. The cost of producing OQ_2 cookies is Q_2EBO.

Another perspective on why supply curves are upward sloping has to do with how efficient the inputs are in producing output. Consider this idea: as a firm gets larger, it is able to produce additional units of output for a lower cost. Compare prices at an organic, local food store to a chain like Albertson's or King Soopers as proof of this theory. This situation is referred to as **economies of scale**. As a firm increases production, it is able to take advantage of large quantities of production and reduce it's per unit cost.

Figure 2.5 indicates that the supply curve has a downward sloping component as well as an upward sloping part. The downward sloping part of the curve represents the economies of scale argument. As the firm increases production from OQ_1 to OQ_2 we observe that the costs of producing additional units of output decreases. The cost of producing the last unit, Q_1, is represented by the distance Q_1A. The cost of producing the

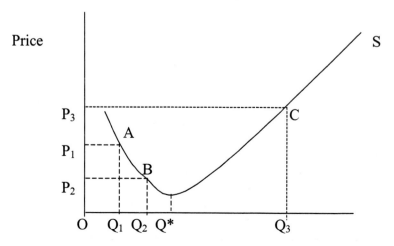

Figure 2.5   Economies of Scale

single unit, Q_2, is represented by the distance Q_2B. This illustrates the idea that as a firm becomes larger; they become more efficient in producing output. However, at the low point of the supply schedule, designated by the point Q^*, the **law of diminishing returns** sets in.

2.3.2. Law of Diminishing Marginal Returns

As you add an additional unit of a variable input (labor) to a fixed workspace—one with a fixed amount of land and capital—output will increase but at a decreasing rate. As more workers are added to a fixed workspace, more production occurs. But, as the workers start getting in the way of one another, each additional worker becomes less productive.

Examples of the law of diminishing marginal returns:

1. As more servers are added to the staff of a restaurant, each server's contribution falls with every new hire as they start to get in each other's way.
2. As more workers are hired to harvest a crop on an acre of land, the smaller the additions to output will be.

When the law of diminishing marginal returns sets in, it becomes more costly to produce additional units of output. This is described by producing any quantity that exceeds OQ^* in Figure 2.5. The supply curve starts to slope upward at Q^*, which indicates that cost of producing additional units beyond this point are increasing. As an example, the cost of producing the unit at Q_3, is greater than the cost of producing a unit at Q^*. It is the upward sloping part of the supply schedule that we typically examine in economics. Firms will maximize their profits when they are producing along the upward sloping part of the supply schedule. We will not prove this claim, so you need to just take it on faith. This principle explains why the supply curve in Figure 2.4 only has an upward sloping part. It depicts the point in time where Maria is experiencing the law of diminishing marginal returns.

2.3.3. Supply Curve as Marginal Cost

The supply curve is also called a marginal cost curve. Marginal cost refers to the extra costs associated with producing an additional unit of output. Therefore, we can draw the supply schedule, or the marginal cost schedule, as the following:

The marginal cost curve reflects the costs of producing additional units of output. The cost of producing OQ_0 units of output is the area OQ_0AB. The cost of producing Q_0Q_1 units of output is the area $Q_0Q_1 CA$. We will use the term "supply curve" and "marginal cost curve" interchangeably throughout the first part of the semester.

2.3.4. Shifts of the Supply Schedule

After several months of being in the chocolate chip cookie business, Maria experienced some unpleasant news about the costs of producing her cookies. Wheat farmers in the Midwest had experienced some very bad weather, which substantially reduced the wheat harvest and drove up wheat and flour prices. Since flour is a very important ingredient in the cookie baking business, it now became more expensive for Maria to bake the cookies.

Maria is experiencing what we refer to in economics as "an increase in the costs of production." We need to understand how we can graphically demonstrate this idea. Consider the following:

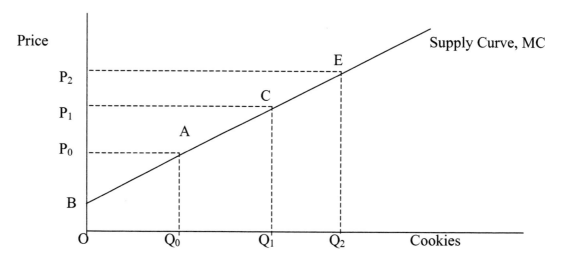

Figure 2.6   Supply Curve (Marginal Cost)

Before the price increase of flour, Maria's cost of production was represented by the supply curve S (Figure 2.7). Therefore, the cost of producing OQ_1 units of cookies was the area OQ_1AB. When Maria experienced the price increase, her costs of production increased. That change is reflected by the upward shift in the supply curve to S'. We now can observe that the cost of producing OQ_1 units of cookies has increased, and is now represented by the area OQ_1EF. Notice that $OQ_1AB < OQ_1EF$.

When cost of production increases due to increased price of inputs, the supply curve will shift inward and upward due to an increase in the costs of production. For any given price, production will be less. The supply schedule will shift from S to S' (Figure 2.7) with an increase in the costs of production. Alternately, if there is a decrease in the costs of production, the supply curve will shift downward and outward to reflect that the firm can produce each unit for a lower cost.

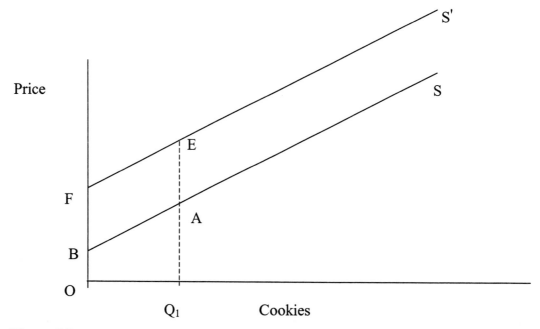

Figure 2.7   Increased Costs of Production

Another factor that causes a shift in the supply curve is changes in **technology**. When there is an increase in technology, we are able to use the same amount of labor and capital more efficiently, therefore producing a greater amount of output. This can be depicted in Figure 2.8 below.

An improvement in technology causes the factors of production to become more efficient in producing output. Recall, that firms purchase both labor and capital as the primary inputs required in production of goods and services. As an example, an improvement in management techniques could result in a better organization of workers and thus, workers become more efficient and can produce a given amount of output in a shorter period of time. With respect to capital, a new machine could be developed that can produce output for both a lower price as well as at a faster rate. In other words, for the same costs of labor and capital, the firm can increase their level of production. The above graph shows how the supply schedule shifts out from S to S′ because of improvements in technology. We observe that the area $OQ1EF$ represents the cost of producing $OQ1$ units. After the improvement in technology, the supply curve shifted out to S′ and the cost of production fell to the area OQ_1AB.

Maria experienced an increase in technology thanks to her mother, Rosa. Rosa watched Maria bake cookies for several weeks before she came to the realization that there was a more efficient approach to cooking baking. Rosa suggested that if Maria used two baking trays instead of one, she could have the second batch of cookie dough ready right after the first batch was removed from the oven. This new method allowed Maria to spend less time baking, shifting her supply curve outward.

2.3.5. The Equilibrium Process

In this section, we will merge the supply and demand curves together on the same graph, and study what we refer to as the **equilibrium process**. We have seen that consumers face a downward-sloping demand curve while firms face an upward-sloping supply curve. When we jointly examine the interaction of the supply and demand curves, we can solve for the equilibrium price and equilibrium quantity.

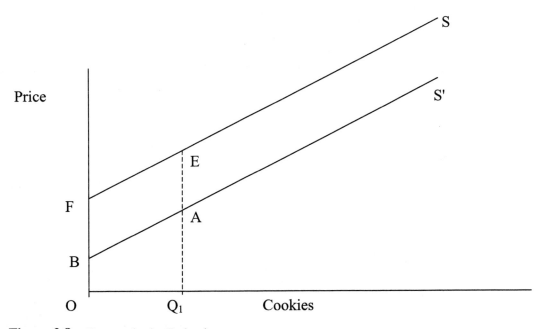

Figure 2.8 Changes in the Technology

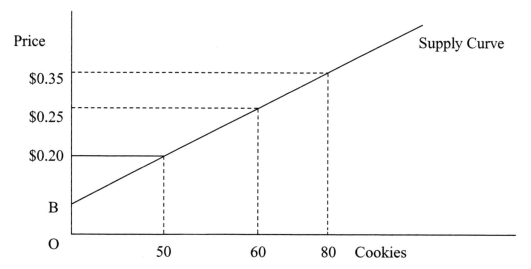

Figure 2.9 Market in the Equilibrium

ECONOMIC PRINCIPLE

A MARKET IS IN EQUILIBRIUM WHEN THE QUANTITY SUPPLIED IS EQUAL TO THE QUANTITY DEMANDED.

This will occur when the equilibrium price and quantity is achieved. In our example, Maria faced the following supply curve.

The Sunday night before her first week in the cookie business, Maria decided on the amount of cookies to bake: 80. This means that she will charge 35 cents per cookie. Monday morning, the following problem arose: the construction workers only demanded 40 cookies. Maybe it was the weather, maybe it was because it was the beginning of the week, but Maria was left with 40 uneaten cookies. This is seen in Figure 2.10. When the quantity demanded is less than the quantity supplied, it is referred to as **excess supply**. When the quantity supplied is greater than the quantity demanded at a given price, there is an excess supply of that good. Maria went home with the extra 40 cookies and much to

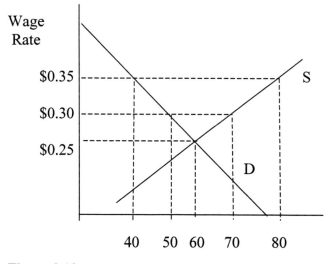

Figure 2.10 Excess Supply of Cookie

Maria's dismay; her family devoured the remaining cookies after dinner (it wasn't only the construction worker who liked her deserts). Although Maria adored her family, she realized that it was costly to bring home the extra cookies. She realized that it was important that the Tupperware container that she transported her cookies in should be empty when she comes home tomorrow.

Cookie-less, Maria decided that she did not want to produce so much of her cookies since her family was all too happy to consume the excess supply. That night, she decided to bake only 70 cookies and sell them at 30 cents each. Referring to Figure 2.10, on Tuesday, Maria was able to sell 50 cookies, reducing the excess supply to 20.

For Wednesday, Maria reduced her production to 60 cookies and reduced the price to 25 cents. That day's sales satisfied Maria: she sold every last cookie. The cookie market could now be considered in equilibrium. The quantity demanded equaled the quantity supplied.

ECONOMIC PRINCIPLE

The above example is a description of the equilibrium process that occurs in all free- functioning markets. Equilibrium is defined as a situation where the quantity supplied by firms at a certain price is equal to the quantity demanded by consumers at that same price. Economists consistently observe in markets that when there is an excess supply of a good (quantity supplied exceeds the quantity demanded) then there is downward pressure on the price of the good until it reaches the equilibrium price.

It is entirely possible that Maria could have chosen a price below the equilibrium on that first Monday morning. In this case there would be an excess demand for the cookies and, in turn, upward pressure on the price of cookies. For practice, outline the equilibrium process that starts out with an excess demand for cookies.

Equilibrium price is the price that equilibrates the quantity supplied with the quantity demanded.

2.3.6. Demand Curve as a Marginal Benefit Schedule

The demand curve is also referred to as a "marginal benefit schedule." The downward demand sloping schedule refers to how much value the construction worker places on each additional cookie. Consider Figure 2.11. The area under the demand curve represents the value that the consumer places on a given number of units. For example, the construction worker is willing to pay Q_1ABO for the first cookie; this is the value the consumer places on consuming the quantity OQ_1. The area Q_2CAQ_1 is the value the consumer places on consuming the quantity Q_1Q_2. We place the term "MB" in the graph to infer the idea of value.

In summary, the demand schedule reflects the maximum value the consumer is willing spend on cookies or any other good, for that matter.

Consider the following graph 2.12, where the equilibrium price is P_0 and the equilibrium quantity is Q_0. With the price P_0 and the quantity sold Q_0, the consumer pays $P_0 \times Q_0$ or the area Q_0EP_0O for the good. Remembering the idea that the demand curve is also a marginal benefit schedule, we can also determine the value the consumer places on Q_0 units. The area, Q_0EBO, represents the value the consumer places on consuming OQ_0 units. This area also implies the maximum the consumer is willing to pay for OQ_0 units. However, the consumer pays the price P_0 and only has to pay the amount Q_0EP_0O. It appears that the consumer was

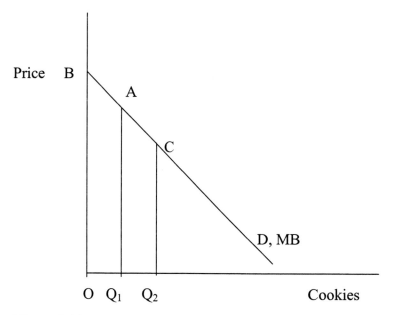

Figure 2.11   The Demand Schedule of Marginal Benefit Schedule

willing to pay more for the good than they had to. The extra amount that the consumer was willing to pay, but did not have is the area EBP_0 represents. This area is referred to as consumer surplus.

ECONOMIC PRINCIPLE

Consumer surplus is the difference between the maximum a consumer is willing to pay and the amount that they have paid to consume the desired units.

The following presents a summary of the supply and demand curve model as presented in Figure 2.12.

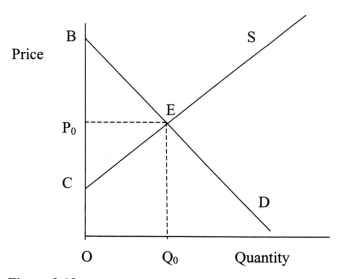

Figure 2.12   The Consumer Surplus

- $P_0 E Q_0 O$—total expenditure for the consumer or total revenue for the firm
- $O Q_0 E C$—Costs of producing $O Q_0$ units for the firm. Remember the area under the supply curve represents the costs of producing a given level of output.
- $P_0 E C$—Producer surplus or profits for the firm. This area represents the difference between total revenue and total costs.
- $B E Q_0 O$—maximum the consumer is willing to spend on Q_0 units
- $P_0 E B$—consumer surplus

Maria   .

As Maria entered her senior year in high school (1967), she was giving a lot of thought about the college she would attend. She chose to attend the Colorado State University (CSU) in Fort Collins. It was a scary world out there. All the boys that Maria grew up with were susceptible to the military draft. The kids who went to college obtained a deferment and the one's who sought jobs ended up in the military and in the Vietnam War. Fort Collins seemed like a good place to go because the anti-war movement was very strong there and that excited her.

By her sophomore year in Fort Collins, Maria had a thriving granola and tie-die t-shirt business. However, this wasn't much better than selling cookies. Cookies, Ben and the wagon, granola, t-shirts were all small time stuff. She needed to go up a level or two in the business world. A friend of hers, Anne had worked at a local pizza place as a cook and that got Maria thinking about selling pizza. But she needed an angle. Pizza was popular but starting a restaurant would be very expensive. You had to rent a building, decorate it, and buy tables and chairs. That was too risky. She needed an angle that could make money. One night, Maria and Anne were discussing how to make money and all of a sudden, Maria came up with the way to be successful. Maria told Anne that the key was to deliver the pizzas right to the home of the customers. Initially, Anne thought that the idea was ridiculous but as they discussed it, and it became more reasonable. Maria emphasized that they would be performing a public service for the city. Delivering pizzas would cut down on the amount of driving by college students and given all the partying that goes on in town, it should make the city safer. Maria told Anne that she need to a couple of days to organize her thoughts about the business and she would get back to her.

Maria first thought about the quality of the product. Anne felt confident about making pizzas and the pizzas at Anne's place were good. Maria realized that the product was good enough. Maria then looked at places that she could rent and since it did not have to be that large, the rent would not be that bad. There would be no tables, no chairs or silverware. Maria looked around town and found several candidates for the store. She next turned to how she would deliver the pizzas. After giving this some thought, she decided that hiring college students to deliver the pizzas would be the way to go.

The next problem was where to get a pizza oven. She could not use a standard oven like she used when she sold baked chocolate chip cookies. She got on the phone (Ebay did not exist) and enquired about pizza places that were either going out of business or expanding and were getting rid of old ovens. Eventually she found an oven that she could afford.

She approached Anne with all the information a week later and Anne was amazed at how quickly Maria moved on the plan. Maria had enough money saved to purchase a used pizza oven and also enough money for the first few months of rent. With their rented space, they set up the oven; hired some drivers and they were in business. Maria started distributing fliers advertising the pizza delivery service. The idea took off quickly as people found this to be a very novel idea. Maria became skilled at making pizzas and enjoyed running a business with a partner. It was a great time and the business paid for college and several trips to Europe.

At the end of her sophomore year, it was time to pick a major. Since she was able to run her own business, so she figured majoring in business was a waste of time. She had read an article in a magazine about the future of computers. The defense department was using computers to process information. Unfortunately, computers took up an entire room so at this time so they were not very practical. The idea was intriguing and she decided that this was the way to go. She investigated further and found out that if one wanted to learn how to build computers you needed to major in electrical engineering. Maria majored in electrical engineering and she found herself to be the only woman undergraduate in the program. She found it very interesting being the only woman in the department. Sexism was rampant but fortunately, there were very few undergraduate men that could match her intellectually and no one worked harder than Maria. By her senior year, the professors in the department realized that Maria was no one to take lightly.

When Maria opened her pizza shop, students were very happy, as now they didn't have to go out to buy pizza. Maria's pizzas were also known to be some of the best pizza in town. There was an aspect of her pricing scheme that Maria would not understand until she had a conversation with Robert many years in the future. Consider Figure 2.13. The typical price Maria charged for a pizza was $6.50 a pizza. The average student purchased 8 pizzas a month. It is possible to calculate the value of consumer surplus. Recall your days as a ninth grader when you learned how to compute the area of a triangle.

$$\text{Area of a triangle} = \tfrac{1}{2} \text{ base} \times \text{height}$$

Referring back to Figure 2.13, total revenue is $4.50 \times 8 = 36.00. It is possible to calculate the value of producer surplus and consumer surplus using the formula for the area of triangle.

$$\text{Producer surplus} = \tfrac{1}{2}\, 4.50 \times 8 = $18.00$$
$$\text{Consumer surplus} = \tfrac{1}{2}\, 5.50 \times 8 = $22.00$$

The calculation of consumer surplus of $22.00 has some interesting implications. The average college student would have been willing to pay an additional $22.00 to consume the 8 pizzas over the month, however, they did not have to because a single price of $4.50 a pizza was charged per pizza.

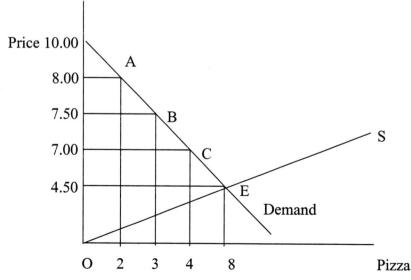

Figure 2.13   The Market for Pizzas

2.3.7. The Impact of Competition

Let's go back to 1967 when Maria was still operating her cookie stand at various construction sites in town. Thad, a checkered shirt- and loafer-wearing preppy had a crush on Maria. And, as common high school crushes go, Thad teased and annoyed Maria at every chance he got. While serving on the school's debate team, Maria considered Thad her nemesis; the kiss-up do-gooder who always argued with her, but rarely won. Also an entrepreneur, Thad decided that setting up an ice cream stand near the construction site would be a good way to make money and see Maria every day. Maria saw his competition as an utter annoyance, and his presence only disfavored Thad even more in her eyes.

But for the workers, ice cream was a suitable substitute for chocolate chip cookies, especially in the hot, Las Cruces afternoons. This means that if the workers consume more ice cream, they will consume less cookies and vice-versa. Because the construction workers can now opt for an alternate snack, there is a shift inward in the demand schedule for Maria's cookies from D to D'. See Figure 2.14. The equilibrium price and quantity both fell since the construction workers are now starting to consume ice cream and reduce their level of cookie consumption. Thanks to Thad, Maria's profits fall from P_0EC to $P_1E'C$.

ECONOMIC PRINCIPLE

Maria has just had her first experience with the consequences of competition. Someone else is starting to supply a good that competes with what she sells. Initially, Maria is harmed by the competition but the construction workers benefit.

Referring to the above graph, the demand curve has shifted downward. A **shift** in the demand schedule means the same thing as a **change** in the demand schedule. A shift or change is different from movement along a stationary demand schedule. As the demand curve shifted downward, we observe that there is a movement along the supply schedule. A movement along the supply schedule is referred to as a decrease in the **quantity supplied**. In Maria's case there is a decrease in demand and a decrease in the quantity supplied.

Maria is facing another business problem. Her parents have decided that she is causing too great a disruption in the kitchen each evening while baking cookies. They tell her that she can only use the kitchen for cookie baking after 10:00 P.M. Now Maria has to give up sleep in order to bake cookies to sell at the construction site. This represents an increase in the costs of production because she has to give up valuable sleep to bake the cookies. Since she is tired,

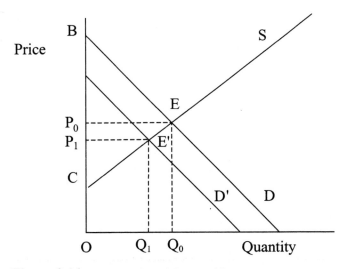

Figure 2.14   The Impact of Competition

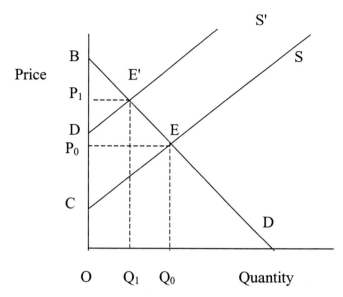

Figure 2.15   Inward Shift of Supply Curve

Maria starts making more mistakes baking which wastes inputs and increases her costs of production. This results in an upward shift of Maria's supply schedule for cookies since it is now more expensive for her to bake cookies. Her parents are being rather harsh. If they only knew that she was destined to be a very wealthy industrialist, then they would probably bake the cookies for her.

After Maria's parents limit her baking time, there is an upward shift in the supply schedule. The upward shift in the supply schedule is also referred to as a decrease in supply. The shift upward in the supply schedule causes an increase in the price of cookies and also a decrease in quantity demanded. To review this idea, we have a shift upward in the supply schedule and a movement along an unchanging demand curve. Therefore, we have a decrease **in supply and a decrease in the quantity demanded**. Her profits fall from P_0EC to $P_1E'D$.

2.4. Economic Modeling

The supply and demand model that we have just developed solves out for the equilibrium price and quantity. These variables are referred to as endogenous variables.

> ***Endogenous variable:*** *a variable that is determined or solved for within the model or system. In our model the two endogenous variables are price and quantity.*

There are also variables that can impact movements in the endogenous variables. These variables cause shifts in the supply and demand schedules. We have looked at changes in income causing a shift in the demand curve and a change in the costs of production causing a shift in the supply schedule. These variables are not solved out by our model but instead are arbitrarily changed by the instructor. These variables are referred to as exogenous variables.

> ***Exogenous variable:*** *a variable that is determined outside the model or system. An exogenous variable will cause a shift in the supply or demand schedule.* Examples of exogenous variables for the demand curve are income, tastes and prices of related goods. Examples of exogenous variables for the supply curve are costs of production and technology.

Robert

At the end of his freshman year at Boston University, the friends Robert hung out with decided they were going to Europe. Fortunately for his friends, they had parents who had no trouble footing the bill for Europe but for Robert, there was no way his parents were going to pay for the trip. He contemplated calling them up but wasting a phone call was not a wise thing to do. Robert had just recently talked to his Dad and the conversation centered around Robert coming home for the summer and working on the farm. Do I go back to Colorado or try to get a job here and save for a trip to Europe?

Robert started thinking job but there was no way he was going to work on the farm. He started scouring the classifieds in the Boston Globe and saw many jobs that had little appeal. Then he came across a job that seemed interesting. It was as a manager of an old apartment house. The advertisement stated that the job required

- Manage the apartment building
- Fix plumbing, electrical, heating and elevator problems
- Free rent
- $400 a month

As Robert looked at the ad, he thought, hey I've done it all in the repair business so that is no problem and he assumed that he could also rent out the apartments. Robert applied for the job and obtained an interview. The owner of the building was named Dale. After initially viewing Robert and realizing he was a college student, Dale said that he was too young and obviously did not have the handyman skills required for the job. Robert stated that he could handle all problems in the apartment house. Dale was suspicious and said that he currently had a sewage backup problem in the basement and if Robert could fix the problem, he could have the job. Four hours later, the sewage problem was fixed and Robert had a job.

Robert started thinking about his high school days when his father made him do all the repair work on the farm. Oddly enough, those skills he developed in high school allowed him to be eligible for this job. Running an apartment house required a fair amount of responsibility but most importantly, he made his own hours. Robert thought that he might thank his Dad for forcing him to do all that work on the farm, but then decided it was premature to do so.

As he learned the first week of the job, this was a rent control building. In the 1960s, in Boston, the mayor's office was concerned that rents in the city were too high relative to people's salaries. There was serious concern that rental rates would become such a large percentage of the average person's salary, that the ability of many families in Boston to maintain a reasonable standard of living would be jeopardized. The plan was to reduce rental rates in a large number of apartment houses throughout the city.

During his freshmen year in college, Robert had taken an introductory class in economics and had learned about the impact of rent control programs. To view this graphically, consider Figure 2.16.

Figure 2.16 presents a supply and demand curve model for the apartment market. For simplicity, let us assume that the supply of apartments is represented by the vertical supply curve S. We are assuming that there is a fixed supply of apartments in the rent control section of Boston. Given the demand curve D, the equilibrium price without rent controls would be R_o and the amount paid by all renters would be R_oEQ_o0. The current consumer surplus would be AER_o.

The rent control program lowered rental rates to R_c. The program expected that the renters would pay the amount R_cFQ_o0, which is lower than the free market price. However, this price resulted in an excess demand since the quantity supplied was $0Q_o$ and the quantity demanded was $0Q_1$. As Robert learned in his economics class, an excess demand would normally cause a rise in the price to R_o and move the market back toward equilibrium. However, in this case the rental rate was not allowed to rise above R_c.

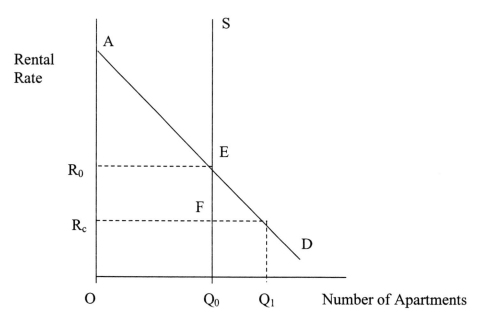

Figure 2.16   Market for Apartments

As apartments in the building would become available, people would bombard Robert to rent the apartment. Since there was an excess demand, Robert would typically have to choose between as many as six people to rent one apartment. As Robert learned in his economics class, non-price criteria could be used to decide whom to choose. It was common to use race, ethnicity, religion, height, weight, etc. as criteria. Robert found all these methods undesirable and decided to rent the apartment to the first one who applied. However, some people would wake up at 3am to be first in reading the classifieds in the paper in order to be first on waiting list for an apartment. Getting up early in the morning was another hidden cost of the rent control program. Robert realized that the rent control program could cause landlords to act in unfavorable ways.

After Robert had been working in the apartment house for several months, Dale approached him with another way to deal with the excess demand for apartments. Dale was very upset that one of his buildings was targeted as a rent control property so he was not able to raise rents to help deal with rising costs. Dale told Robert that they could use a method known as 'key money' to deal with all would-be renters. Dale said that since the renters were getting a great deal on the apartment, they would be willing to pay a non-refundable deposit of $2,000 for the key to the apartment. This program was illegal, but it was difficult for the police to monitor these types of activities.

Robert knew exactly what Dale was talking about. Referring back to Figure 2.16, renters placed a maximum value on the $0Q_0$ apartments of AEQ_00. Without rent controls, the renters would pay the amount R_0EQ_00 and the consumer surplus would be AER_0. However, with a price of R_c, renters thought they would be paying R_cFQ_00 and the consumer surplus would be $AEFR_c$. The use of key money implied that people would be willing to spend part if not all of their consumer surplus to get the apartment. If Robert used the key money approach, theoretically, renters would pay the area R_cFEA as key money, to get he apartment. In fact, the key money was a method to extract out the consumer surplus from the renters. As Robert learned in class and was witnessing before his very eyes, the costs of the apartments could be higher with the rent control program.

Robert would battle with Dale about the key money approach since Robert did not like to auction off the apartments. Regardless, Dale was a good person who more often than not helped out his renters.

Rachel

Rachel loved to read and was also a gifted writer. In the fourth grade she read Gone With the Wind and fell in love with the written word. Her parents were very proud and expected her to excel in school. Rachel did not disappoint her parents as she excelled in school and was admitted and attended Dartmouth. Rachel graduated from Dartmouth with a degree in English literature and a minor in biology. Her father would have loved her to go to medical school while her mother hoped for at least the hint of a profession. Rachel did not disappoint and told her parents that she was going to Park City, Utah to ski. She wanted to become a freestyle skier and thought this to be a good profession. Rachel had skied a great deal during the last 10 years and if one wants to get real good at skiing that one has to ski everyday. Her parents were disappointed but not surprised that graduate school was not the choice.

She arrived in Park City with her friend Donna in August of 1972 and they were set to ski. Her parents told Rachel that she was now responsible for her own costs and the money from home would stop. Her parents said that for her first 22 years, she was given the opportunity to see the world, vacation in exotic places, hike in Nepal, blah, blah, blah. It was time to be on your own. Rachel was taken back but her parents were right.

Rachel first job in Park City was as a minimum wage dishwasher at a resort hotel. She and the other four dishwashers were earning \$1.65/hr. Although Rachel wasn't paying attention, the predominately Democratic Congress was talking about raising the minimum wage in order to make minimum wage earners better off, while then-President Richard Nixon and his Republican following were trying to dissuade them from such action. Would raising the minimum wage make Rachel better off?

2.4.1. Labor Market for Minimum Wage Earners

Consider Figure 2.17. The demand schedule represents the demand for labor by firms. At a lower wage rate, the firm will demand a greater quantity of labor. The supply curve represents the supply of labor by all minimum wage workers. As the wage rate increases, minimum wage workers will offer a greater quantity of labor in the market place. For our purposes, let us assume that the labor market is originally in equilibrium at the minimum wage of \$1.65 set by the government and N_0, which is the equilibrium level of employment.

The Democratic Congress offers a new law that would raise the minimum wage to \$2.00. The logic of the proposal is that as the minimum wage rises, workers will be better off as they are paid a higher wage. However, as the minimum wage rises to \$2.00 an hour, we find that the quantity demanded for labor falls to $0N_2$ even though the quantity supplied for labor rises to $0N_1$. Firms will hire only the $0N_2$ workers and employment falls. The only people to benefit are those who keep their job. Congress succeeds in raising the minimum wage. Rachel loses her job and has to look for new employment.

The point of this story is that the wage rate should only change when there is a shift in either the demand or supply of labor. When the government attempts to influence market, it will commonly drive the market out of equilibrium. In this case, the government will not permit the wage to fall below \$2.00 an hour and therefore, the labor market is not allowed to achieve equilibrium.

Rachel decided that she needed to exploit her skills, which were writing and not washing dishes. It was now the end of September and she needed a job. There was a monthly city newspaper that was operated by a guy named Alamo Dave. Rachel decided to approach Alamo about a job.

Alamo had been in Park City since he was released from the military in 1945. He came to Park City to mine silver and live in the mountains. The mining days were coming to an end and the town was quickly becoming a ski town. Alamo was not very happy with the change in the town from a primitive mining town to a fast paced ski town. He would write editorials

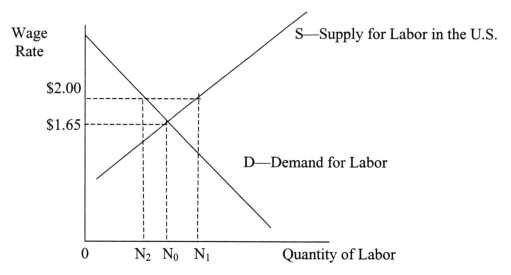

Figure 2.17   Labor Market and Minimum Wage

every now and again criticizing the change but no one cared as his breed was quickly dying off. As the town changed, Alamo realized that if his paper were to survive, he needed to change along with the town. By the way, Alamo was the coach of the Park City Rugby team.

Rachel met Alamo Dave in an apple juice tavern named the Alamo. Alamo Dave's real name was Dave Sawyer but since he spent so much time in the tavern drinking apple juice, he was called Alamo Dave. Rachel introduced herself and told Alamo that she really liked his newspaper and wondered whether she could work with him. Alamo thought about it and realized that this was a golden opportunity. This young woman seemed bright and he needed help. Rachel was hired and she became a newspaperwoman. She learned how to run the entire business from fixing the printing press, to renting advertisement space, writing scathing editorials to paying the bills.

Rachel arranged with Alamo that she needed off from 7:00 A.M. – 5:00 P.M. from early November to late April off and the rest of the time she would work for the newspaper. Alamo said fine and a great relationship began.

During her first winter in Park City, Rachel was walking down Main Street with several friends and saw a sign in the Window of Muldoon's Apple Juice Tavern. The sign said "Nickle Juice Night".

It was typical that Muldoons sold a glass of apple juice for 35 cents, but for this night only; a glass of juice was 5 cents. You could drink a lot of juice for one dollar. This scenario is described in the following graph.

With the price falling from 35 cents a glass to 5 cents a glass, the quantity demanded increased from OQ_0 to OQ_1. With respect to Muldoons, it was much more crowded than usual as Rachel, her friends and many other people had a fine time. There was also a piano player who entertained the crowd for the evening. He was also a fine singer and he really got into the evening.

On the following Monday, Rachel was walking down the street and Muldoons was advertising that they would have another nickel juice night on that Friday. Rachel decided right then that she would cancel her plans for Friday night and frequent Muldoons again.

On Friday night, Muldoons was packed. Since it was advertised in advance, more people heard about the event and chose not to go to the movies, dinner or anything else and come to Muldoons. This is displayed graphically in the following manner.

The demand curve has shifted from D to D′ or has become flatter. The demand curve has become flatter or more responsive to the price change. Since there is more time for people to respond to advertisement, there will be a larger increase in the quantity demanded. Instead of

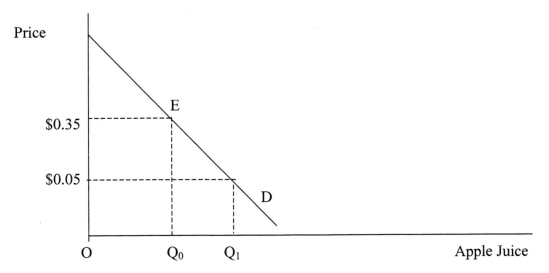

Figure 2.18   Movement along the Demand Curve

going to the movies, dinner or out to a play, people decided to go to Muldoons. We have described the concept known as the:

> ***Second Law of Demand***—*given some price change, as more time elapses, consumers can make more adjustments and respond in a greater way to the price change. This is reflected in a flatter demand curve.*

In the Muldoons example, since people had more time to respond to nickel juice night, more people went to Muldoons on the second Friday night. Figure 2.19 indicates that on the first night, the quantity demanded was $0Q_1$ but on the second Friday night, the quantity demanded increased to $0Q_2$. The same piano player was there and he played long into the night. After the second Friday night, Muldoons advertised again the following Monday that they would have nickel juice night again. Rachel and her friends realized that they better show up early if they wanted to get a table. The line out the door was significant as the demand curve became even flatter (D''). The quantity demanded increased to $0Q_3$. The piano player was

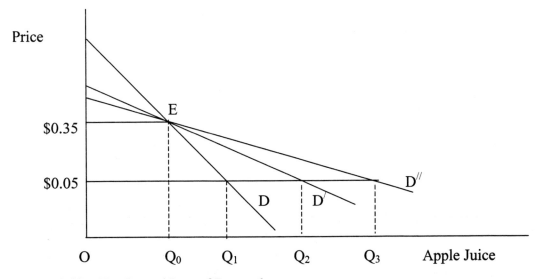

Figure 2.19   The Second Law of Demand

there the third Friday night as well. Things however, got out of hand and Muldoons never had nickel juice night again. Rachel never realized that the second law of demand was in effect over those three weeks but she sure did have a good time.

In the summer of 1974, Rachel decided to go home for a couple of weeks and to appease her parents. Rachel's Mom and Dad picked her up at the Hartford airport and they proceeded to grill her about life in Park City. They were not impressed with the amount of time she spent skiing but they were intrigued with her work at the Park City Times. Rachel told them that she was writing numerous articles on local politics about the expanding influence of the ski corporation in Park City. She also told them about Alamo Dave. Her Mom was concerned.

They pulled off the highway and her Dad said that they needed to get some gas. As they went to the local gas station, her Dad moaned and said that the gas line was longer than usual. Rachel looked up and saw that the line to get gas consisted of about 15 cars. Rachel asked what was going on and he said don't you ever read a real newspaper. "Real funny Dad", Rachel responded. Her Dad said that he would drop Rachel and her Mom at home and he would spend the hour or two getting gasoline for the car.

That evening Rachel realized that if she was serious about being a newspaper woman, she needed to find out why gas lines were very long all over the country. Even though she did not own a car, this was not a problem in Park City but it was a problem all over the country. The next morning she went to the Yale library and started reading newspapers from all over the country. The problem started in the summer of 1973 when the oil producing countries of the Middle East (Iran, Kuwait, Saudi Arabia and Iraq) decided to reduce the production of oil. These countries were responsible for producing close to 50% of the world's supply of oil and therefore, a collective decision by these countries could have a significant impact in the world oil market.

With a reduction in the production of oil, Figure 2.20 displays that the supply curve shifts inward from S to S' and the price of oil (and gasoline) increases from P_0 to P_1. From what we have learned this semester, the quantity demanded should fall and a new equilibrium condition should be obtained. But why were there long lines at the gas pumps?

As Rachel did more research at the library, she started to understand the history of the U.S. and these oil-producing countries. In the 1950s, it was recognized that there was an abundant amount of oil in the Middle East but there was no capability to mine the oil. U.S. oil companies created working arrangements with the governments of these countries to develop

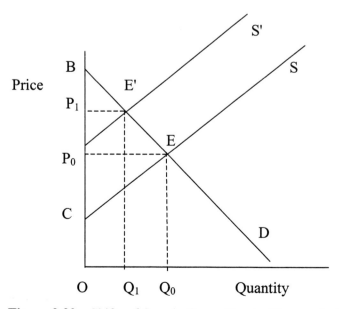

Figure 2.20   Shifts of Supply Curve Due to Changes in Oil Price

the infrastructure to mine for oil. The U.S. oil companies spent millions of dollars investing in the capital needed to mine and refine oil. In the 1950s and 1960s the U.S. government along with the oil companies played a significant role in the amount of oil that would be produced in the Middle East and the prices that would be charged.

The U.S. government believed that it was important to keep oil prices relatively low since oil was the primary source of energy in the world. At that time, the U.S. also produced much of its oil domestically in states such as Wyoming, Texas and Oklahoma. Combining local production with Middle Eastern production allowed the U.S. to keep oil prices at the targeted price of P* in Figure 2.21.

The plan of keeping oil prices at the targeted price of P^* was successful for many years. If there was an increase in demand for oil to D', then oil production (domestically or in the Middle East) would increase and the supply curve would shift outward to S' and keep oil prices stable at E'.

As Rachel continued to read, she discovered that the cultural values of the Muslim society were always at odds with the values of the oil companies and U.S. government. As it turned out, oil producing countries in the Middle East formed an alliance called the OPEC nations and decided that the U.S. should no longer play any role in determining oil production and prices. In the summer of 1973, the OPEC nations reduced the production of oil but the U.S. was determined to keep the price of oil at the targeted value of P^*. The plan was to increase domestic production enough to offset the reduction in oil production in the Middle East. This policy was unsuccessful because the U.S. was unable to generate enough domestic production of oil to offset the production in the Middle East. This story can be seen by inspecting Figure 2.22.

Before the OPEC nations implemented any change, the oil market was a point E and at the targeted price of P*. The federal government kept the market price for oil at P^* and did not allow oil to be traded at any other price. As the OPEC nations decided to decrease the production of oil, the supply curve shifted to S' and normal market forces would cause the price of oil to rise to a new equilibrium price of P_0. The quantity demanded should have declined to OQ_1.

However, the federal government did not allow the price to rise but kept it at P*. Therefore, there was an excess demand for oil and gasoline at the targeted price of P^*. The distance EF represents the excess demand. The quantity supplied at P^* is OQ_2 and the quantity demanded is OQ_0, which results in more people wanting to purchase the good than is

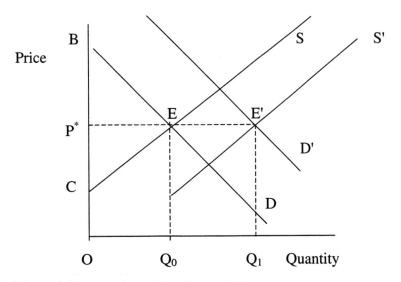

Figure 2.21   Supply of Oil at Targeted Price

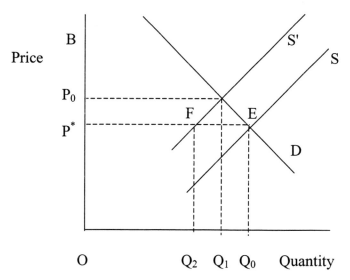

Figure 2.22   Oil Supply in U.S. after OPEC

available. This is why there were long lines at the gas stations. The price of gasoline was kept artificially low at P^*.

As described in the rent control topic, suppliers of gasoline came up with innovative ways of getting around the price control. They advertised that with a tune up for your car, you tank would be filled when you picked up your car. So instead of waiting on line, people would drop off their car, go to work and come back later to pick up their car. They had to pay to have their car tuned up but they did not have to wait on line for gas.

Arthur

Arthur had a great time in college. He went to the State University of California (SUC) on an athletic scholarship to play basketball. His parents were unsure about mixing basketball and academics but basketball was going to pay for his college education, so it was hard to turn down. Before he left for school, Arthur's Dad sat down with him to explain that college was going to be a much larger challenge academically than he was used to. Arthur listened and gave the impression that the lecture had meaning.

Arthur showed up to school in August of 1968. He was unsure about what to major in and in fact gave it little thought that first year. All his thoughts were on basketball but what he was surprised at was that during the first week of the semester, which was two months away from official practicing, his basketball coach mapped out a conditioning regiment that required working out six days a week. Conditioning involved, sprints, long distance running (Arthur had never done that before), swimming and weightlifting. By the time practice started in October, Arthur was in better shape than he had ever been and he thought that basketball practice was going to be a snap. He was wrong, as practice was brutal.

Arthur's academic experience in college took on many different facets. Arthur's real skill was public speaking as he had a real ability to talk about a wide range of topics even if his background knowledge was limited. By the end of his sophomore year, Arthur decided to major in speech communications; however, he realized that he needed a minor, which could supply him with enough information to speak on any topic. This was no easy task but he sensed it was important.

When the spring semester of 1970 was done, he needed to find a job for the summer. One of his teammates, Walt, was from Salida, Colorado and Walt told him that his father owned a rafting company and he needed more guides to run the commercial trips down the Arkansas River. Walt had been running rapids since he was eight years old and said that it were one of the best things he ever did. At first, Arthur did not think that learning how to guide rafts through rapids would be fun. However, Walt convinced him and Arthur told his parents that he was moving to Colorado for the summer to run the rapids. Arthur's father just listened in amazement but realized that there was nothing he could say or do to convince him to not go to Colorado.

Arthur learned pretty quickly that safely guiding a raft through the rapids of the Arkansas was non trivial but Walt was right, it was a blast. Arthur became intrigued with one of the drivers of the bus that would transport the guides and customers from the end of the rafting trip back to the rafting headquarters. The name of the bus driver was Bigsbey. Bigsbey was 65 years old and had just recently decided to settle down in Salida. As it turned out, Bigsbey had spent the last forty years traveling all over the world. Bigsbey loved to tell stories about his travels and Arthur was fascinated with all the places that Bigsbey had lived. Bigsbey told of living with a tribe in Cameroon that had no electricity, books, no shoes, in fact, they had nothing but some rudimentary clothes and hunted wildlife with antiquated spears. Bigsbey live with this tribe for five years and told Arthur that it was similar to what life was like in the U.S. over two hundred years ago. Bigsbey also lived in a country called Iraq and became knowledgeable about the Muslim religion. Arthur had never heard of Muslims before.

As Bigsbey told stories throughout the summer, Arthur became more and more fascinated with different cultures and different times. At the end of the summer, Arthur asked Bigsbey why he had never asked Arthur about what it was like to play college basketball. Bigsbey explained that Arthur needed to learn more from him than the other way around. The summer was short and Arthur needed to learn a lot. The summer ended and as Arthur traveled back to Los Angeles to spend a week with his family, he reflected on the summer. He had learned how to navigate a raft down a river with class 4 rapids but more importantly learned that there is a whole world out there that he knew nothing about. At the beginning of his junior year, Arthur still majored in speech communication but decided to minor in history. History would be a great way to at least begin to understand the world around him. But let's not be crazy, he also needed to work on his 15-foot jump shot.

Arthur ended up as the starting point guard on the team all four years and gained much recognition nationally for his play on the court. During his senior year in college, he led his team to the final four for the national championship. He was considered one of the best players coming out of college that season. The Boston Celtics drafted him into the NBA in 1972.

During Arthur's second year with the Celtics he signed one of the first shoe contracts for an NBA player in 1972. He signed a two- year agreement with the shoe company EKIN. After signing the contract with EKIN, he became interested in how EKIN produced their basketball shoes. He found out that until recently, EKIN produced the shoes in the U.S. but rising labor costs caused the company to consider producing the shoes in Japan. Labor costs were considerably lower in Japan. Consider Figure 2.23.

Figure 2.23 displays the supply and demand for labor in the basketball shoe market. This model should be interpreted in a similar fashion to all of our other supply and demand curve models. The vertical axis represents the wage rate or the price of labor. The horizontal axis represents the quantity of labor. The demand curve represents the demand by EKIN for workers. As is typical with the first law of demand, the lower (higher) the wage rate, the greater (smaller) the quantity demanded for labor. The supply curve represents the amount of labor that is willing to be employed at a given wage rate. When the wage rate increases, more people are willing to work.

Up till 1971, EKIN was paying a wage rate of W_0 but this wage is becoming too high relative to production costs and EKIN that basketball shoes will become too expensive for the

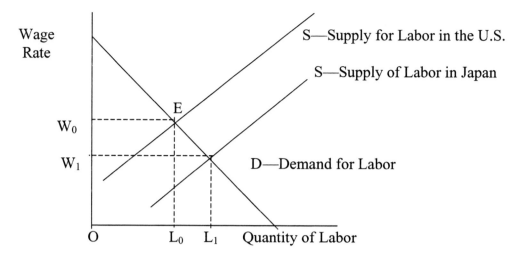

Figure 2.23   Supply and Demand for Labor in the Basketball Shoe Market

American consumer. EKIN investigates and realizes that basing their operation in Japan will result in lower wage costs.

In the above graph, we see that the supply curve for labor in Japan is shifted further out to the right than the supply curve for labor in the U.S. This implies that Japanese workers in the early 1970s were willing to work for a lower wage rate to produce basketball shoes than in the U.S. With W_1 & W_0, EKIN decided to switch their production of basketball shoes to Japan. Arthur understands the logic of the EKIN decision but he does wonder whether the work conditions in a Japanese basketball shoe factory will be the same as would exist in the U.S.

2.4.2. Forecasting Price and Quantities

During her last semester in college, competition in the pizza delivery business was becoming fierce. Besides other pizza places, Chinese and Italian restaurants started to deliver their food products too. After carefully reviewing the situation, Maria saw that the demand for pizza was shifting inward due to the greater opportunities for consumers to have food delivered to their houses. In addition, Maria found it more difficult to hire delivery people since more restaurants attempted to hire drivers. This had the impact of shifting inward Maria's supply curve since she had to pay higher wages to the drivers. Maria then attempted to predict what should happen to the price of her pizzas and the quantity sold. Consider Figure 2.24.

Let the equilibrium price and quantity be P_0 and Q_0, respectively. Since the demand for Maria's pizzas was declining, the demand curve shifted inward to D', which would cause a fall in the price and quantity sold. However, the supply curve had also shifted inward which made it a little more complicated as to the effect on price and quantity. Suppose the supply curve had shifted inward to S', and then the price would have fallen to P_1. A second option would have been for the supply curve to shift to S'', which would have resulted no change in the price of pizzas. In this case, the inward shift in demand, which causes a fall in the price, would have been exactly offset by a decrease in supply, which causes an increase in the price. The third option would have been that the supply curve shifted to S''', which would have caused an increase in the equilibrium price. As we can see, when both the supply and demand curve shift simultaneously, you can only predict the direction of change for one variable. The shift in the demand curve causes the price to decrease and the shift of the supply curve causes the price to rise. We do not have enough information as to the relative sizes of the two shifts.

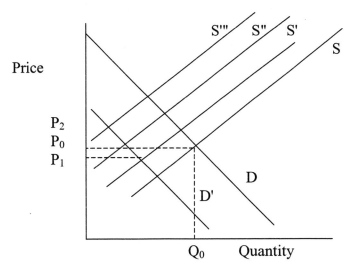

Figure 2.24 Maria's Supply Curve Shifting Inwards

We cannot determine what happens to price in this example but we can predict the directional impact on quantity. The shift inward in the demand curve causes a reduction in the equilibrium quantity and the shift inward in supply also causes a reduction in the equilibrium quantity. Since both shifts cause a reduction in quantity, it is straightforward to predict the movement in quantity.

Whenever both curves shift at the same time, it is only possible to predict the movement in one of the endogenous variables. In this case we predict that quantity will fall but the change in price is ambiguous. In other examples, quantity could be ambiguous while the prediction for quantity could be certain. It depends on the shifts of the supply and demand curves.

In 1972, Maria graduated with a degree in electrical engineering from CSU and took a job with IBM. Eventually, she was put in the research division looking at the possibility of building computers that were small enough to sit on a desk and be totally self-contained. The primary issue was to build a micro computer that had sufficient capacity to hold enough information to be of value to a user. By 1975, Maria felt that she understood what was needed to build such a computer. She left IBM and enrolled in the MBA program at Harvard in the fall of 1975. She always wanted to live in a big east coast city and Boston seemed as good as any. While in the program, she would work on developing the computer.

1976

Robert graduated from Boston University in 1972 and enrolled in the Ph.D. program in economics at M.I.T., in Boston. He excelled as an undergraduate and was excited to get into M.I.T. By 1976, Robert was a year away from getting his Ph.D. done but he was still working for Dale. As it turned out, Dale owned buildings all over Boston.

By 1976, Arthur is in the middle of a great career as a point guard for the Boston Celtics. Arthur has explored the club scene over the last year looking for opportunities to play the guitar. Being an NBA star helps him make inroads into the club scene and he gets a gig at the Café Wha. He loved playing basketball but playing the blues in some dark club in Boston was equally exciting.

Maria has also become intrigued with the club scene in Boston as it presents a very different culture than she has ever seen before. Maria has visited a number of clubs in town but finds the Café Wha to be the best. On a slow Wednesday evening, Maria is sitting in a near empty Café Wha when Arthur comes on the stage and starts playing. After his performance, Arthur introduces himself to Maria since she is the only one in the place. Over the next few months, Maria and Arthur became friends.

As it turns out, Dale owned the Café WHA and was constantly having electrical, plumbing and sewage problems. In fact, the Board of Health was a constant visitor to the establishment and it wasn't due to Arthur's performance on the guitar. One day when Maria was there listening to Arthur play, Robert showed up with his tools in order to fix the backed up sewer in the café. After he was done, he looked for Dale and found him sitting with Maria and Arthur. Dale motioned for him to come over to the table. Dale introduced Robert to Maria and Arthur. Maria said that she was an MBA student at Harvard and Arthur said that he shot twenty footers and played the guitar. Robert told them that he was at M.I.T. earning his Ph.D. in economics. Dale left and Maria, Robert and Arthur started to talk.

$ Chapter 3

3.1. Constructing the Macroeconomic Model

The objective of this chapter is to construct a macroeconomic model that can be used to study the performance of the entire economy. We are interested in understanding what factors influence the overall growth of our country's economy. Instead of looking at individual markets as we did when we introduced supply and demand analysis, it is our objective to examine the behavior of all markets simultaneously.

Maria started the MBA program at Harvard in 1975 and graduated in 1977. She found the MBA program to be challenging on an intellectual level and provided important, practical lessons, which she learned from successful business people who were regularly invited as guest-lecturers. She did note, however, that there were many more men invited to speak than women and that always bothered her. This was not the first time she realized that she lived in a male-dominated society. When she was at Colorado State University, she was one of the only female undergraduate electrical engineering majors. It was this observation about men and women that would affect her life substantially in the future.

While in graduate school at Harvard, Maria spent most of her free time tinkering with the capacity issue for a personal computer she had started working on at IBM. She had recently expanded the memory so it could hold 50 pages of text. She had heard rumors from friends in the industry that 50 pages were 20 more than IBM. Hence, she was getting close to making the machine work. Turning it into a moneymaking proposition, however, would be a daunting task. She would need a factory, trained workers and money.

Maria had known Arthur for over a year now and she had actually gone to one of his games. Maria was never a sports fan and found it difficult to understand why grown men would be willing to run up and down the court for over two hours every game. Arthur and Maria became good friends; their conversations covered parents, siblings and dreams about the future.

One evening during the summer of 1977, Arthur finished one of his sets at the Cafe Wha, and his communicative friendship with Maria took a fortuitous turn: they began talking about computers. Maria explained to Arthur that most computers were attached to something called a "mainframe," (remember, it's the late 70s). To use a computer, you had to work in a specific room where a number of monitors were attached to this mainframe, and word processing and statistical analysis were two of its primary uses. Furthermore, these mainframes were not hooked up to one another so there was no Internet. Maria went on to explain that when she worked for IBM from 1972–75, she worked in the division that was doing research on developing personal computers, which could be used at home or for business. In fact, over the last two years while she was completing her MBA, she worked steadily at night, creating a personal computer that could be purchased by individuals and firms. She wanted her invention to become a reality. Arthur was intrigued with the idea and realized that Maria was not to be taken lightly. She had an exciting vision of the future.

Maria told Arthur that she lacked the money to hire additional people to help her solve hardware problems and software issues related to the computer. She wondered if Arthur would be interested in investing in her company considering he had earned a fair amount of money over the last five years. He had even helped pay for college for his two sisters and one brother. After Arthur agreed to invest in the project, Maria had another proposition for him. Since Arthur had tremendous presence and was very articulate, Maria asked him to be a spokesperson for her company. At this time in her life, Maria liked to be behind-the-scenes and had no desire to play a public role. Arthur decided that he would get involved in Maria's company because it offered him a new direction to pursue when he finished playing basketball.

Eventually, Arthur became a skilled spokesman for Knowledge Inc., Maria's firm. Robert graduated from Boston University in 1972 and enrolled in the Ph.D. program in economics at M.I.T. in Boston that same year. He excelled as an undergraduate and was excited to move onto such a prestigious school. Despite his scholastic progress, Robert still worked for Dale. He had to spend quite a bit of time keeping the Boston health officials satisfied about the sanitary conditions at the Café Wha. It seems that the health department was concerned about the sewage problems in the kitchen where food was prepared. Robert thought it added a nice touch to the establishment, but the health officials thought otherwise. Dale, on the other hand, just wanted Robert to fix the problem.

By August 1977, Robert earned his Ph.D. in economics. Graduate school proved to be an interesting experience for Robert. Instead of taking classes in history, English, and biology, as you would as an undergrad, all he had to do was take classes in one area. Robert liked economics as a class in undergraduate school because all the ideas could be expressed using graphs. At the introductory level, his professors used very little math, but as the semester progressed to intermediate macroeconomics and microeconomics, it required more mathematics. However, at the graduate level, mathematics is the primary tool to use as one explores the uses of production functions and supply and demand curves. Not surprisingly, the mathematical representations for these graphical models can tell more sophisticated stories than the graphs alone. As an example, the math can tell you how far the demand curve shifts out when there is an increase income.

At first, Robert had a lot of difficulty dealing with the mathematics. He realized that his one calculus class as an undergraduate was insufficient to prepare him for the rigors of graduate school. He ended up taking two more calculus classes as well as a class in linear algebra and differential equations. After two years of pounding his head against the chalkboard, the use of mathematics became clear. It was no longer an obstacle for him, but a tool.

Robert eventually finished his Ph.D. in the summer of 1977. After the final defense of his thesis, he wanted to celebrate since he was starting a new job in September of 1977. He had arranged to meet Maria and Arthur at the Café Wha in order to celebrate his graduation and new job. As Robert arrived at the café, Maria and Arthur were just finishing their conversation regarding the creation of a new computer company. Maria and Arthur filled Robert in on their plans, but they were very interested in the job that Robert just took. They wanted the full story. Robert ordered some apple juice and started talking.

"I am now working for the Federal Reserve System or as it is commonly called, the Fed," Robert said. He continued to inform them that the primary responsibility of the Fed is to determine how much money will circulate in the economy. The Federal Reserve actually controls the printing press that prints the money. Robert continued to explain that the Fed uses the ability to control the money supply to:

i. To help promote economic stability

ii. To help promote a stable price level or low inflation rates

To accomplish these goals, the Fed divides the country into twelve parts or districts. Each district has its own Federal reserve bank: one in Boston, New York, Richmond, Atlanta, Chicago, St. Louis, Minneapolis, Cleveland, Philadelphia, Kansas City, Dallas and San Francisco. Each bank is responsible for evaluating the economic conditions in their district and reports their findings to the Federal Reserve Board, headquartered in Washington D.C. The Federal Reserve Board collects all this information and constructs the appropriate monetary policy. It was the Federal Reserve Board that had offered Robert a position.

Robert went on to explain that the economy is made up of a large number of components and while economists have a good understanding of the individual parts of the economy, having a working knowledge of how all the parts interact is still a challenge. The first important component in the economy is the relationship between households and firms. This is displayed in Figure 3.1. Households perform two primary functions in the economy. First, they provide labor services to firms, which aid the production process. The arrow that flows from households to firms (Figure 3.1) is referred to as **labor supply**. Second, the households earn and receive labor income, which is represented by the arrow going from firms to households. It is called **labor income**. With this income, households make expenditures to the firms and in return, the households receive goods and services.

Firms and households pay taxes to the federal government, also displayed in Figure 3.1. In return, households and firms receive government services such as national defense, domestic programs and interstate highways. It is also necessary that households and firms deposit their income in either a checking or savings account at a commercial bank. In return, households can borrow money from banks in order to finance purchases for a new home or car. Firms may also borrow money from the banking system so that they can expand their businesses.

The Fed oversees the operations of the commercial banks and makes sure that the commercial banks loan money to qualified households and firms. In addition, the Fed can supply banks with more money so that it is easier for households and firms to borrow money. This is done when the Federal Reserve wants the economy to expand. Robert continues to explain that the Fed can also manipulate interest rates, which is highly related to influencing the money growth rate. We will address this issue later on.

In addition, the Federal Reserve acts as a clearinghouse for checks. They ensure that a check from one bank will be honored by another bank. As an example, consider Arthur who was on a road trip with the Boston Celtics in New York City when decided to buy his parents an anniversary gift. He went to an exclusive jewelry shop and bought them matching watches. Arthur used a check from his local bank in Boston to purchase the watches. The jewelry shop deposited the check in their bank (Chase Manhattan). After the deposit, Chase Manhattan needs to collect the money from the First Bank of Boston, which is Arthur's bank. It is the case that both Chase Manhattan and the First Bank of Boston have bank accounts with the Federal Reserve. Chase Manhattan wires the check to the Federal Reserve who then transfers the money from the First Bank account to Chase Manhattan. The Federal Reserve charges bank for this service, which is referred to as **check clearing.**

Maria wanted to know what Robert would specifically be doing at the Federal Reserve. Robert explained that the Federal Reserve employed a large number of economists and he would be starting at the bottom of the food chain. However, if he could publish enough articles that contributed to the understanding of the economy, he would move up and hopefully have input into monetary policy. Both Maria and Arthur were impressed. Robert, Maria and Arthur finished one glass of apple juice after another in celebration of Robert's new career.

One month later, Robert left for D.C. Maria elected to stay in Boston to work on her computer company. Arthur was getting ready for his fifth NBA season.

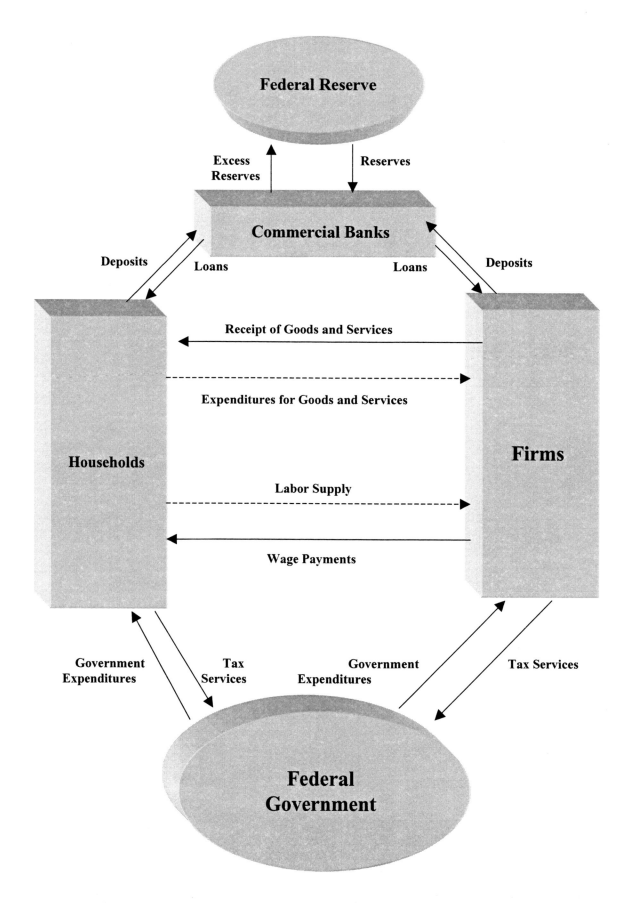

Figure 3.1 Flow Diagram of the U.S. Economy

3.1.1. Washington, D.C.

As Robert was putting the finishing touches on his new office, he gazed out the window (at his clear view of the Capitol) and let his thoughts wander back to the long hours he used to spend working on the farm. Back then, he had a strong desire to live in a big city. He smiled about his father's insistence that he learn carpentry, electrical, plumbing, cement work and everything else that was required to keep a farm going. This knowledge allowed him to get a job managing the apartment house for Dale, which contributed substantially to financing college and graduate school. In addition, he had met Maria and Arthur at the Café Wha who had become lifelong friends.

Robert's thoughts, as they always did, meandered back to economics. He was fascinated with macroeconomics, which studies the behavior of economic variables over time. Consider, for instance, the supply and demand curve for microcomputers that Maria faced in the early 1980s, represented in Figure 3.2.

By 1983, Maria had one of the few companies that built and sold personal computers to firms. Figure 3.2 presents the equilibrium solution for the microcomputer market in 1983. The equilibrium price is P_{83}, or the price that computers sold for in 1983. The quantity, Q_{83} represents the number of computers sold in 1983. There were several other competitors in the business and competition was intense, but Maria was having a great time.

Figure 3.3 above presents the market for computers in 1984. Consider point E, which describes the equilibrium condition in the 1983 computer market. The quantity produced was Q_{83} and the average price charged was P_{83}. In 1984, the demand curve for computers shifted outward to D' as computers became more desirable. At the same time, technological breakthroughs continued to propel the industry, which caused the supply curve to shift outward. In this case, the supply curve shifted outward to S'. The equilibrium quantity sold in 1984 was Q_{84} and the price of computers fell to P_{84}. It has been the case in the computer market that the supply curve has shifted outward at a greater rate than the outward shift of the demand curve. In other words, the increase in technology has always been greater than the computer's increase in popularity. The result has been annual reductions in the price of computers.

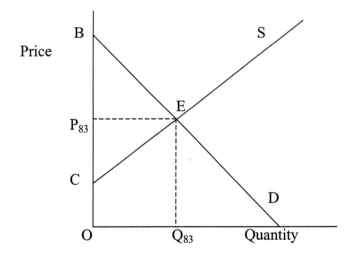

Figure 3.2 The Computer Market in 1980

Robert's fascination was not what caused the relative shifts in the supply and demand curves, but the behavior of the prices and quantities over time. In the case of the computer market, economists examine the behavior of:

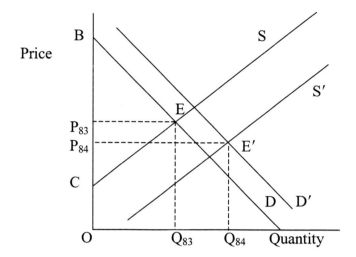

Figure 3.3   The Computer Market in 1984

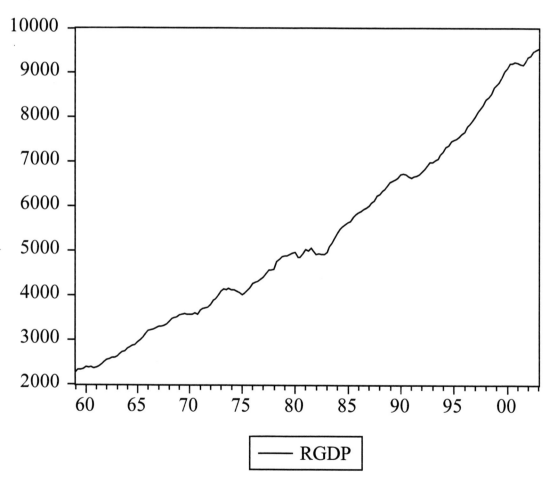

Figure 3.4   Real Gross Domestic Product Trend

- Prices (P_{80}, P_{81}, P_{82}, P_{83}, P_{84}, P_{85},) etc. and
- Quantities (Q_{80}, Q_{81}, Q_{82}, Q_{83}, Q_{84}, Q_{85},) etc.

Robert's fascination with macroeconomics impelled him to focus on the actual statistical behavior of economic variables over time.

By 1984, Robert had been with the Federal Reserve for seven years and had become a prominent economist at the Federal Reserve. In February of 1984, he was at a ritzy hotel in

Washington D.C. preparing a discussion of the performance of the overall economy with local business people and reporters. He had done this many times and always enjoyed interacting with the public since they are directly impacted by what the Fed does. He began by presenting the following figure.[1]

Robert continued his presentation by stating that the total production of goods and services for the entire economy is represented by the term **real gross domestic product (real GDP)**. Real GDP can be characterized by two distinct patterns. First, it is apparent that there is an upward trend in the movement of real GDP. From 1959 to 1984, there appears to be steady growth in the production of goods and services. This upward trend reflects the growth in population, the work force in our country, as well as the accumulation of factories, machinery (capital stock) and the development of new technologies. All of these factors are responsible for an upward trend in real GDP, or the increasing ability of the economy to produce larger amounts of goods and services. We will refer to this component as the **natural level of GDP (Y_n).**

Robert pointed out that a second characteristic of real GDP is that there are cyclical swings around the natural level of GDP. For example, we see that in the mid-1970s, there was a downturn in real GDP. This period lasted for about year-and-a-half during which the GDP fell by almost 2.5%. Many people attribute this contraction in economic activity to the dramatic increase in the price of oil and energy. There were also contractions in GDP during 1979, and between 1981 through 1982 and 1990 through 1991. Economists also blamed the 1979 contraction on oil price increases while the contraction in the early 1980s was attributed to reductions in the growth rate of the money supply engineered by the Federal Reserve System. Later on in the semester we will analyze these periods in greater detail.

The second component of GDP is referred to as the **cyclical** or **transitory component of GDP (Y_c)**. It is not related to the long-run accumulation of capital stock and technology, but is more sensitive to short-run factors in business conditions, which are only temporary in nature. The prime factor associated with causing movements in Y_c is changes in the money supply. This relationship will be one of primary objectives of study later on in the semester.

Given the above descriptions, GDP (Y) can be written as:

$$Y = Y_n + Y_c \tag{3.1}$$

At any point in time, we may observe that Y, or the observed level of GDP represents the value of GDP currently produced. It is the job of an economist to decompose Y into its two, unobserved components: Y_n and Y_c. It should also be out that contractions could occur in *both* components of GDP. Many people claim that the 1973–75 recession saw a decline in Y_n while the 1981–82 decline was due to a fall in Y_c. This distinction will be a very important task that we will undertake later on in the semester.

Contractions in GDP are also called **recessions**. An extreme recession is referred to as a **depression**. The last depression the U.S. had was the Great Depression, which began in 1929 and lasted until 1934. During this historical economic downturn, almost 25% of the labor force was unemployed.

The first time Robert really understood the significance of the Great Depression was in 1972, during his senior year in college. He was still managing the Imperial where he met a 75-year-old tenant named Hank. Hank spent most of his life in New York City and was 32-years-old in 1929. When the Depression began, he was working in a clothing store selling men's pants and shirts. He lost his job in August of 1931 and did not find another job for almost two years. Robert was amazed at the stories Hank told about scavenging for food to help feed his parents. Hank recalled that the great depression was very unsettling because people did not know when it would end. Living in economic despair for several years definitely imposes serious burdens on families as well as psychological problems on the individual.

---

[1] Even though Robert is presenting movements in GDP in 1984, from an instructional perspective, the author has included the behavior GDP until the early 2000s.

A more general term that encompasses downturns in economic activity and the eventual expansion that ultimately follows is referred to as the **business cycle**. The business cycle describes the decline in economic activity, the eventual bottom of the decline, the start of the expansion out of the recession and the leveling of GDP back to its long-run trend.

The basic tools that we will use to analyze business cycles in the economy are an expanded version of supply and demand analysis.

3.2. Developing Some Macroeconomic Terminology

Gross Domestic Product (GDP): the total value of final goods and services produced and sold in the economy over a period of time. By final, we mean the product or service that is sold to the consumer.

The production process is broken up into many components before it reaches the final stage where the goods and services are sold to the consumer. Let us consider the production of an automobile. Careful inspection of the automobile-building process reveals many intermediate steps before the consumer can purchase the car. Raw materials such as steel, rubber, plastic and electronics have to be purchased by the automobile company, which are then used to produce the automobile. These intermediate steps, which involve the transactions of goods and services, are not counted in GDP figures. Consider the following table:

Table 3.1   Intermediate Expenditures for the Construction of an Automobile

Input	Cost
Steel	$5,000
Plastic	$2,000
Electronics	$10,000
Labor	$5,000
Profit	$3,000
Total	$25,000

This example assumes that the automobile company has to purchase the above inputs in order to construct the car. The final sale price of the car is $25,000, and this price reflects the costs associated with building the car. The purchase price of the car takes into account the costs of purchasing the steel, plastic, the electronics and the labor. There are two methods to calculate GDP. In the first method, one could add up all the purchases of the intermediate inputs, or the **value added**. In this case, it would equal $25,000. In the second method, one could just use the final sale price. Obviously, it is easier to just use the final price of the good. If we were to add up the sale price of all the intermediate purchases as well as the final price of the automobile, we would be counting the intermediate purchases twice. By just counting the value of all final goods sold (the automobile), we are counting all intermediate stages only once. As another example, when a retail store purchases clothes from a manufacturer, this purchase is not part of real GDP. The only transaction that contributes to GDP is the sale to the consumer who purchases the article of clothing for personal use.

GDP is calculated by adding up the value in dollars of all final goods and services that have been purchased by consumers. Unfortunately, this GDP figure leaves out some very important elements. All of us spend time throughout the year on housework. GDP figures do not take into account the value placed on the housework. This could be evaluated by determining how expensive it would be to hire someone to perform household chores.

3.2.1. Nominal GDP, Real GDP, the Price Level and the Inflation Rate

In order to understand the workings of the overall economy, it is necessary to define a series of terms: *Nominal GDP, Real GDP, the Price Level, and the Inflation Rate.* It is important to understand how these four variables are related to one another. To facilitate the understanding of these variables, we will join Rachel on one of her vacations to Bali.

It is 1975 and Rachel has just completed her third year of skiing at Park City. Rachel entered a number of freestyle contests over the last two seasons. In the mid-1970s, mogul skiing was the primary event in freestyle contests while aerials and ballet were still relatively new to the sport. Rachel was not very good at ballet or aerials but she could ski the bumps. Skiing in Utah also allowed her to ski powder on a regular basis. As she found out early, skiing ice or skiing powder was not very different. The idea is to never sit back on your skis.

From 1972–75, skiing was all that mattered to Rachel. She was often one of the first skiers on the lifts in morning and one of the last skiers coming down the mountain for the day. There were many young people that lived in Park City, and although all of them came to ski their devotion to the sport varied greatly. Rachel was one of the more obsessive skiers. The two people she skied with the most were her friends, Stephanie and Donna. Stephanie was studying to be a ski instructor, but had many days off to ski with Rachel. In fact, most of the people that were really into skiing became ski instructors or joined the ski patrol. Rachel was the exception as she chose to just ski.

During the last month of the season during her third year in Park City, Rachel was skiing down a steep mogul run and took a bad fall. Rachel did not get hurt physically, but she was definitely shaken up. Rachel realized that she had never been so scared as during the fall. Stephanie was skiing with her and said that the three or four cartwheels Rachel did during the fall were impressive. Rachel skied down to the bottom of the area after the fall. The next morning she dutifully got up to go skiing. That day, the difference was the memory of the fall. Rachel realized she was done skiing.

Rachel needed something else and she realized it was the newspaper business. She had virtually taken over the paper by the summer of 1975. Alamo Dave had decided that Park City was becoming too crowded. He could not handle the growth and was preparing to leave town for good. Alamo told Rachel that since she had done such a great job with the newspaper, that the entire operation was hers. By late 1975, Rachel had hired two news writers and a printer to run the printing press. Advertising space was a critical part of the paper. It was the primary source of revenue so Rachel spent a large percentage of her time making sure this was done right. She still loved to write and made sure she wrote all the editorials as well as approved all the stories. By the summer of 1976, the *Park City Times* had become well known in the state of Utah for penetrating editorials and the reporting of several scandals in the Park City Ski Corporation.

By September of 1977, Rachel realized that Park City was too small for her to reach her potential so she applied for a job with the *The Washington Post* in Washington D.C. After several interviews, she accepted a job on the economic news beat for the *The Washington Post*.

Rachel had one month before her first day at the *Post* and during that time, she decided to vacation in Bali in the South Pacific for three weeks. She arrived in Bali on November 1, 1977 and was planning to spend 21 days there. Instead of staying in a hotel, Rachel opted to rent a small bungalow so it would be easier to get to know the locals. Shortly after arriving, she met Weena, a 23 year-old local woman who quickly became a good friend. It was good fortune for Rachel that Weena was very active in swimming and all sorts of boating activities since that was a main reason Rachel was attracted to Bali. Rachel and Weena would spend the days snorkeling, kayaking, sailing, scuba diving and eating.

One day while they were sailing, Rachel noticed a distant island that she wanted to sail and eat lunch at. Weena warned that it was a very bad idea to visit that island because the Morlocks lived there and it was dangerous. Rachel was alarmed since the Morlocks were a product of centuries of evolution tied to the decay of human existence.

Weena confided in Rachel that her parents were considering running for mayor of their village. The incumbent mayor claimed that the village was prospering economically and that everyone in the village should be thankful for the strong local economy. However, Weena's parents had difficulty accepting this claim because many of their friends lived in poverty. Weena's parents needed to obtain the information that would either support or reject this claim.

As Rachel listened to Weena's concerns, she thought of her experiences with economics. She took her first economics class during her sophomore year and recalled all too vividly the boring subject matter as well as the dull professor who taught the class. Rachel had recently seen the movie "The Night of the Living Dead" and had thought that her economics professor should have played one of the living dead. Her next experience with economics took place in a writing class during her junior year. The required topic was to write about the impacts of an increase in minimum wage. Surprisingly, she enjoyed doing the research on this topic and found the analysis to be exciting. She earned an A in the class and afterward, started to look for economic stories to write about. She never took another economics class in college, but learned by reading newspapers, magazines and attending public talks on current economic issues.

Rachel realized that Weena was talking about understanding the difference between nominal and real GDP. Rachel could remember the specifics about the topic and realized that she would need to look at an economics textbook if she were to help Weena's parents. A smile came across Rachel's mouth as she realized that she was going to need her principles economics textbook, a book she initially hated. Rachel had a parents mail out her textbook to Bali.

After the book arrived in the mail, Rachel spent a great deal of time reading the chapter on GDP. Rachel discovered that specific information would be needed if an objective approach could be used to determine the economic strength of the town. The procedure was fairly straightforward since there were only two products produced in Weena's village: pineapples and kiwi fruit. Therefore, all the income earned in the village was due to selling these two products.

Table 3.2   GDP Calculations for 1976

	Quantity	Price	Total Revenue
Pineapples	2000 crates	$20/crate	$40,000
Kiwi Fruit	3000 crates	$10/crate	$30,000
GDP			$70,000

Table 3.3   GDP Calculations for 1977

	Quantity	Price	Total Revenue
Pineapples	1800 crates	$30/crate	$54,000
Kiwi Fruit	2800 crates	$20/crate	$56,000
GDP			$110,000

Rachel collected the following data from all the villagers that sold pineapples and kiwi fruit.

Rachel determined that in 1976, the village sold 2000 crates of pineapples at a price of $20 a crate. The village also sold 3000 crates of kiwi fruit at a price of $10 a crate.

The formula for nominal GDP is;

$$GDP = P_1Q_1 + P_2Q_2 + ... + P_nQ_n,$$

The variable n refers to the number of goods and services that are produced in an economy. For the U.S., n is in the millions, but in this village there are only two products. In fairness, Rachel offered the current mayor of the town access to all the information she collected. Rachel sat down with Weena's parents to examine the data while the mayor used his staff to analyze the data.

CALCULATIONS FOR NOMINAL GDP

The mayor made the following calculation for GDP: in the first row, we see that 2,000 crates of pineapples were sold in 1976 at the price of $20 per crate. Revenue for pineapples in 1976 is $40,000. By adding revenues for pineapples and kiwi fruit together ($70,000), we obtain a measure of GDP for 1976. For the year 1977, GDP is calculated to be $110,000.

The mayor then calculated the growth rate of GDP over the two years. The percentage increase is calculated by subtracting GDP in 1976 from GDP in 1977, and then dividing that value by GDP in 1976:

$$(110,000 - 70,000) / 70,000 = 0.57 \text{ or } 57\%$$

The mayor concluded that GDP increased by 57% from 1976 to 1977 and also stated that the average growth rate of GDP in the United States was about 3.5% per year. Therefore, our community is thriving compared to the decadent U.S., and his leadership is essential to the village.

It was time for Weena's mother's time to present her analysis. She was suspicious of the mayor's result because everyone knew he was sleazy. In addition, the textbook stressed that the figure computed by the mayor was referred to as **nominal GDP**, which can be a misleading indicator of economic wellbeing.

Nominal GDP: the dollar value of final goods and services produced over a given period of time. It is standard to use a year as the measure of time. Nominal GDP is measured using current prices.

CALCULATIONS FOR REAL GDP

Weena's mother presented the following: The two factors that cause nominal GDP to change are changes in the price of goods as well as change in the quantities of the goods sold. It is of interest to decompose the percentage change of nominal GDP into the percentage change in prices, and the percentage change in the actual output or the quantity of pineapples and kiwi fruit sold. The former is a measure of inflation whereas the latter is a measure of economic growth. It is the growth in real output that is the better measure of economic growth. This measure of economic growth is called **real GDP**.

Real GDP: measures the growth in nominal GDP that is strictly determined by the change in the production of goods and services. The impact of price changes is ignored or held constant.

In order to compute the value of real GDP for 1977, we have to evaluate the quantity of production in 1977 using 1976 prices. We use 1976 as the **base year**. The base year is a reference point for which to compare all other years. The choice of what year to use as the base year involves several issues, all of which are not relevant to the class (other than to say the choice of a base year is usually dependent on choosing a year that depicts stable economic growth). After selecting a base year, we then multiply 1976 prices by 1977 quantities. The logic of this approach is that we are not allowing prices to change for 1977 so we end up comparing the level of production over two years with the only difference being the change in production of the two goods.

The formula for real GDP is the following:

$$\text{Real GDP for 1977} = (\text{1977 quantity of pineapples}) \times (\text{1976 price})$$

$$+ (\text{1977 quantity of kiwi fruit}) \times (\text{1976 price})$$

$$(1800)(\$20) + (2800)(\$10) = \$64,000.00$$

$64000 is a measure of real GDP for 1977.

Weena's mother then presented the percentage in real GDP from 1976 to 1977.

$$(64,000 - 70,000)/70,000 = -0.08 \text{ or } -8\%$$

It was the case the real GDP actually fell from 1976 to 1977 by 8%. These results caused a tremendous reaction among the villagers as they realized that the village as a whole was worse off. It is important to point out for the base year that *nominal GDP exactly equals real GDP.*

DEFINITION AND CALCULATION OF THE PRICE LEVEL

Weena's parents also presented the change in the **price level** over this same period.

> ***Price Level:*** *the average price of goods and services at a given time*

In this example we could obtain a measure of the price level by simply averaging the price of pineapples and kiwi fruit. If we averaged these two prices, it implies that we are assigning equal weight or importance of each good in determining the price level. In this case, 1976 the price level would be 15 and the 1977 the price level would be 25.

However, taking a simple average is *not* correct. The above analysis ignores important aspects of our nominal GDP calculations. As an example, expenditures for pineapples in 1976 are $40,000 while expenditures for kiwi fruit is $30,000. It is obvious that pineapples play a larger role in Bali's economy and thus in determining nominal GDP. Therefore, pineapples should play a larger role in determining the price level than kiwi fruit.

In order to calculate the price level, we must first calculate the weight of each good to the economy.

The weights are determined by the following:

$$\text{Weight for pineapples} = \frac{\text{Total Revenue for pineapples}}{\text{GDP in base year}} = \frac{40000}{70000} = 57\%$$

$$\text{Weight for kiwi fruit} = \frac{\text{Total Revenue for kiwi fruit}}{\text{GDP in base year}} = \frac{30000}{70000} = 43\%$$

Average price level in 1976;

$$= (\text{Weight for pineapples x price of pineapples})$$

$$+ (\text{Weight for kiwi fruit} \times \text{price of kiwi fruit})$$

$$= (.57 \times 20) + (.43 \times 10) = \$15.70$$

Average price level in 1977 (use weights from base year);

$$= (.57 \times 30) + (.43 \times 20) = \$25.70$$

When we calculate price level for all years, we always use the base year weights multiplied by the prices for a given year. In our example, the 1976 base year weights are used to calculate the price level for 1977. In the U.S. economy, the base year weights are changed every three or four years. Due to the large number of items in the U.S. economy, it is too costly to compute the new weights each year. Only when the base year changes do the weights change.

DEFINITION AND CALCULATION OF THE INFLATION RATE

Weena's parents also presented the change in the **price level** over this same period.

Inflation rate: the percentage change in the price level

$$\text{Inflation rate} = \frac{1977 \text{ price} - 1976 \text{ price}}{\text{Average price in 1976}} = \frac{10}{15.70} = 63\%$$

Weena's parents compiled all this information and presented it to the villagers as her mother ran for mayor. They were able to explain to the villagers that the community was not growing at as fast a rate as the incumbent mayor claimed. The village was actually experiencing hardship. Weena's parents did point out that inflation was fairly high but before they could suggest a policy to combat it, they would have to do further reading in the textbook. They won the election.

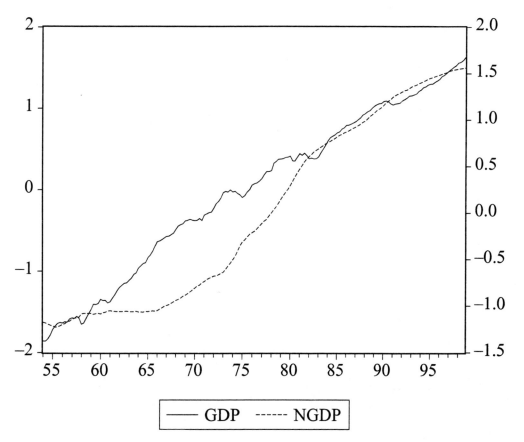

Figure 3.5 Real and Nominal GDP Movements from 1959 to 1992

Weena arranged a party for Rachel before her departure back to the United States. Weena thanked her for her friendship and her help. Rachel realized that she played the role of an economic advisor in the village. Rachel was now anxious to get back to Washington D.C. and start her career as an economic journalist. Oddly enough, economic news was becoming exciting to her and she looked forward to the people she would meet as well as the stories she would cover.

Figure 3.5 displays the behavior of real GDP and nominal GDP for the United States from 1954–1998. Inspecting these figures reveals that nominal GDP has been more stable or smoother over the years than real GDP. This is because nominal GDP is influenced by both quantity and price. During a recession, real GDP will fall, which will cause a departure of real GDP from its trend. However, during most recessions, there is still an upward movement in the price level. It has been the case in the U.S. economy that increases in the price level has been larger than downturns in real GDP. The consequence is that nominal GDP appears smoother over time because the price effect overwhelms the quantity effect. As an example, we can observe a decrease in real GDP during the 1973–75 period, but nominal GDP continued to grow during this period. Rising prices during this period were large enough to offset the decline in real GDP.

3.3. The Theory of Aggregate Demand

It is 1983 and Robert has been working at the Federal Reserve for six years and things had been going well. He was learning how to balance his time between two different aspects of his job. The first component was to write research papers. Economists that taught at universities and colleges wrote about economics from a more theoretical perspective, and did not typically have opportunity to interact with senators, members of congress and the executive branch. However, university economists and Fed economists were expected to publish their ideas in academic journals. Robert was fortunate enough to publish a number of papers in these journals. The other component of his job was to study real world problems and advise the policymakers on what policies should be implemented. The primary objective is to construct policies that result in promoting economic stability.

One of the current controversies was the cause of the 1981–82 recessions. On one particular day, Robert was answering a number of questions posed by the media. It was common for the journalist to mention their name before stating the question. As Robert motioned to a reporter in the back of the room, she said her name was Rachel. Rachel asked the following question:

> There is talk in academic circles that the Federal Reserve policy decisions to slow down the growth rate of the money supply was at least partially responsible for causing the 1981–82 recession. Is this true?

Robert was not happy given that the prior questions were pretty benign and required little effort to answer. But this question raised all the issues that were slowly becoming a concern of the Federal Reserve. It had to do with understanding the different components of aggregate demand. **Aggregate demand (AD)** is a concept that describes the different components that make up the demand for goods and services in the economy.

> **Aggregate Demand:** *Represents the total demand in the economy by households, firms, all levels of government and sales to countries around the world. In effect, the aggregate demand curve is just like any other demand curve, but represents the sum of total of all goods and services in an economy.*

3.3.1. Components of Aggregate Demand

There are five components that constitute aggregate demand. In order to understand each component, we should first look at the way aggregate demand is presented in an equation.

$$AD = C + I + G + M + EX \qquad (3.1)$$

AD is aggregate demand
C – consumption by households
I – investment by firms for factories, tools, computers, etc.
G – government expenditures
M – the money supply
EX – net exports

The aggregate demand schedule is drawn as the following:

As you recall, a standard demand curve for a particular good would have the price of that good on the vertical axis. The aggregate demand is drawn with the price level for the economy on the vertical axis since we are representing demand for all goods and services. On the horizontal axis, real GDP represents the amount of all goods and services consumed in the economy. The downward sloping shape of AD suggests that as the price level falls, all goods and services are becoming less expensive. Therefore, the quantity of aggregate demand will increase.

Referring back to Rachel's question, Robert realized that it was a common belief that the 1981–82 recession was caused by an inward shift of the aggregate demand curve. The controversy was which component was responsible for the inward shift. Robert considered exploring the potential role of a decline in consumption as the cause of the recession.

CONSUMPTION

Consumption: Captures money spent by individuals and households on goods and services. Consumption is a function of income that households have access to.

ECONOMIC PRINCIPLE

Consumption function: $C = f(Y)$

C = consumption

Y = income or real GDP

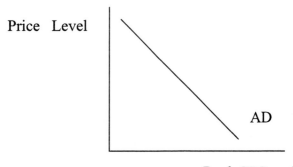

Figure 3.6 Aggregate Demand

The above relationship suggests that an increase in income allows the consumer to increase their expenditure on consumption goods. From the standpoint of the entire economy, C represents total consumption in the entire economy and Y is real GDP. The above relationship suggests that consumption decisions are based on current income.

However, it is often the case that when people make consumption decisions, they take into account what they will be spending in the future. As an example, many college students take out loans to pay for tuition, food and housing. The decision on the amount of money to borrow is influenced by the person's perception of what they believe they can afford to pay back in the future. Medical students typically borrow large sums of money because they expect to have a high income. Graduate students in English typically do not borrow large amounts of money because their expected future income is lower.

In this sense, the above relationship becomes more complicated since consumption decisions are not just contingent upon current income but are also influenced by what people expect to earn in the future. These issues can be examined by looking at Arthur when he was attempting to negotiate his first NBA contract during the summer of 1972. He decided to negotiate his own contract.

	Arthur's proposal	Team's proposal
1st year	$100,000.00	$ 40,000.00
2nd year	$150,000.00	$ 50,000.00
3rd year	$200,000.00	$375,000.00
	$450,000.00	$465,000.00

The first column is the contract offer that Arthur proposed to the NBA team. The size of the contract proposal is $450,000 over three years. The NBA team countered with a different contract amount in the second column. This offer is valued at $465,000 over the three years. Not having a business agent, Arthur goes home to ponder the two salary structures. Through simple addition, Arthur realizes that the team's offer is for $15,000 more than his proposal. Should he then take the counter offer? In order to determine which offer is better, Arthur must perform **present value analysis** of both proposals.

ECONOMIC PRINCIPLE

Present Value Analysis: *converts future sums of money into the value of the money in today's terms.*

Present Value analysis assumes that a dollar received today is worth more than a dollar received tomorrow. This is because a dollar received today could begin to earn interest if it was deposited in a bank. A dollar received in the future cannot earn interest until it is received. Another factor about why a dollar in the future is worth less than a dollar today is that the price level typically increases year to year, so a dollar in the future can buy a smaller amount of goods and services.

An example of the present value analysis is as follows:

If you put $100 in the bank today at an interest rate of 10%, over the year you will earn;

$$100 \times 0.1 = \$10.00 \text{ in interest income.}$$

At the end of one year the $100 has grown to a value of $110. From this we see a general formula:

$$P(1 + R) = FV.$$

Where

P = principle or the original amount of the deposit

R = interest rate

FV = future value

$$P(1 + R) = FV; \ 100(1 + 0.1) = 110$$

From above calculations we see that $100 will grow to $110 if it is invested in the bank for one year at an interest rate of 10%. From another perspective, we can ask what $110 to be received one year from now is worth at the present time. Formally, we are asking what is the present value of $110 to be received a year from now. The answer is found by solving our general formula for something called **present value (PV)**.

$$P(1 + R) = FV$$

$$P = \frac{FV}{(1 + R)}$$

Instead of using P as in the above formula, we could use PV, which represents present value. Therefore we write the formula as;

$$PV = \frac{FV}{(1 + R)}$$

The computation of present value is:

$$\$100 = \frac{\$110}{(1 + 0.1)}$$

If you are expecting to receive $110 one year from now at an interest rate of 10%, that $110 is worth $100 today. It is the case that PV represents the present value of the sum that will be received in the future.

What if you decided to save your $100 into the bank for two years?

$$P(1 + R)(1 + R) = P(1 + R)^2 = FV$$

$$100(1 + 0.1)(1 + 0.1) = \$121.00$$

We see that $100 will grow to $121 if it is invested in the bank for two years at an interest rate of 10 percent. From another perspective, we can ask what $121 that would be received two years from now is worth at the present time. The formula is

$$P(1 + R)^2 = FV$$

$$P = \frac{FV}{(1 + R)^2}$$

$$P = \frac{121}{(1 + .1)^2} = \$100$$

The general formula for determining the present value of a future income stream is

$$PV = I_0 + \frac{I_1}{(1+R)} + \frac{I_2}{(1+R)^2} + \frac{I_3}{(1+R)^3}$$

Where, I_1, I_2, I_3, represents income in consecutive years. I_0 represents income that is received today and I_1 is income that will be received a year from now, etc.

Arthur needs to use the above formula to determine which of the contract proposals has the highest present value. The computations are as follows:

Arthur's proposal calculated at an interest rate of 10 percent

$$PV = 100,000 + \frac{150,000}{(1+.1)} + \frac{200,000}{(1+.1)^2} = \$401,652$$

The team's proposal calculated at an interest rate of 10 percent.

$$PV = 40,000 + \frac{50,000}{(1+.1)} + \frac{375,000}{(1+.1)^2} = \$395,371$$

Much to Arthur's credit, he remembered something vaguely from his introductory economics class in college, so he dragged out his textbook and relearned the above formulas. Arthur realized that the present value of his salary proposal was higher, so through some clever negotiation, Arthur was able to obtain his proposal.

By using the above formulas, Arthur was able to derive a reliable approximation of the value of his income over the next several years. In this manner, Arthur could plan out his ability to consume over the next the three-year period.

An important aspect of the above analysis concerns the relationship between current income and expected future income. Economists maintain that expected future income is much more stable than current income. The reason for this claim is that the economy over time is relatively stable, but any given year could be subject to substantial swings in economic activity. However, over time those downturns are offset by upswings in economic activity, which results in perceptions of expected future income being relatively stable. Since economists maintain that consumption is influenced by expected future income, then consumption should be more stable than current real GDP.

Therefore, economists maintain that consumption should be written as:

$$C = f(Y^e),$$

$$\text{Where } Y^e = I_0 + \frac{I_1}{(1+R)} + \frac{I_2}{(1+R)^2} + ... + \frac{I_n}{(1+R)^n}$$

Y^e represent the present value of the expected life term earning stream. If there is a downturn in income for a year due to a recession in the economy, it will only have a minor impact on Y^e. The result will be that consumption will only change by a small amount, whereas, current income may change by a greater amount.

Inspecting Figure 3.7 supports this claim. Consumption is much more stable over time than is real GDP. It is not subject to the wide swings that real GDP is subject to. Therefore, when there are upturns and downturns in economic activity, households realize that these deviations are temporary. As an example, if there were an unusual increase in economic activity such that the average person's income increases above its long-run trend, this change would be viewed as temporary. The person is not going to go out and make a permanent

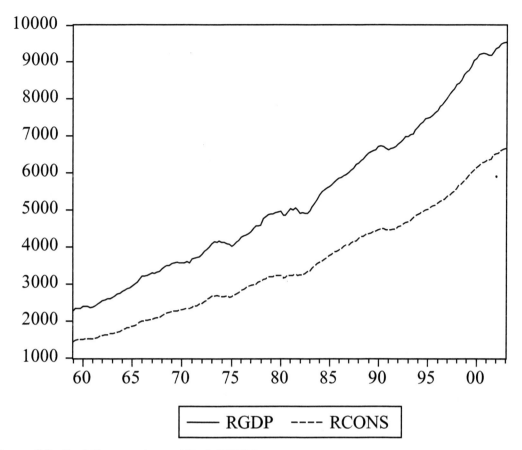

10000
9000
8000
7000
6000
5000
4000
3000
2000
1000

60   65   70   75   80   85   90   95   00

——— RGDP   ---- RCONS

Figure 3.7 Real Consumption and Real GDP Movements

change in their consumption behavior. Consumption may increase by a small amount but not by the full amount of the change in income. Inspecting Figure 3.7 once again reveals that the upturns and downturns in real GDP are much greater than movements in consumption. It appears that people average out large changes in income and believe that their expectations of expected income will not be influenced to any significant degree by temporary changes in real GDP.

The last time we visited with Arthur, it was 1972 and he had just negotiated a three-year contract with the NBA. All was going well for Arthur (he was averaging 15 points a game and 9 assists in his rookie season). However, near the end of 1973 things turned upside down for him – and all the other U.S. citizens – by an unexpected event in the Middle East. The OPEC nations rejected the setting of oil prices by the United States and implemented their own pricing scheme. Within a few months, oil prices skyrocketed by close to 50%. Since oil was a primary source of energy used in the U.S., costs of production increased across all markets in the United States economy and of course, so did the price level. The price of oil rose steadily until 1975 causing an increase in the inflation rate. Naturally, Arthur never anticipated OPEC's pricing scheme, especially the year prior to negotiating his salary contract. With the increased inflation rate (remember that inflation results in the reduction of the value of money), his contract had decreased in real value; the dollars Arthur was earning purchased less goods and services. When negotiating his salary, Arthur should have taken into account what the inflation rate was going to do over the length of his contract. He should have used the Fisher Equation to determine what the value of his money would be.

ECONOMIC PRINCIPLE

Fisher Equation: relates the nominal interest rate to the inflation rate.

$$R = r + \pi^e$$

R = nominal interest rate
π^e = expected inflation rate
r = real interest rate (the rate of return adjusted for inflation or the real purchasing power of one's money)

Typically, $r < R$
Example: Assume that $R = 4\%$ and that $\pi^e = 3\%$
$4\% = r + 3\%$ and $r = 1\%$

Since R does not take into account the impact of the inflation rate during the length of the contract, it is misleading. In the above example, the nominal interest rate of 4% represents the nominal return. However, a positive inflation rate will reduce the purchasing power of that return. By adjusting for inflation, the real interest rate represents the real value or purchasing power of the return. Arthur should have used r.
Instead of:

$$PV = I_0 + \frac{I_1}{(1+R)} + \frac{I_2}{(1+R)^2}$$

Arthur should have used:

$$PV = I_0 + \frac{I_1}{(1+r)} + \frac{I_2}{(1+r)^2}$$

By using r, Arthur would have adjusted for the rate of inflation and had a better estimate of the value of his contract. However, don't forget that π^e is an estimate. The best Arthur could do was predict the inflation rate and since he knew that predicting the future is difficult if not impossible, Arthur hired an agent who was able to accurately forecast the rate of inflation, and thus negotiate his second contract. Arthur learned quickly, albeit the hard way.

The above analysis indicates that having an accurate measure of expected inflation is important. Consider a bank that is willing to lend money to a firm, with an ideal real-rate of return of 5%. This implies that if the expected inflation rate over the length of the loan is 3%, the bank has to charge a nominal interest rate of 8%. Suppose the loan is made at a nominal interest rate of 8%. During the loan period, suppose the inflation rate unexpectedly increased to 6%. The real interest rate or the real rate of return would decrease to 2%. In this example, the bank is worse off. Likewise, the borrower is better off since they will be paying back money that can purchase a smaller amount of goods and services. The real cost of borrowing the money has gone down.

As Robert considered exploring the role of consumption as the cause of the 1981–82 recessions, he realized that most economists did not believe that there was a downturn in expected income. Therefore, consumption was most likely not the cause of this recession. Robert thought about investment.

INVESTMENT

Investment: Expenditures made by businesses for factories, machinery, tools, computers, etc.

It is 1985, and Knowledge Inc. has been very successful, but the market is changing. Any advantage Maria had in the early 1980s in terms of producing the high- quality computers was quickly disappearing. Large companies such as IBM were quickly gaining ground on small companies in their ability to produce high-quality computers. Most computer companies had finally mastered the current level of technology, so the early advantages that Maria had were gone. She had made millions of dollars, but it was time to get out of the computer-building business.

Maria had some expertise in developing software programs, and she decided to specialize in this side of the business. Unfortunately, she had to layoff a number of her employees that did not have skills in developing computer programs and had to hire people that could help her develop software. It was hard to say goodbye to many of her employees, but it was no longer possible to profitably produce computers.

As Maria started to organize this new endeavor, a journalist (Rachel) from *The Washington Post* asked Maria what it was like to be the only female entrepreneur in the computer business. This journalist raised some issues that had plagued Maria for many years. During her undergraduate years at Colorado State University (CSU), she was the only female undergraduate in the electrical engineering department and all the professors in the department were male. It was something that always bothered her, but there was nothing she could do about it until now. Rachel wanted to interview Maria for part of her story since Knowledge Inc. was one of the top computer companies in the early 1980s.

They spoke for many hours during which Rachel told Maria that she had interviewed a group of women in New York City that were attempting to create a small women's college. It would emphasize mathematics, science and engineering. Maria was intrigued with this prospect and contacted the group. After several phone conversations, Maria traveled to New York to take a close look at the enterprise. The women were very excited to have Maria since she was an engineer, an entrepreneur and had money. Millions of dollars had already been raised, but more money was still needed. Maria spent a week in New York then went back to Boston to consider her next step.

Maria was considering two business ventures. The first was to allocate most of her time writing software and making large inroads into the software business. She was confident that the future for computer software was astronomical. However, being involved in starting a college that emphasized the technical training of women was also a very exciting prospect. The only problem with the college was that any monetary return would be was a distant thing and could possibly not happen at all. Maria was at a crossroads in her life. The software company was a good prospect in terms of making money, but the college idea represented something more important. Maria chose to scale back her software business and allocated almost half of her resources to help develop the women's college.

A year later, Maria's software business was doing very well and she was faced with what to do with her profits from the software business. She was thinking about building a larger facility with the gains. A friend of hers owned an athletic shoe company called Kober and was considering opening up a factory in South Korea, where labor costs were much lower than in the U.S. Her friend needed additional resources to help open the factory and asked Maria if she wanted in as a partner. Maria only had enough money for one of the projects. What criteria should Maria use to decide between the two ideas? Maria must forecast the potential rates of return of the two investment projects. In addition, she has to take into account the difficulty of operating each endeavor in terms of time commitment, hiring and firing workers, etc. Maria has to estimate the economic returns of building a larger facility to write software programs compared to a factory in South Korea that would sell footwear.

ECONOMIC PRINCIPLE

Marginal productivity of capital (MP$_K$): *measures the increase in output due to the addition of one more unit of capital.*

The marginal productivity of capital is a downward sloping curve as shown in Figure 3.8. The curve is downward sloping for a similar reason that the supply curve is upward sloping and for the same reason the production possibility frontier is bowed outward. As additions to the capital stock are made (the factory becomes larger), it becomes more difficult to coordinate and manage a larger facility. Therefore, output increases, but at a decreasing rate. Make sure that you understand the connection between the law of increasing cost, the upward sloping supply schedule, and the downward sloping MP$_K$ curve. Maria is needs to estimate the MP$_K$ for both projects. Consider Figure 3.9.

After careful research, Maria determined the marginal productivity schedule for the factory in South Korea is represented by MP$_{KF}$ and the marginal productivity schedule for the software expansion is MP$_{KS}$. Her analysis indicates that the rate of return should be higher for the software expansion, so Maria decided to not get involved in the athletic shoe business.

Her next decision was to decide how large of an expansion to the software factory she should make. To help with the decision, she compared the rate of return of different sizes of the factory to another investment opportunity that carried almost no risk, such as government bonds. It is common for the federal government to borrow money from its citizens to help pay for the deficit. The government offers a rate of return that makes it attractive for people to loan money to the government. The government guarantees the safety of these loans so Maria knows that if she lends a certain amount of money to the government, she will be paid back.

To determine the optimal size of the factory, Maria uses the rate of return for government bonds, a safe investment. Let this return be R$_G$, which is the opportunity cost of the money that Maria is investing in the software factory. Inserting the return on government bonds with the MPK results in the following:

It pays to invest in a store the size of K$_1$ since the return is greater than the opportunity cost R$_G$. It also pays to invest in a building the size of K$_2$ for the same reason as the size 0K$_1$. However, investing in a store the size of K$_4$ does *not* make sense because the rate of return when increasing the capital stock from K$_3$ to K$_4$ is the area K$_3$K$_4$AB. The rate of return on the government bond for the same resources is the area K$_3$K$_4$CB. Going beyond K$_3$ implies that the

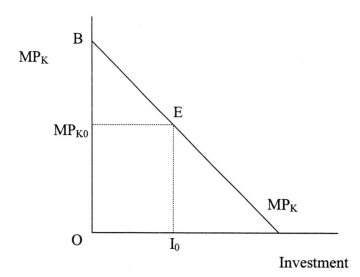

Figure 3.8 Marginal Productivity of Capital

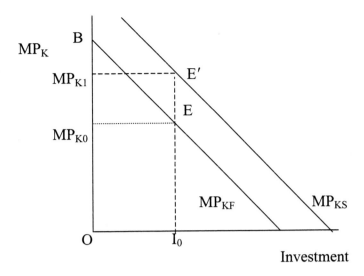

Figure 3.9 Marginal Productivity of Capital for the two projects

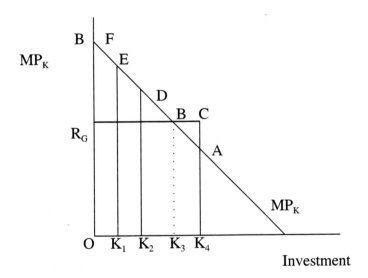

Figure 3.10 Government Bond and MPK

opportunity cost of the investment is greater than the return on the investment. The optimal level of investment is K_3. The decision rule is to invest up to the point where the MPK = R_G.

More generally, all firms, whether small or large, go through the same basic process when deciding on how large a capital stock to employ. The demand for investment schedule for the entire economy looks identical to the one that Maria faced.

The real interest rate, r, and the marginal productivity of capital, MPK are the primary determinants of investment in the economy. Expectations of the MPK are influenced by a larger number of factors such as expected demand, competition, population growth, etc. We have now explored the primary factors that influence investment (I), one of the components of aggregate demand.

Historically, investment has been a volatile component of economic activity. Figure 3.10 presents investment and real GDP from 1960–1990. One can see that investment is much more cyclical than real GDP. Economists maintain that 75% of all business cycles are due to movements in investment.

Robert decided not to go into the theory of investment because most economists did not believe that a slowdown in investment was the cause of the recession.

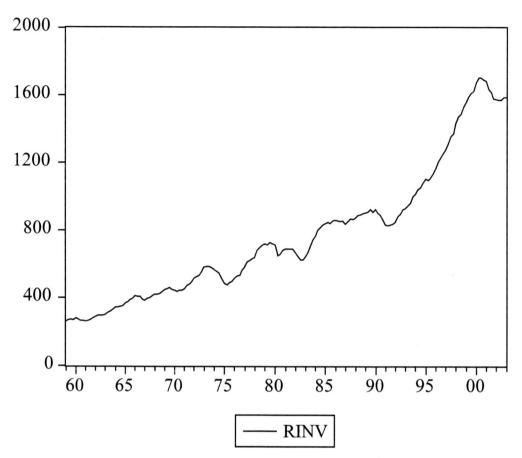

Figure 3.11   Real Investment

Robert then considered the role of the Federal Reserve, government expenditures or exports as possible causes of the recession, but realized that it would be difficult to justify such an argument. He realized that he needed to address the money supply. This reporter could be a pain in the neck.

MONEY SUPPLY

Another component of aggregate demand is money supply. **Money supply** can be defined in two ways:

$$M1 = currency + demand \ deposits$$

Currency—the amount of paper currency and coins that are currently circulating in the economy
Demand deposits—the amount of money that is currently contained in all checking accounts in the economy

The above definition is for the money supply referred to as M1. There are broader measures of the money supply such as M2.

$$M2 = M1 + time \ deposits$$

Time deposits—refer to deposits made to savings accounts. This measure of money is tied to savings decisions for retirement and/or purchases anticipated to make in the future.

Our objective is two fold. First we need to understand how the Fed manages the growth rate of the money supply. The second is to examine how the growth rate of the money supply is used to promote economic stability. **Stability** is defined as stable economic growth for real GDP and a low inflation rate.

Federal Reserve Mechanisms for Controlling the Money Supply

Late in the 1980s, Maria's software business was proving to be very profitable. Her thoughts wandered back to her time as a child in Las Cruces where her business ventures started. Maria decided she wanted to go back home and help generate economic activity in order to bring higher paying jobs to her home town. She started an investment house where people could invest their money in her business and she would guarantee a minimum rate of return on that investment. How could Maria make such a guarantee? Maria knew that she could take that money and loan it to local businesses that were already successful and wanting to expand. In addition, Maria could loan money to people who wanted to purchase a home. Maria saw the value in collecting large sums of money from the inhabitants of Las Cruces and then loaning these funds out to the private sector. Maria decided to open a bank.

First, Maria guaranteed some interest rate or rate of return to the people who were interested in depositing money with her. Maria offered the interest rate of R_M. In 1984, when Maria was setting up her bank, R_M was equal to approximately five percent. Maria would provide loans to selected local businesses and potential homeowners at an interest rate of R_L, with

$$R_M < R_L.$$

The difference between R_L and R_M represented the rate of return that Maria charged to bring lenders and borrowers together. This difference in these interest rates was the rate of return that Maria charged for performing this service.

In order for Maria to be a clearinghouse for money and to be able to meet the guaranteed rate of return she promised to investors, she had to make wise loans, i.e., the owners of the businesses to whom she lent money were people certain to pay back their loans in a timely manner.

With this new investment opportunity, Maria thought it was a good idea to establish a check-writing policy for the people who were willing to invest their money in her bank. In other words, the people who were willing to invest money with her could write checks at any time to spend their money. The question Maria faced, however, was how much money did she need to keep on hand in order to satisfy the check writers' needs for ready cash for any given deposit? Maria knew that people would continually write checks that Maria had to honor. Any amount of the deposit that did not have to be kept on hand could then be loaned out.

Maria contacted Robert to get some guidance on the finer points of running a bank and the role the Fed plays in monitoring bank activities around the country. Robert referred her to the people who managed the commercial banking system. Maria learned that the required reserve ratio around the country was between 10 and 20%. She found out that the Fed actually has guidelines on the minimum amount of reserves that a bank has to hold for every dollar of deposits. The percentage required by the Fed is 20%. Let us call this percentage, the **required reserve ratio (rr)**. In other words, if $1,000 was deposited in her bank, Maria would have to keep 20% of deposit in the bank at all times to meet daily transactional needs of the depositor. Maria could then loan out the remaining 80% of the deposit. Let's look at a simple T-account to see what this means. Maria's neighbor opened a checking account at the bank. In it she deposited $1,000.

Assets	Liabilities
RR $200 ER $800	$1,000 DD

Assets: the wealth or money obtained by the bank.
Liabilities: the money deposited in the bank, which the bank has the responsibility to pay back to the depositor.
DD (demand deposit): A demand deposit is the deposit made by the individual (depositor). At anytime a depositor has the right to withdraw the money he or she placed in the bank. This is commonly referred to as checking account.
RR (required reserves): that amount of deposits that must be kept on hand at the bank to meet daily transactional needs.
ER (excess reserves): that amount of the deposits that the bank can loan out to potential borrowers such as families and firms. Families will borrow money to purchase a house and firms will borrow money to expand their business.

Of that $1,000, Maria must keep $200 on hand in the bank. She can lend out $800. After reviewing loan applications, Maria decided to lend the $800 to Thomas, the local car mechanic, for the purchase of some new tools. Instead of having $800 in excess reserves, the bank now has $800 in loans under assets. This is seen in the T-account below.

Assets	Liabilities
RR $200 Loans $800	$1000 DD

Thomas purchases $800 of equipment from Rosa's mechanical tool shop and she deposits the $800 in her bank. Of that $800, $160 must be kept as required reserves and $640 can be loaned out. The T-account looks like this:

Assets	Liabilities
RR $160 ER $640	$800 DD

The $640 can be loaned out to another small business. Suppose the business uses this money to purchase inventories that it wishes to sell in the future. The firm that sold the inventories will deposit the $640 in their bank and the T-account will look like the following:

Assets	Liabilities
RR $128 ER $512	$640 DD

The loan process continues until there is no money left. The expansionary process is determined by the **money multiplier (mm)**.

$$mm = 1/rr$$
$$1/0.2 = 5$$

Where rr represents the required reserve ratio, which in this case is 20% or 0.2. This implies that the original deposit of $1,000 will grow to $1,000 x 5 = $5,000. From another perspective, the amount of deposits grows in the following manner:

$$\$1,000 + \$800 + \$640 + \$512 + ... = \$5,000$$

We can see that the stability of Maria's bank, as well as all banks in our country, depends upon everyone not withdrawing all their money at the same time. If this occurred, the banks would have to call in all their loans, which could be very difficult and costly.

Maria was intrigued with the potential instability inherent in the banking system. Maria asked Robert about it and he informed her that in our history there have been several occasions when there was a banking panic and large numbers of people did attempt to withdraw their money. The most recent example of this was during the Great Depression in the early 1930s. With large numbers of people attempting to withdraw their money from banks across the country, the banking community was unable to honor all these withdrawals simultaneously. President Roosevelt, in reaction to this panic, closed all the banks in the country for several days. The "banking holiday" was used to quiet people's concerns about the stability of the banking system. President Roosevelt was successful in relieving people's concerns, and the banking system survived. Fortunately, large-scale banking panics are almost nonexistent in our country today.

How does the Federal Reserve use the banking system to influence the supply of money in our economy? The Fed primarily uses a technique called **open market operations**. To explain, consider the following T-account for a given bank.

Assets	Liabilities
RR $20,000	$100,000 DD
ER $80,000	

This bank has the ability to loan out $80,000, which will grow into demand deposits of an additional $400,000. If the Fed does not wish for these loans to occur, they can chose to borrow the money from the bank. The Fed sells the bank a bond or a security. This is referred to as an **open market sale** of securities or bonds. The bank is required by law to enter into this transaction with the Fed. The Fed, in turn, offers a rate of return on this bond, which we assume is for one year and after that year, the Fed will pay the bank back the $80,000 plus interest on the $80,000. This transaction prevents the expansionary process from occurring because when the Fed deposits the money in their account; they do not let it circulate. The bank's T-account now looks like the following:

Assets	Liabilities
RR $20,000	$100,000 DD
Bond $80,000	

The bank is unable to loan out the $80,000 to the private sector. When the Federal Reserve sells securities, it reduces the supply of money.

Suppose that six months later, the Fed wants to increase the supply of money to help stimulate economic growth. This is accomplished by buying back the securities from the bank, a transaction referred to as an **open market purchase**. The Fed will offer the bank the $80,000 plus all the interest the bond would have earned over the year, but six months early. This is an excellent opportunity for the bank to get $80,000 and all the interest income. The bank can then loan this money out and the money multiplier process will continue. Where does the Fed obtain the money to pay for the interest on the $80,000? The Fed controls the printing presses to produce new ones, fives, tens, twenties, etc.

The Federal Reserve can also influence the money supply by using the **discount window**. Using this method, the Federal Reserve can loan money to the banks at the interest rate called the **discount rate**. We will refer to this interest rate as R_D. It is the case that $R_D < R_M$. As an example, Maria's bank is permitted to borrow money from the Federal Reserve and then turn around and lend it out at a higher interest rate. If the Federal Reserve wants the money supply to rise, they lower R_D. If they want the money supply to fall, then the Federal Reserve raises the discount rate. Consider Maria's Bank's T-account.

Assets	Liabilities
RR $200	$1,000 DD
Loan $800	

Maria's bank has no excess reserves to loan out. Suppose a customer, Johnny Cool, enters the bank and proposes that the community needs a skateboard shop. Having never heard of a skateboard, Maria asked a variety of questions, and became convinced that this could be a profitable endeavor. Realizing that she had no excess reserves to loan out, Maria borrowed the money from the Federal Reserve at the interest rate R_D and then loaned the money to Johnny Cool at the interest rate R_M. The expansionary process would work exactly as before.

As we outlined in the last section, the banking system's survival depends on confidence in the system. If everyone simultaneously decided to withdraw his or her money, the banking system would collapse.

The Federal Reserve monitors the behavior of the banks across the country to ensure that banks make loans that are relatively secure and do not compromise the safety of the deposits. The Federal Reserve uses knowledge of the expansionary loan process to control the supply of money in the economy. The money supply can be represented as the following:

$$M1 = mm \times B$$

M1 = currency and demand deposits
mm = money multiplier = 1 / rr
B = the monetary base = currency plus reserves held by banks

The Federal Reserve can control the amount of the monetary base by using either open market operations or changes in the discount rate. Using the required reserve ratio of .2 implies that if the Federal Reserve increases the monetary base by $100,000 (purchasing securities), the money supply will rise by $500,000.

To summarize the above discussion, consider the following T-account:

Assets	Liabilities
RR	DD
ER	
Loans	
Securities	

At any point in time, a bank will have their assets divided into four components. The Federal Reserve requires the bank to have a certain amount of required reserves (RR). The bank will also have excess reserves (ER), which can be either loaned out or held as emergency funds. ER can be used when the bank has an unexpectedly large number of withdrawls, and their RR fall below the minimum. If the bank has ER on hand, they will not fall below the minimum level of reserves mandated by the Federal Reserve. In addition, banks will also have a certain amount of loans lent out to their customers and a particular amount of securities that have been purchased from the Federal Reserve. Over time, the assets of the bank will move into the four different categories.

Robert thought long and hard on how to answer this reporter's question. He could talk about a reduction in the money supply causing a decrease in output, which was becoming a popular view as the cause of the 1981–82 recessions. It could be complicated if she was aggressive.

Robert's thoughts wandered over to **government spending.** This includes all expenditures made by the federal government. Examples of government spending include: salaries to government employees, defense spending, welfare, social security programs and foreign aid. Robert realized that a reduction in federal government expenditures was not a remote explanation for the cause of the 1981–82 recessions.

Robert was getting desperate. He considered the **international market**. U.S. companies sell a significant amount of their output to countries around the world. Farmers sell wheat worldwide and much of our manufactured goods are also sold around the world. These sales are referred to as **exports**. Unfortunately, there was not a significant reduction in exports in the late 1970s and early 1980s to explain why the aggregate demand curve shifted inward and caused the 1981–82 recession.

The other aspect of the international market is when U.S. citizens purchase goods that are produced outside of the U.S. For example, people can purchase foreign-made cars or clothes. This is referred to as **imports**. As U.S. citizens purchase more foreign made goods, it shifts the aggregate demand curve and can hurt the U.S. economy. Again, Robert realized that an increase in imports had not occurred to the extent that one could argue it caused the 1981–82 recession.

Robert was getting tired and frustrated. He had just reviewed all the components of aggregate demand*: consumption, investment, the money supply, government expenditures and the exports and imports.* He did not want to discuss the role of monetary policy as a potential cause of the 1981–82 recession. Robert could see that all the reporters were getting bored except Rachel whose eyes only seemed more intent on discussing the role the Fed had in the recession. Robert took a bold chance. He told Rachel that he was tired and if she was interested in discussing her question or anything else, how about it over dinner. Rachel thought about it for a few seconds and said sure. The rest of the reporters in the group realized that the briefing was over. Robert and Rachel went to dinner.

Maria's software company did well over the late 1980s. With the continued growth in the computer industry, the demand for new and innovative software was strong. Maria decided that trying to compete in the word processing market was not worth it. The spreadsheet market, on the other hand, was virtually untapped. She had been using a simple spreadsheet program for almost 10 years while she ran her businesses. Oddly enough, the spreadsheet was still not popular by the mid-1980s. Maria allocated most of her resources in this area and was very successful. She also worked on a graphics program that could produce charts and figures.

Maria also invested in real estate all over the country. She went into partnership with a number of investors to expand the mall in Las Cruces. It was important to her to give back to her hometown, and it was especially fun to invest money in the expansion of a mall. She recalled when she sold chocolate chip cookies to the construction workers who built the foundation of the mall almost 30 years ago. Maria also got involved in some real estate deals with Dale in Boston. By the early 1990s, Maria owned several apartment buildings in the Boston area.

The Women's College of New York was doing well. By 1992, the average entering freshman class was 150 young women. The graduating class of 1992 produced 30 engineers, and 90 students who went to graduate school in medicine, engineering and mathematics.

Maria also taught one class a year. She lectured on how to combine technical skills with entrepreneurial endeavors. Almost half the student population would do some type of internship at one of Maria's companies before they graduated.

Robert was still at the Federal Reserve in the early 1990s. By then he was on the personal staff of the Chairman of the Federal Reserve. Robert was directly involved with all major changes in Federal Reserve policy. He also took several one-year positions at different universities around the country. It was good to get out of D.C. every three years or so. The Federal Reserve encouraged their economists to take leaves from the bank and teach and do research. Robert spent a year at the University of Washington, the University of California at San Diego and at the University of Michigan. Robert loved the university life, but the excitement of being directly involved with economic policy was too much of a draw to give it up. Robert realized that working at the Federal Reserve was the job for him.

In 1985, Robert bought an old brownstone in Georgetown, which was desperately in need of repair. Over the years, he repaired sewage problems, put down an oak floor, tore down walls and, in the end, had remodeled almost the entire building. His home became an outlet; while he was hammering and hanging sheet rock, he forgot about his day job. His parents would visit once a year as his dad started to appreciate the wonder of D.C. During one visit, his dad commented on all the work Robert had done on the house.

"As I recall, whenever I made you do plumbing, electrical work or concrete work, you would complain. In fact, when you were 15-years-old, I was pretty much convinced that this type of work was not for you, and your mom and I decided to not have you do any more of it," Robert's dad said. Robert was shocked that his parents had contemplated such a change and he said that he was glad they made him do that work. His Dad said that the reason he didn't let up on Robert was that he needed the work done and he could not have done it by himself.

Robert became friends with Rachel over the years. He loved the Park City stories she would relay. Robert also maintained his friendship with Maria and Arthur. Maria would always complain that Federal Reserve monetary policy was hurting her businesses. Robert told her that it was good for business in the long run.

Arthur stopped playing basketball in 1980 and became more involved with Knowledge Inc. As we established earlier, Maria never liked the limelight so Arthur would represent the company in most public sessions. He learned some of the computer jargon and became fairly knowledgeable about computers at a basic level. The technical side, contrastingly, really bored him.

Arthur's parents were continually amazed at his good fortune. From NBA basketball player to vice-president of a major computer company, Arthur seemed to just float through life.

By 1987, Arthur started to become restless and was looking for a new opportunity. Maria's business ventures were getting old although they were usually successful. He needed something else. He was visiting his alma mater, the State University of California (SUC) and was talking to his basketball coach, Coach Gooden, who was still at the school. Coach Gooden surprised him by asking if he was interested in coaching at SUC. Arthur was immediately interested. His coach then stated that the coaching job was with the women's program and not the men's team. His coach said that the women's team needed a Head Coach. At first Arthur was not impressed since the few women's games he had seen at the college-level were not very good nor was the level of athleticism. Coach Gooden realized that Arthur was not impressed by the offer, but he continued to encourage Arthur anyway.

Coach Gooden told Arthur that there is more here than meets the eye. "Do you remember, Arthur that you used to complain that most of your teammates at the college and even at the pro level didn't think enough about how to play correctly? They depended on their athletic ability and forgot about the fundamentals of basketball," Coach Gooden said. Arthur did recall that his dissatisfaction with teammates was frustrating. Coach Gooden told Arthur that the women play a different type of ball than the guys; it was the type of ball you played in college and the pros. The women really understood the game of basketball. They were very coach-able. They want to learn and they really enjoyed playing as a team. Coach Gooden told Arthur that four of the players were in the gym shooting around right now and that he should have a look.

Arthur went to the gym and started to watch a pickup game of two-on-two. Arthur was surprised at the ball-handling skills and two of the players had nice perimeter shots. Arthur watched the women play for about 20 minutes before he went over to introduce himself. They all knew who he was since Arthur held many basketball records at SUC. Coach Gooden observed as Arthur starting working on some shooting drills and ball handling drills he learned with the Celtics. Arthur was impressed for two reasons. First, the players actually listened, and second, they mastered the drills quickly.

An hour later, Arthur walked into the Coach's office. Arthur said that he was interested in the head coaching job. Coach Gooden said the job was his. Coach Gooden said that the level of support for the women's team was only 25% of what the men were allocated. There were a few programs around the country that took women's basketball seriously: the University of Tennessee, the University of Georgia and the University of Connecticut. As Arthur found out, the attendance for women's games was very low and the program was not well funded. Coach Gooden showed Arthur to his new office and it was obvious that his office was not as nice as Gooden's office, but he would deal with that later.

Rachel showed up in D.C. in 1977 and by 1990, she was one of the top economic journalists for the *Post*. She traveled all around the world reporting on economic happenings. She still owned the Park City Times, but did not have much time to monitor it. Rachel loved traveling and always made sure to stop off in any tropical environment to sail, scuba or snorkel.

Rachel also got involved with the Women's College of New York (WCNY). She was able to convince the executive committee to develop a journalism department for the school. As it turned out, just having math, science and engineering was not broad enough. Rachel became one of the most prominent spokespersons for the college. She was active on the admissions board and she often met with young women from all over the country and even the world to find them spots at WCNY. Rachel and Maria became very good friends. They both spent a lot of time working with the young women at WCNY as well as continually monitoring the quality of the school.

Rachel emphasized to Maria that all the students at WCNY needed strong writing skills. Computer, science and math skills were important, but these students needed to know how to write. Maria agreed, and all graduates were required to take a freshman, sophomore, junior and senior-level class in writing.

3.4. Theory of Aggregate Supply

This section is best presented in conjunction with Robert's early experiences in graduate school. The first semester of the program, all students took a microeconomics, macroeconomics and a statistics class. For the second semester, students took a second class in microeconomics and macroeconomics, and took the first class in econometrics. Robert found these classes to be very difficult and quite often would be up well past midnight studying. Each class required at least three problem sets per semester and his professors often gave the students two to three weeks to complete one problem set. Groups of graduate students would work together to complete each set. The only two activities that kept Robert sane during that first year was fixing plumbing, electrical and other problems with the Imperial apartment building, and playing pick-up basketball games. Sometimes, while he worked on a problem set or studied for an exam, Robert would wish for a phone call from Dale telling him that he needed to fix something.

At the end of the first year, all of the students who wanted to stay on track in the Ph.D. program studied for the microeconomics and macroeconomics theory exam. Each exam was six hours in length and would be given a week before the fall semester during the students' second year. Students were expected to study the entire summer for the two exams. As the exam dates crept nearer, Robert's stress level started to rise and he realized that it was critical that he passed both exams. If a student failed one or both of the exams, the next scheduled attempt was in January of the following year. Robert knew that if he failed an exam, he would have to study again during the upcoming semester as well as take three new classes.

Two weeks after Robert and his peers took the two exams, the results were released. Robert failed both exams. Needless to say, he was despondent over his inability to pass the exams. To make matters worse, he was the only student in the first-year group that did not pass at least one of the exams. As Robert navigated through his third semester in graduate school, he struggled with the new set of classes he was taking and the thought that he would have to take the microeconomics and macroeconomics theory exams over again. By the middle of November in his third semester (1973), Robert had his first economic epiphany. Between the three classes he was taking and his preparation for the macroeconomics and microeconomics theory exams, the fundamentals of economic analysis were becoming clear to him. Regardless of whether he was studying macroeconomics, microeconomics, international economics or econometrics, the approach was the same: all economic agents (firms and consumers) were assumed to make decisions that were always in their best interest. Although it was a simple idea, it was the fundamental aspect of economic analysis.

Robert did well on his final exams for the Fall 1973 semester and also passed the microeconomics and macroeconomics theory exams in January 1974. He was starting to figure it out. Robert had to take classes for another year and take two more major exams. He completed all his class requirements by August of 1975 and was now ready to start the most demanding part of the program: a dissertation, which involved doing original research. Robert had to develop some unprecedented ideas that would contribute to the body of economic analysis. Robert's primary interest was macroeconomics and he wanted to pursue a topic in this area.

While Robert was trying to figure out a topic and determine what professor would direct his dissertation, he was approached by a professor in his department who wanted Robert to get involved in a research project that was going to explore a new macroeconomic model developed in 1973 by an economist named Robert Lucas. Lucas published a paper in 1973 in the top economic journal called the *American Economic Review*. In that paper, Lucas had developed a new mathematical approach to studying business cycles. Robert's initial task was to completely understand the Lucas paper, which required Robert to reproduce all the mathematics used by Lucas. It took Robert two months of steady work to solve out the model in the Lucas paper.

Robert's next task was to construct a graphical representation of the Lucas model. Lucas's critical contribution was the development of macroeconomic supply curve. Fortunately, the theory of aggregate demand had already been developed so this task only related to supply. In one sense, the new curve was similar to the typical market supply curve, but there were two components. The first component was called the **Long-Run Aggregate Supply (LRAS) curve** and it represented long-run growth in the economy. This curve emphasized factors such as technology and population, which had *permanent* effects in the economy. The notion of long-run equilibrium was associated with this idea. The second component was called the **Short-Run Aggregate Supply (SRAS)** curve and it represented *temporary* movements in the economy. The concept of a short-run equilibrium was associated with this curve. These two supply curves, along with the aggregate demand curve, would solve out for the price level and real GDP.

As Robert considered how to graph these ideas, the lead professor of the project told Robert that he had to also develop the labor market along with the market for real GDP. The labor market determined the level of employment in the economy as well as the wage paid to workers. The problem was how to integrate the labor and output markets into one cohesive story.

The connection to both markets was the concept of the long-run and the short-run. Lucas initially decomposed output or real GDP into the following two parts:

$$Y = Y_n + Y_c$$

From the supply side, it is common to divide GDP into factors that cause permanent changes in real GDP and the factors that cause temporary changes in real GDP. The permanent component of real GDP is referred to as the **natural level of output (NLO or Y_n).** You may recall from Figure 3.3 that real GDP had an upward trend, and Y_n represents that trend. It is argued that growth in technology and population is the primary reason for the upward trends in GDP over time. There is also some cyclical variation around the trend, which is referred'to as the **cyclical component of real GDP (Y_c).** This represents variations of output around Y_n. The variations are due to temporary shocks, which typically emanate from the aggregate demand side of the economy. This is an important point that we will elaborate on below.

When the economy is operating at the NLO, the economy is in **long-run equilibrium** and $Y_c = 0$. Long-run equilibrium implies that consumer surplus across all markets is maximized, and that profits across all sectors are also maximized. From a microeconomic perspective, all markets such as computers, apples, shoes, cement, etc. would have to be in equilibrium. When we covered supply and demand analysis, it was stated that markets are not always in equilibrium, but have a tendency to always be moving toward equilibrium. Long-run equilibrium suggests that all of these markets are either in equilibrium or moving toward equilibrium.

The macroeconomic perspective on long-run equilibrium does not look at individual markets, but instead at the sum of all markets, which is referred to as real GDP. We refer to long-run equilibrium when the economy is at the natural level of output.

The economy will also experience shocks to the aggregate demand curve that will cause output to deviate from the NLO. In this case, $Y_c \neq 0$; however, the economy would then be in a state of **short-run equilibrium**. It was necessary for Robert to capture these concepts in a graphical framework.

Robert started by introducing the following productions function:

$$Y = f(K, L, T)$$

As you recall from earlier in the semester, a production function describes the relationship between output (real GDP) produced by the economy and the inputs labor (L) and capital (K) used in the production process. In addition, technology (T) is also important in determining the level of output. From a macroeconomic perspective, L represents total employment in the economy while K represents the entire capital stock in the economy. Technology is the ability to coordinate L and K in producing output.

The problem Robert faced was how to model employment. Robert did come up with a labor market while working on this project in graduate school, but a better explanation came to him many years later while he was having dinner with Maria. It was the early 1990s and Maria's business holdings had become widespread. She owned a large software company, considerable amounts of property all over the world and had become a major player in the clothing and footwear business.

Maria had flown to D.C. in order to talk with representatives from Southeast Asia about starting a clothing factory. On that evening, Maria told Robert that she had been reflecting on the all the people she had hired over the years and how the productivity of these workers had changed over time. Maria had marveled how her own work on software programs allowed people to write quicker, become more organized in their work habits and, therefore, her work had become more efficient. Maria agreed that the implementation of computers in all aspects of her business allowed people to do more work. From an economist's perspective, Robert said that increased efficiency in the work force meant an increase in the productivity of labor. We can simply refer to this as an increase in technology.

Maria pointed out that she viewed a large percentage of her employees as permanent in the sense that it was unlikely this group would be let go. Robert responded that from an economist's point of view, her staff was viewed as the *permanent level of employment*. Maria did acknowledge that a small percentage of her employees varied due to economic conditions, and Robert said that this group could be viewed as the *temporary component of employment*. Robert then went into lecture-mode. He wrote on his napkin the following equation:

$$L = L_n + L_c.$$

Robert explained that from the perspective of the entire economy, the variable L represents the current level of employment in the country, also referred to as the *observed* level of employment. Observed employment can then be decomposed in the **natural level of employment (L_n)** and **the cyclical component of employment (L_c)**. Similar to the interpretation of output, it is reasonable to divide employment into these two components.

Robert turned his napkin over and started writing a series of graphs. Maria always found this amusing about Robert, and she also enjoyed listening to Robert talk about economics. Maria did observe that Robert was writing on very expensive cloth napkins as they ate in a very upscale D.C. restaurant. Maria planned on correcting the situation when they paid the bill.

3.4.1. The Labor Market

Robert developed the following story. The labor market consists of firms that demand to hire workers. The firm's desire to hire workers results in the demand curve for labor. The other half of the labor market consists of workers who offer their labor services to firms. The workers represent the supply curve of labor. It is the interaction of labor suppliers and labor demanders that plays a large role in the determination of the equilibrium level of employment. The long-run equilibrium solution in the labor market will determine the natural level of employment, L_n. The interaction of L_n with the capital stock (K) in the economy and the current level of technology (T) will determine the natural level of output, Y_n. This can be written as the following:

$$Y_n = f(L_n, K, T)$$

As you recall from before, the observed level of output in the economy is written as

$$Y = f(L, K, T)$$

It is instructive to first analyze the labor market at the firm level, and then aggregate up all the labor markets to derive the labor market that represents the entire economy.

THE LABOR MARKET AT THE FIRM LEVEL

This idea is best explained by examining some of Maria's business interests. As we have seen, Maria was one of the major investors in the expansion of the mall in Las Cruces. What surprised Maria was her interest in the construction companies that contributed to the building of the mall. She started to interact with concrete workers, steel workers, plumbers, electricians and carpenters. Her interest in these professions was partially due to her relationship with Robert. All of Robert's stories about fixing this and that always amused Maria, but now her business interests directly intersected with these professions.

In the early 1990s, Maria became involved in a large construction project in Seattle, Washington. The plan was to build a huge shopping center north of the University of

Washington. Even though there were a number of investors in the project, Maria became the point person to contact all the different types of builders needed to complete the project.

THE SUPPLY OF LABOR

Maria was well aware that the wage rate offered to workers is a prime determinant of how willing people are to work. The amount of money that a worker is paid is referred to as the **nominal wage**. We will call this wage W. A rise in the nominal wage induces people to supply more labor. In other words, as wages increase, so does the willingness of individuals to work. The labor supply schedule is drawn in the following manner:

W—nominal wage

L^s—represents labor supply

At a wage rate of W_0 workers are willing to supply L_0 amount of work. If the wage rate rises to W_1 then the quantity of labor supplied rises to L_1. We are suggesting that as wages rise, there is a greater incentive for workers to work.

Of course, when looking at the nominal wage, implicit assumptions are being made about what wage can purchase. Whenever a labor supply schedule is drawn, the expected price level is taken into account. When workers agree to work for a specific wage, that agreement could last upwards of a year before any changes to the wage may occur. As the worker considers entering into the work agreement with the employer, the worker must have some idea about what those wages can purchase. In a sense, they have to make a guess or prediction about what they think the price level will be over that year before they enter the work agreement. Let us represent that guess or prediction as the **expected price level, P^e**. Consider Figure 3.13.

When the labor supply L^S is drawn, it assumes an expected price level, P^e. We now introduce a new concept called the **expected real wage**, which is written as

$$W_0 / P^e$$

When workers decide to offer the amount of labor L_0, they expect to earn the real wage. From a common sense perspective, this idea represents what workers are able to purchase with their labor income.

Suppose workers believe that the expected price level will rise tomorrow to $P^{e\prime}$. They realize that at the wage rate W_0 they are worse off. Consider the following:

$$W_0 / P^e > W_0 / P^{e\prime}$$

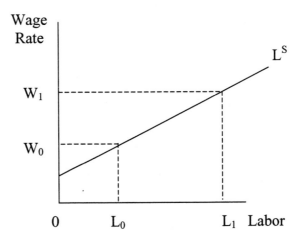

Figure 3.12 Labor Supply

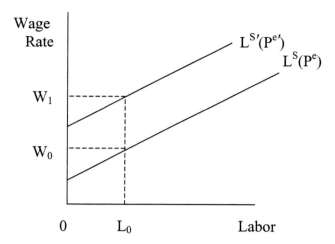

Figure 3.13   The Expected Price Level on Labor Supply

When the expected price level increases to $P^{e\prime}$, workers realize that their original wage W_0 will purchase a smaller amount of goods and services. From another perspective, when prices rise faster than wages, workers are able to buy less goods and services, and are worse off.

When the expected price level rises, the labor supply slope will shift upward and inward to $L^{S\prime}$. It is the case that to offer L_0, workers want to be compensated with a nominal wage of W_1. *The inward and leftward shift in of the labor supply curve represents workers demand for higher wages to compensate them for the higher cost of purchasing goods and services.* This is a very important assumption made in macroeconomic analysis.

When workers demand higher wages, we assume that the increase in wages is identical to the increase in the expected price level. In other words, we assume that

$$W_0 \, / \, P^e = W_1 \, / \, P^{e\prime}.$$

One of the problems Maria dealt with was how to forecast the expected price level. As she negotiated with different unions, she found varying estimates of the expected price level. Every trade union had a different economist predicting a different future price level. We will deal with this issue later in the semester.

Another factor that can cause the labor supply schedule to shift is work preferences. Suppose workers across the economy experience a change in the perception of the value of work, and this change decreases their desire to work. This implies that at each wage, workers are less willing to work. The labor supply curve would shift upward and inward from L^S to $L^{S\prime}$ as presented in Figure 3.13. Let us represent preferences toward work as PRF.

A third factor that causes the supply of labor to shift is changes in population. Suppose the federal government were to relax immigration laws so that it was much easier for international people to enter the U.S., gain citizenship and look for employment. This would represent an increase in population and shift the labor supply curve outward. Let us represent population as POP.

THE DEMAND OF LABOR

As construction started on the Seattle project, Maria was constantly re-evaluating the type and number of workers that would be needed to complete the project. She realized it was important to coordinate all the workers with the size of the project in order to have a well-functioning enterprise.

As we have stated before, firms hire labor in order to perform important roles in the production process. Maria has to determine how many workers she needs to hire. To make this determination, Maria has to evaluate the productivity of each worker in the different positions within the project. In addition, the wages that Maria is willing to pay her workers depends on the worker's productivity. The more productive a worker, the higher the wage he or she can earn.

The concept that describes the productivity of the worker is referred to as the **marginal productivity of labor (MP$_L$)**. The MP$_L$ describes the productivity of each additional unit of work effort.

ECONOMIC PRINCIPLE

Marginal productivity of labor (MP$_L$) __ Is the increase in output due to working an additional unit of time. It can also be viewed as the output attributed to one more people working one additional hour.

From Maria's time at the MBA program at Harvard, she learned that the MPL was impacted by the *law of diminishing returns*. In other words, as a firm hires additional workers, output increases but at a decreasing rate. This is why the MPL schedule or the labor demand schedule is downward sloping. The MPL curve is drawn as follows:

The MPL curve is downward-sloping for similar reasons that the supply schedule is upward sloping; for the same reason the production possibility frontier is bowed out and the same reason the demand for investment schedule is downward-sloping. As the work effort increases, the contributions to production increase, but a decreasing rate. This result assumes that all the other factors of production (capital and technology) are held constant. Increases in the work effort will result in diminishing contributions to output.

Referring to Figure 3.14, consider the first worker Maria hires. This worker can help produce a certain amount of output, represented by the area 01BC. When the second worker is hired, the additional amount of output produced is represented by the area 12AB. Since the second worker produces less output than the first worker, Maria will only be willing to pay the second worker a lower wage than the first the worker. The MPL curve is also called a *labor demand schedule*. It describes the quantity of labor demanded for different wage rates.

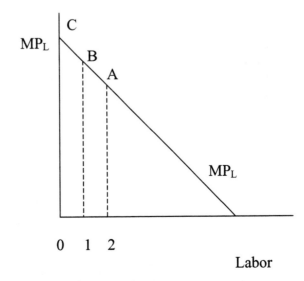

Figure 3.14 The Marginal Productivity of Labor

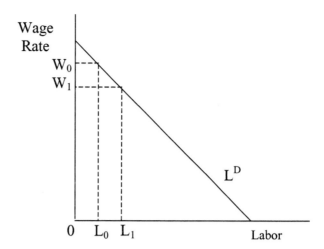

Figure 3.15   The Labor Demand Schedule

We have augmented Figure 3.15 by inserting the wage rate on the vertical axis. The wage rate represents the cost of purchasing labor. The above graph introduces an additional concept that is related to the MP_L. As the MP_L of a worker increases, the worker becomes more valuable to the firm and therefore merits a higher wage rate. Consider the first worker as represented by distance $0L_0$ and the second worker is represented by the distance L_0L_1. As discussed above, the MP_L of the first worker is greater than the MP_L of the second worker. Therefore, Maria is willing to pay a higher wage to the first worker. The above graph reveals that the first worker would be paid a wage rate of W_0 while the second worker would be paid a wage rate of W_1.

We have traced out the labor demand schedule, represented by the term L^D. Similar to the first law of demand, a decrease in the wage rate will cause an increase in the quantity demanded for labor. It is important to point out that this curve represents two concepts that are highly related. First, the MP_L curve represents the productivity associated with hiring each additional worker. Since the MP_L is downward sloping, firms would only be willing to hire additional workers if there was a decrease in the wage rate. Since the wage rate also appears on the vertical axis, we see that a falling MP_L is associated with a falling wage rate. Therefore, the wage rate that the firm is willing to pay its workers is directly related to the MPL of that worker.

Factors That Shift the Labor Demand Curve

As Maria has noticed over the years, the productivity of a worker has changed. In her own case, the dramatic improvements in her own ability to be productive have also changed. During the summer after eighth grade, she was making about $20 a week in profits operating her mobile retail store. Selling chocolate chip cookies increased her profits to $25 a week. Her drastic increase in profits occurred during college when she came up with the idea of delivering pizzas. That was still one of her fondest memories because the proceeds from that business paid for college, room and board and three substantial vacations to Europe and Asia.

Describing these changes over Maria's life graphically can be done in the following manner:

As you can see, the demand for her labor had definitely changed over the years. In college, Maria earned a wage of W_0 selling pizzas, but at IBM during the 1972–75 period, her wage increased to W_1. By the mid 1990s, it was at times difficult to evaluate her wage because of her business interests, but it is safe to say she was earning at least W_2.

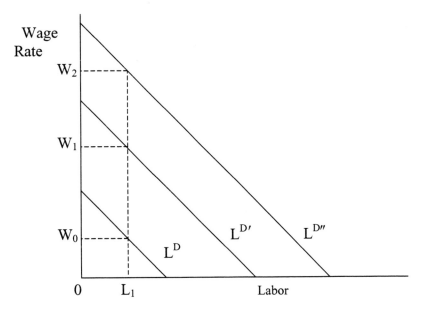

Figure 3.16 Changes in Maria's Productivity

From a more formal perspective, the demand curve for her labor was continually shifting outward from L^D to $L^{D'}$ to $L^{D''}$ and will probably shift outward for quite a while. The following factors all contribute to shifts in the labor demand curve:

- Changes in the capital stock
- Changes in technology
- Changes in the value of the goods produced by the worker

Capital Stock

Suppose a worker is able to benefit from using new capital, which results in an increase in productivity of the worker. As an example, a faster computer, or better tools can improve the productivity of a worker. This will result in a shift outward in the labor demand curve as shown in the above figure.

Technology

Improvements in technology also result in worker productivity increases and thus, a shift outward in the labor demand schedule.

Changes in the Price of Goods Produced by the Worker

After Maria had been operating one of her stores in Las Cruces for about a year, the store became very profitable. She was able to purchase a wide variety of clothes from numerous manufacturers back on the east coast and sell them for relatively low prices in Las Cruces. In fact, no other local store could compete with her. One day her employees requested a meeting with Maria concerning their current wages. They argued that the high profits Maria earned could be partially attributable to the performance of the workers. Therefore, Maria should give everyone a raise in wages to reflect the higher profits earned. After further discussion, Maria told her workers that she would get back with them in a few days.

Maria started to dwell on the situation. She realized that the success of the store depends upon a multitude of factors starting with her vision of the store. However, profits were high and the workers probably deserved a share in the success by receiving higher wages. Maria had recently raised the prices of most of the goods in the store due to the high demand. Since the demand curve for her clothes had shifted outward, the market price increased from P_0 to P_1. This is shown in the graph below.

At the market price of P_0, Maria paid a wage of W_0 to hire L_1 amount of workers. This is shown in Figure 3.18 below.

After the shift in the market demand curve from Figure 3.17, the price of the output increased from P_0 to P_1. It is now the case that Maria's workers produce output that is sold for a higher price. Therefore, the workers have become more valuable to Maria. The increase in the value of the workers is shown by the shift outward in the demand curve from L^D to $L^{D'}$. Since her workers are now producing output that has a higher value, they should receive W_1 instead of W_0. After contemplating this situation for a while, Maria acknowledged that all of her employees in the retail clothes should get a raise.

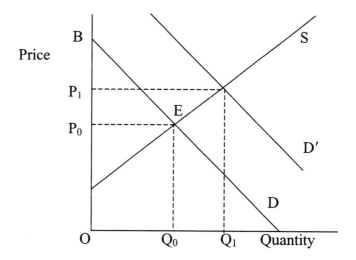

Figure 3.17   Shifting Maria's Clothing Demand Curve

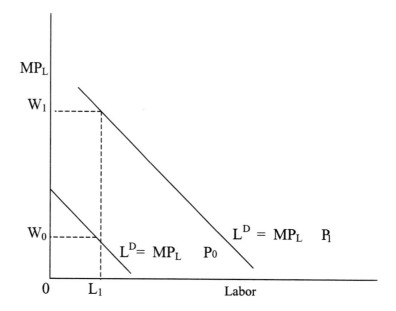

Figure 3.18   Shifting Maria's Labor Demand Curve

It is typical to multiply the MPL curve or the demand curve for labor by the price of the good that is being produced or sold. The labor demand schedule is also

— represented by (MPL $\times$ P) or (the amount of output $\times$ price of good)
— (MPL $\times$ P) is the value that a worker is creating
— (MPL $\times$ P) = L^D

If the price of a good increases from P_0 to P_1 as shown in the figure above, the demand curve for labor shifts outward. This implies that, when the price of the goods produced by workers increases, the value that is created by workers increases. From the standpoint of the firm, the worker has become more valuable and therefore, merits a wage increase. As the labor demand schedule shifts outward, the wage paid to any number of workers increases.

EQUILIBRIUM IN THE LABOR MARKET

In equilibrium, the labor market looks like the following:
As expected, the labor market functions in a similar manner as any market for a particular product.

The Labor Market for the Entire Economy

One of the most important markets that must to be in equilibrium for the economy to be operating at the NLO is the labor market. The NLO acts as a reference point, which reflects the optimal level of output for the economy. Even though it is unlikely that the economy will ever be at the NLO, it is assumed that the economy is always moving toward the NLO.

As we suggested above, the overall labor market is the most important market for solving out the NLO. Let's reconsider the aggregate labor market.

The labor supply schedule, L^S represents the supply of labor for the entire economy while the labor demand curve represents the demand for labor by all firms in the economy. The intersection of both curves results in an estimate of the natural level of employment, L_n. The labor supply curve will still shift due to changes in the preference to work, changes in the expected price level as well as population changes. The labor demand schedule shifts because of changes in the capital stock, technology and the current price level.

We take L_n and insert it into the production function for the entire economy, which results in the NLO (Y_n):

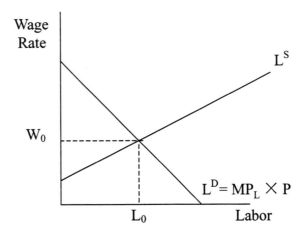

Figure 3.19 The Labor Market

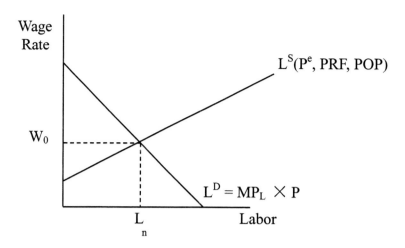

Figure 3.20   The Labor Market of the Entire Economy

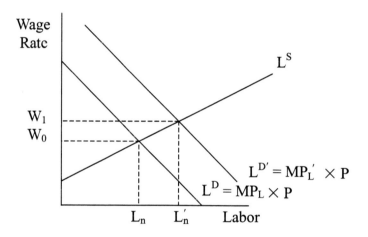

Figure 3.21   Effects of Improvement in Technology on Labor Market

$$Y_n = f(L_n, K, T)$$

L_n = Natural level of employment

K = Capital stock

T = Technology

One of the most common factors that cause changes in the NLO are changes in the level of technology (T). Economists have not developed a theory about why changes in technology occur, so we consider this variable to be exogenous, or outside, in our model. Suppose there is an increase in the level of technology. The following graph describes the impact in the labor market.

An improvement in technology means that all workers become more productive. The marginal productivity of labor has increased from MP_L to $MP_L{}'$. We represent the increase in technology as T′ which is greater than T. The labor demand curve shifts out from L^D to $L^{D'}$. The curve shifts outward to represent the increase in productivity of each additional work effort. We also observe an increase in the natural level of employment from L_n to $L_n{}'$. It is the case that Y_n will increase with an improvement in technology as demonstrated by the following equation:

$$Y_n{}' = f(L_n{}', K, T') > Y_n = f(L_n, K, T)$$

Given that $L_n{}' > L_n$ and $T' > T$ implies that more output can be produced, and also results in $Y_n{}' > Y_n$.

The above analysis makes a very important assumption. Sometimes, when there is a technological change, it can reduce the importance of workers. Suppose new machinery can be implemented into a manufacturing process, which in turn, improves the speed and efficiency of output. It could, however, completely oust the worker. For example, machinery will replace the need of assembly line workers. In this case, the MPL of workers has decreased and the labor demand curve will shift inwards. To simplify our analysis, we will assume that any technological change will enhance the productivity of workers.

Changes in the Capital Stock

An increase in the capital stock is assumed to have a similar impact as an improvement in technology. An increase in the capital stock allows workers to have greater access to machinery, tools, etc., which increases the productivity of all workers. Therefore, an increase in the capital stock from K to K′ causes the labor demand schedule to shift outward. It follows, of course, that the natural level of employment will rise. Using our production function analysis reveals the following

$$Y_n = f(L_n, K, T) < Y_n{}' = f(L_n{}', K', T).$$

The natural level of employment would increase to $L_n{}'$ and the equilibrium wage rate would increase. In addition, since the natural level of employment increases, the NLO will increase also.

3.5. The Determination of Output and the Price Level

We need to develop a graphical model that will solve out for the current level of output (Y), the NLO (Y_n) and the cyclical component of output (Y_c). Recall the following relationship:

$$Y = Y_n + Y_c$$

We now need to construct the remainder of our model in order to understand the causes of business cycles and changes in the inflation rate. Consider the following graph.

On the horizontal axis we have output, which represents real GDP produced in the economy. On the vertical axis we have the price level, which represents the average price of all goods and services produced in the economy over a specified period of time.

At any given point in time, the NLO will be a certain value, which assumes that technology and the capital stock are held constant. Recalling our mathematical representation

$$Y_n = f(L_n, K, T) = NLO$$

We can draw the NLO as a vertical line, which states that for a specified period of time, the NLO is a certain value. This suggests that the level of technology, the capital stock and the

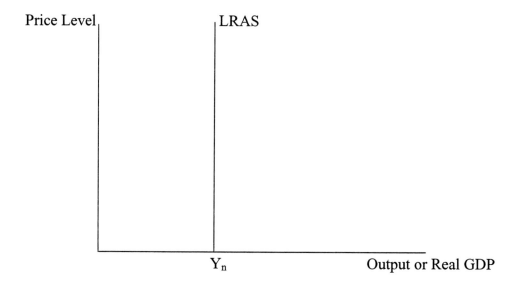

Figure 3.22   Long-Run Aggregate Supply (LRAS)

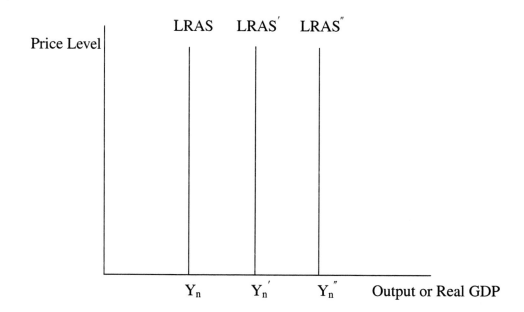

Figure 3.23   NLO Movement with Techonology Improvement

price expectations are held constant. The term LRAS refers to the long-run aggregate supply curve. This is another way of referencing the NLO. We will elaborate on this idea later in the semester.

It is the case that the NLO grows over time since our economy experiences improvements in technology on a continual basis. As technology grows, so does the NLO. This is seen in the graph below.

With an improvement in technology, the LRAS curve shifts to the right to LRAS' or Y'. As technology grows over time, the natural level of output will also grow. It is important to point out that the NLO shifts over time as there are increases in technology, the capital stock and population.

3.5.1. Short-Run Aggregate Supply (SRAS)

The SRAS curve represents departures of output around the natural level of output, which we have referred to as the cyclical component of output (Y_c). The SRAS is an upward-sloping curve just like a typical supply schedule. It reflects the costs of producing additional units of output and since the law of diminishing marginal returns is still a very relevant concept, the SRAS is upward sloping.

SHIFTS IN THE SRAS

As we have previously stated, the SRAS curve behaves in a very similar manner as the typical supply schedule. An increase in the costs of production (increase in wages, for example) will cause the SRAS to shift upward and inward. An increase in productivity will cause the SRAS to shift outward and downward. An additional factor that causes shifts in the SRAS is expectations about future inflation or higher future prices.

Expectations

An important aspect of the above model is the role of expectations in the economy. This is best introduced by reviewing some of Robert's experiences.

In 1976, Robert was in the middle of graduate school, attempting to obtain a Ph.D. in economics. Since Robert had always been intrigued with magic and illusion, he had attempted to introduce illusion in his classes to help enhance the learning process. One Monday morning, he announced to his class that there would be a major exam on the following Wednesday. The class was annoyed since Robert only gave them two days to study. On Wednesday, Robert stated that there would be no exam. The class erupted with significant displeasure since they had studied for an exam they wouldn't take. Robert countered with the claim that everyone was better off since they had studied and knew the material. In addition, Robert reminded them that it is important to continually study economics and not wait to study right before the exam.

The next Monday, Robert made a similar announcement and on the following Wednesday he didn't give an exam again. The students were even more irate this time. Robert attempted

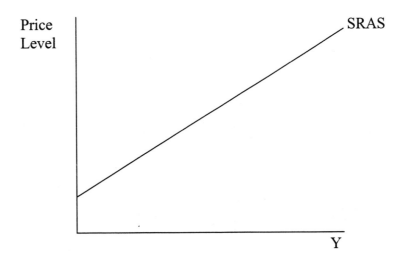

Figure 3.24 Short-Run Aggregate Supply

the same technique the third Monday, but the students did not take him seriously, and most refused to study.

Robert learned something very valuable from this lesson. People can only be temporarily fooled. It is in the best interest of people to correct mistakes that are costly. People are rational in the sense that they attempt to correct past mistakes. Students were allocating time to study for an exam that was not to be. With correct information, the students would not have increased their study time on those Mondays and Tuesdays.

Robert wondered that since the average person corrected their mistakes, should economic models do the same thing? In other words, should economic models be constructed in a manner that the models learn from previous mistakes?

These are issues that we need to address from Robert's experience and implement them into our model. Expectations about higher future inflation will cause workers and firms to change their current behavior. An increase in expected inflation will cause workers to demand higher wages so that their real wage will not fall. This will cause the labor supply schedule and the SRAS to shift upward.

LONG-RUN EQUILIBRIUM

We have constructed the aggregate demand curve and the short-run and long-run aggregate supply curves. Referring to Figure 3.25, the intersection of all three curves at point E is called **long-run equilibrium**.

ECONOMIC PRINCIPLE

> ***Long-Run Equilibrium***—*is the level of output when the economy has fully adjusted to all economic shocks.*

Any economy is constantly responding to aggregate shocks that will cause shifts in all three curves. Some of these shocks will be temporary, which will cause shifts in AD or SRAS. As an example, changes in the money supply will cause an initial shift in the AD curve. We will argue that the impact on real GDP will be temporary, but there will be a departure from long-run equilibrium. We are interested in how the economy moves back to long-run equilibrium. When the economy fully adjusts to the change in the money supply, we return to long-run equilibrium.

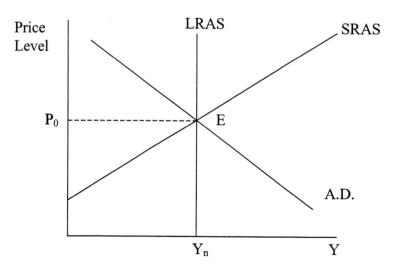

Figure 3.25 Long-Run Equilibrium

Point E represents long-run equilibrium in the economy. Long-run equilibrium implies

- Consumer surplus is maximized for all individuals
- Profits for firms are maximized
- The economy has fully adjusted to all economic shocks.

3.5.2. Underlying Assumptions of the Model

As we have explained before, an economic model solves out for a number of endogenous variables. In the aggregate supply and demand curve model, those variables are the price level, the inflation rate and real GDP. Real GDP is divided into Y_n and Y_c. The exogenous variables are:

- Technology
- Capital Stock
- Energy Costs
- Money Supply
- Government Expenditures
- Taxes
- People's preferences for work verses leisure
- Population

We will explore how changes in any of these exogenous variables impact the aggregate supply and demand curve model.

The model is divided into two parts. The first is aggregate demand, which is represented as:

$$AD = C + I + G + M^S + (EX - IM)$$

Where C is consumption by households, I is investment by firms, G is government expenditures M^S is the money supply, EX is exports and IM is imports. The second is Aggregate supply which is written as:

$$Y^S = Y_n + Y_c$$

$$Y_n = f(L_n, K, T, EC)$$

Y_c is a function of temporary shifts in the AD and SRAS schedules

Where L_n is the natural level of employment, K is the capital stock, and T is technology and EC represents energy costs. Energy costs represent the costs of all forms of energy such as oil, electricity, natural gas and nuclear power. It has been common in the past to just concentrate on the oil industry, which we will also do.

K and T determine the natural level of output from the supply side. We will see that EC can have both permanent impacts causing changes in Y_n, and temporary impacts on Y_c. At times, the impact of changes in energy costs can be confusing. The demand side also contributes to the natural level of output in terms of consumption, C, and investment, I. The demand by households for consumption goods reflects permanent spending patterns, which aids in output growth over time. This is the case because the number of households has been growing over time due to standard population growth in the economy. Investment by firms is similar in that growth in the economy is also reflected in the expansion of the size of existing firms and the addition of new firms in the economy.

The cyclical component of output, Y_c, reflects changes in temporary factors in the economy. This is usually associated with changes in the money supply and government expenditures from the demand side and temporary changes in energy costs from the supply side. We will now explore the impact of these permanent and temporary changes in the economy.

Changes in Technology

Suppose there is an improvement in technology. We have assumed that an increase in technology increases the marginal productivity of labor. Therefore, the labor demand schedule shifts from L^D to $L^{D'}$ and the natural level of employment rises from L_n to L_n'. Remember that $L^D = MPL \times P$. The reason why the labor demand schedule is shifting outward is due to the increase in productivity, which makes labor more productive. The MPL increases to MPL', which causes the labor demand curve to shift from L^D to $L^{D'}$.

The natural level of employment increases from L_n to L_n'. The original natural level of output was:

$$Y_n = f(L_n, K, T)$$

And now the new natural level of output is:

$$Y_n' = f(L_n', K, T')$$

Where $T' > T$

Viewing Figure 3.27, we see that the LRAS shifts outward to LRAS'. In addition, the costs of producing output will fall causing the short-run aggregate supply curve to shift outward from SRAS to SRAS'. The overall price level will fall from P_o to P_1. A new equilibrium is established at E'.

Starting at Y_n, the economy is in long-run equilibrium at point E. The increase in technology causes the LRAS to shift outward to LRAS' and the SRAS to shift outward to SRAS'. This results in a new equilibrium solution at E'. Depending on the type of technological change, the movement from E to E' could take years.

Changes in the capital stock would be treated in a similar fashion, but it is much more common to analyze changes in technology.

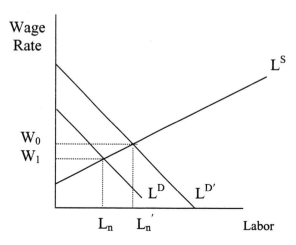

Figure 3.26 Technological Improvement Analysis

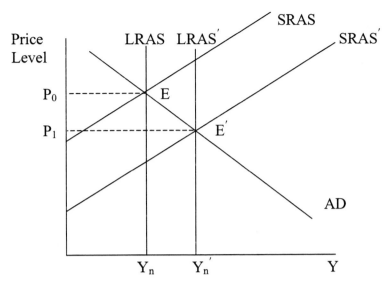

Figure 3.27   Changes in Technology in Aggregate Supply Curves

3.5.3. Theoretical Issues Concerning Monetary Policy

The objective of this section is to explore how changes in the money supply are captured in the AD and AS curve model. Suppose the Federal Reserve decides to increase the money supply through the use of open market operations. The Federal Reserve purchases securities from the commercial banks, which in turn allows the banks to increase their loans to firms and households at a lower interest rate. As more loans occur, there is an increased demand for goods and services by the firms and people that borrow the money.

Consider Figure 3.28. The increase in the money supply causes a shift outward in the aggregate demand schedule from AD to AD'. Graphically, we observe that there is an increase in output to Y_1. This increase in output occurs because as more money is loaned out, the borrowers spend that additional money, which causes output to grow. As the demand for goods and services grows, there is upward pressure on prices, resulting in the price level rising from P_0 to P_1.

At the same time, the production of goods and services increases and output rises to Y_1. In the labor market (see Figure 3.29 below), the demand for labor increases since the price level is increasing. The demand for labor increases from L^D to $L^{D'}$ because workers are now producing output that is worth more. Since the price level increases from P_0 to P_1 the labor demand curve shifts outward. With an increase in employment to L_1, firms are able to increase output to Y_1.

There is also an increase in the nominal wage from W_0 to W_1, which leads us to an important assumption: the increase in the price level is larger than the increase in the nominal wage. This assumption is consistent with what all of us experience in the real world. We typically see prices changing for food, gasoline, clothes, athletic equipment, etc. on a monthly or even more frequent basis. However, our wages are much more stable and may not change more than once a year. Since prices are more flexible than wages we assume that

$$W_1 / P_1 < W_0 / P_0.$$

At point E' the real wage in the economy has fallen although output and employment have increased at E'. Workers are now worse off because the price of goods and services has increased more than their wages. At point E', the economy is now in *short-run equilibrium*.

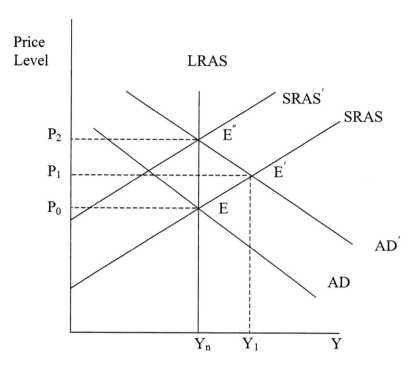

Figure 3.28 The Long-Run Neutrality of Money

As the workers in the economy realize that prices are rising, they adjust their expectations of the price level and assume the price of goods will be more expensive. When workers are able to renegotiate their wage agreement, they will demand higher wages to keep pace with the rising price level. This will cause the labor supply curve in Figure 3.29 to shift upward to $L^{S\prime}$. In other words, the demand for wages increases. The renegotiation of wages upward will increase the costs of productions, which will also shift the SRAS in Figure 3.28 upward and inward to SRAS'. Both the labor market and output market move to E″ and now are back to long-run equilibrium. After the shift, the employment level moves back to L_n and output returns to Y_n. The wage rate increases to W_2 and the new price level is now at P_2.
It is now the case that

$$W_0 / P_0 = W_2 / P_2.$$

It is assumed that in the long-run, prices and wages have increased by the same amount and the real wage returns to its original level. Workers are now as well off as they were before the money supply increased. This condition is the *long-run* result. The real wage in the economy as well as the level of output remains unchanged.

The long run is defined as the period of time when the economy has fully adjusted to all economic shocks. The initial shock to the economy was the increase in the money supply. In the short-run, there is a temporary increase in output and the level of employment. However, over time, the economy adjusts by nominal wages rising and the economy moves back to the natural level of output and employment.

We have seen that monetary policy only had temporary impacts on the economy. In the example above, an increase in the money supply causes a temporary increase in output, but no impact on output in the long run. Therefore, monetary policy is viewed as a technique that can only impact real factors in the short-run. This is also referred to as the **long-run neutrality of money**. Changes in the money supply can influence output and employment temporarily or in the short-run. However, money is neutral in the long-run.

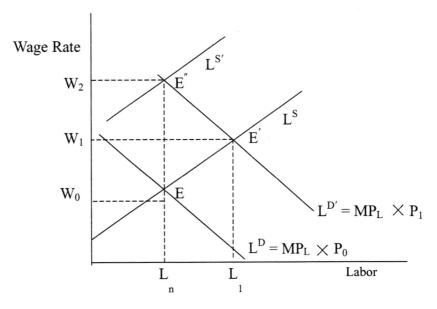

Figure 3.29   An Increase in the Money Supply on the Labor Market

3.6. Wage Contracts

Related to the above analysis, is the type of wage agreements which workers and firms enter. It is costly to negotiate a wage agreement and firms would like to enter into relatively long-term wage agreements with workers. Workers on the other hand, would like to have the opportunity to renegotiate their wages more frequently. In the 1950s and 1960s, the price level was fairly stable in the U.S., so it was safe for workers to enter two- to three-year wage agreements because unexpected changes in the price level were somewhat uncommon.

This worked well for most firms and workers. With respect to the firm, setting wages for all its workers will give it a good idea about the cost structure it will face in the future. Workers also benefit from knowing their future wages since they will be able to make more informed decisions regarding their spending patterns. In this case, workers cannot easily renegotiate their labor agreements. Therefore, when referring to Figures 3.28 and 3.29, it could take several years before the labor supply curve could shift to $L^{S\prime}$ in response to an increase in the money supply.

When the price level became more unstable and harder to predict in the 1970s, workers started to enter shorter term wage agreements. Wages could now be renegotiated annually or sometimes more frequently. By the mid 1980s, the U.S. price level became more stable and workers felt safe to enter more long-term wage agreements again.

An important point arose out of the length of a wage contract. During times when there were long-term wage agreements, an increase in the money supply caused output to increase for a longer period of time. Referring back to Figure 3.28, an increase in the money supply caused the economy to move to $E\prime$, and stay there until workers could renegotiate their wage agreements. The longer workers had to wait to demand higher wages, the longer the economy stayed at $E\prime$. When the economy was dominated by short-term wage agreements, the impact of monetary policy was reduced as the economy moved more quickly to $E\prime\prime$.

$ Chapter 4

4.1. History of the U.S. Economy

In the spring of 2004, Robert was assigned by the Fed to summarize the economic history of the U.S. from the 1950s to 2002. He was told to focus on business cycles and to gain an understanding of what role monetary policy played in these recessions. Robert was enthusiastic about the project since a lot of his research focused on these issues. He had until the fall of 2004 to finish the study. He was to focus on the following recessions:

- 1973–75 recession
- 1979 recession
- 1981–82 recession
- 1990 recession
- 2001–02 recession

Robert had to also incorporate the different approaches to monetary policy over the years, including:

- Interest rate targeting 1950–72
- Response to the oil price shocks 1973–79
- Minimize the inflation rate 1980–present

Over the years, Robert had spent multiple summers mountain climbing in Colorado, Utah, Wyoming and Alaska. During the summer of 2004, Robert decided to spend a couple of weeks in Breckenridge, Colorado with the objective of climbing a number of "fourteeners," as well as to work on the project. He had purchased a time share at Grand Timber Lodge so he could spend two weeks every summer there and reside in a "five star" resort. It was a good deal and besides he could revisit some of his favorite climbs. Robert loved to camp, but after a strenuous hike, he relished in the comfort of a condominium with a hot tub, access to good food and a DVD player to watch old movies. He planned to spend the next month climbing up mountains.

The first climb he had his eyes set on was Mt. Quandary, widely accepted as a moderately difficult. He started hiking at 5 a.m. on a Wednesday morning. As they often did, his thoughts wandered to the latest project he had been assigned. The chairman of the Federal Reserve, Alan Greenspan, wanted a concise history of monetary policy since the 1950s. Robert needed to combine the different monetary policy philosophies over the last fifty years as well as determine how these policies impacted the five recessions that the U.S. economy had experienced in 1973–75, 1979 and 1981–82, 1990–91 and 2001–03. His task was to put all these recessions into perspective in terms of causes and evaluate the policies that were enacted to offset these recessions.

4.2. Monetary Policy

Robert recalled that the objective of monetary policy is two-fold. The first objective is to help promote sustained economic growth and minimize variations in output around the natural level of output. The second objective is to maintain a relatively low growth rate in the price level or minimize the inflation rate. Related to stabilizing output growth and the inflation rate, is the Federal Reserve's concern about interest rates. A secondary objective has also been to create policies that would result in stable interest rates. As we have previously discussed, the economy has several different types of interest rates.

The **federal funds rate** is the interest rate that banks charge other banks for borrowed money. It is often referred to as the overnight rate, as these are very short-term loans. The **discount rate** is the rate of interest that the Federal Reserve charges commercial banks to borrow money. The **prime rate** is the rate of interest that large banks charge their best customers, and **mortgage rates**, which are the interest rates for borrowing money to finance a home. It is the case that all these interest rates move closely together. Consider Figure 4.1 which displays the federal funds rate and the prime rate. It is clear that these two interest rates move together.

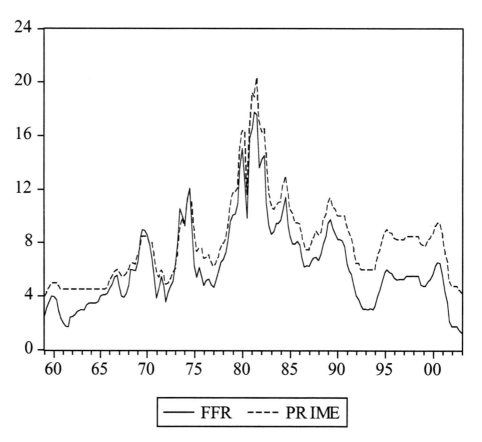

Figure 4.1   The Federal Funds Rate and the Prime Rate of Interest

4.2.1. The Federal Funds Market

As we have discussed previously, commercial banks are required to hold a percentage of their reserves on hand to meet daily transactional needs. It is quite common that a bank will bump up against the minimum amount of reserves due to several factors. One factor is that there could be unexpectedly large withdrawals by their depositors as people choose to increase their purchases. Another reason might be that the demand for loans made by customers has been strong due to a growing economy. In either case, the bank could find itself in a position that it would have to borrow from another bank in order to keep above the required reserve ratio. These loans are typically for a day or two.

The demand for reserves schedule in Figure 4.2 represents this concept. Not surprisingly, demand curve is downward sloping. The demand curve will shift outward when there is strong economic growth. Strong growth usually results in banks making a large number of loans to firms and households, so it is common that banks loan out a large percentage of their excess reserves. In addition, customers may be writing a large number of checks during good economic times, putting an additional strain on required reserves. Each of these factors can cause the demand curve for reserves to shift outward.

The supply of reserves represents the excess reserves that large commercial banks hold in expectation of making loans to small banks that may have run short of reserves. Figure 4.3 presents the supply curve for reserves. As the interest rate rises, banks are willing to loan out a greater amount of their excess reserves. Therefore, the supply of loans is upward sloping. Open market operations engaged by the Federal Reserve directly influence supply reserves. When the Federal Reserve sells (buys) bonds from commercial banks, the supply of reserves schedule shifts inward (outward).

The impact of inflation has an important effect on the supply curve for reserves. As we have discussed earlier in the semester, holding the nominal interest rate constant, an increase in inflation rate will reduce the real rate of return on the loan. Recall the Fisher equation:

$$R = r + \pi^e,$$

Where R is the nominal interest rate, r is the real interest rate and π^e is the expected rate of inflation. When there is an increase in inflation, banks will want to charge a higher nominal interest rate so that the real rate of interest or return does not decline. Referring to Figure 4.3, an increase in inflation will cause the supply curve of reserves to shift from S to S'. The intuition is when the

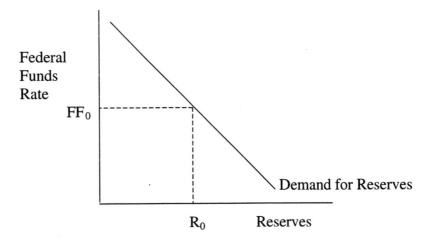

Figure 4.2 The Demand Bank Reserves

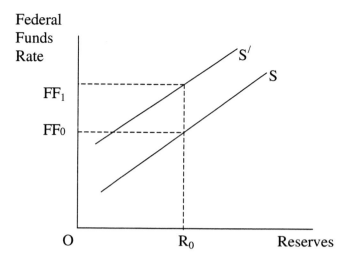

Figure 4.3   The Supply of Bank Reserves

inflation rate increases, banks will increase the federal funds rate from FF_0 to FF_1 when offering R_0 amount of reserves.

Consider an open market purchase of bonds that causes the supply schedule to shift outward in Figure 4.4 to S'. The federal funds rate will fall from FF_0 to FF_1. Since commercial banks have access to more reserves, the cost of lending money to all customers will decrease, and we will see a fall in the prime rate as well as mortgage rates. This is how all interest rates are related.

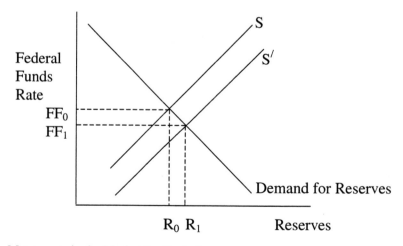

Figure 4.4   Movements in the Market for Bank Reserves

4.2.2. Targeting Interest Rates

From 1950–75, the Federal Reserve's objective was to target interest rates at a relatively low level. The logic of this policy was that if interest rates were low and stable, firms and households could benefit from the low costs of borrowing money, as well as the knowledge that interest rates would be low in the future. The Federal Reserve believed this would help sustain economic growth. The policy is known as **interest rate targeting**, and would work in the following way: Let FF_T be the targeted federal funds rate. Suppose the economy is experiencing substantial growth and a number of smaller banks have made enough loans such that their excess reserves are falling below minimum required amount. In this case, these banks may have to borrow reserves from larger banks in order to have enough reserves to meet daily transactional needs as well as satisfying Fed requirements. The increase in the demand by smaller banks to borrow reserves from larger banks is represented by a shift outward in the demand for reserves from D to D' in Figure 4.5. This would cause upward pressure on the Federal funds rate from FF_0 to FF_1. However, the Fed would then engage in an open market purchase of securities to increase the supply of reserves to S', and keep the federal funds rate at FF_T.

The Fed pursued this policy from the 1950s to the early 1970s. However, referring back to Figure 4.1 indicates that there was a slow but upward movement in the federal funds rate over this period. Many economists considered the policy successful even though the Fed had to constantly revise upward the targeted federal funds rate. This policy was considered pro-cyclical in the sense that as the economy expanded, the Fed would increase the money supply in order to facilitate economic growth. The Federal Reserve made sure there was enough money in the economy to help the economy grow.

The policy worked well from 1950–72, as can be seen in Figure 4.6. The left-hand-side of Figure 4.6 indicates the positions of AD, SRAS and LRAS in 1960. They all intersected at point E, which resulted in a price level of P_{60}. The solution for the price level in 1961 was P_{61}, which was a very modest increase compared to P_{60}. Over the 1950–72 period, the increases in the price level or changes in the inflation rate were very small. This fact contributed to the success of the interest rate targeting as the changes in expected inflation were also very small. We will see why this is true below.

Milton Friedman was one of the only economists that objected to the Fed policy of interest rate targeting. His claim was that it had the potential to cause significant amounts of inflation since an increase in the money supply would eventually result in an increase in the price level, and an increase in inflationary expectations. Recall the Fisher equation:

$$R = r + \Pi^e$$

R = nominal interest rate
Π^e = expected inflation rate
r = real interest rate (the rate of return adjusted for inflation or the real purchasing power of one's money)

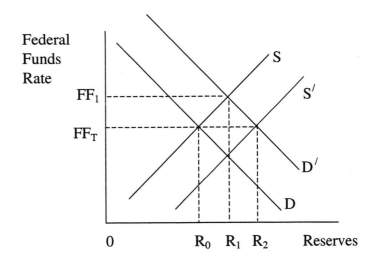

Figure 4.5 Changes in the Market for Bank Reserves Due to Growth

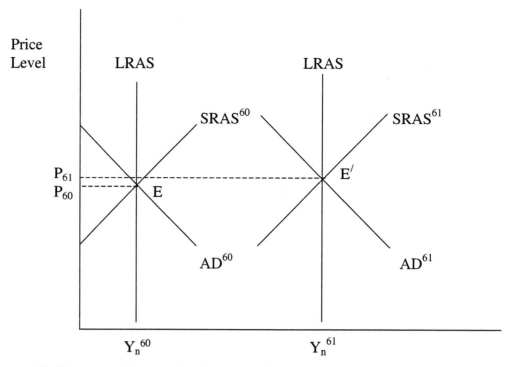

Figure 4.6   Illustration of Interest Rate Targeting Policy

Friedman's concern was that an increase in the money growth rate would cause an increase in the expected inflation rate, Π^e, and then an increase in the nominal interest rate, R. Referring back to Figure 4.4, the Federal Reserve engaged in open market operations, which caused the supply of reserves to increase and the supply curve to shift to S'. If Π^e increased, it would cause banks to raise nominal interest rates in order to maintain a constant real rate of return. In this case, the supply curve would shift back to S, and the federal funds rate would be pushed back to FF_1 and make the interest rate-targeting policy difficult to achieve.

Friedman's concerns were realized, but the upward pressure on the federal funds rate target was slow at start. Figure 4.1 depicts that the federal funds rate did rise slowly over the 1960s, which reflects Friedman's concerns but the increases in the federal funds rate were small enough such that many economists viewed the policy as successful.

4.2.3. The 1973–75 Recession

Robert had been hiking for about an hour and a half, and was making good time. The U.S. Forest Service had recently altered the direction of the lower trail due to overuse of the original trail. Robert always marveled at the amount of work involved in breaking a new trail. He had recently purchased a new Osprey daypack, which was very high tech. He though, that since he could afford nice things, why not purchase high quality equipment?

The cause of this recession is well understood. The OPEC nations had recently expelled the U.S. from the Middle East and ended all U.S. influence in determining oil prices. In 1973, the U.S. economy was heavily dependent on oil related products. This dynamic was due to U.S. policy in the Middle East and the domestic production of oil within the U.S. Consider Figure 4.7, the market for gasoline in the U.S.

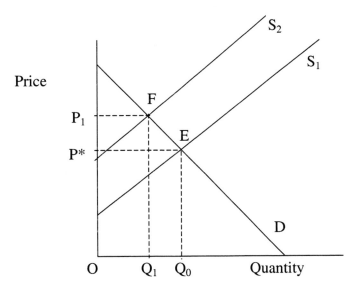

Figure 4.7 Market for Gasoline in the U.S.

In the U.S., there were price controls on gasoline in the early 1970s. However, the U.S. government had some success since they were able to influence oil production in the Middle East. The combination of Middle East oil production and U.S. oil production created the position of the supply curve labeled S_1. The targeted price of gasoline in the U.S. was P*. Whenever there was an increase in demand for gasoline, which put upward pressure on gasoline prices, the government would respond with one of the following two actions. They would either encourage an increase of domestic oil production, shifting the supply curve outward or return the price to P*. The other policy would be to encourage Middle East oil production to increase. This policy worked well in the 1960s and early 1970s.

Gasoline prices around the world were much higher than U.S. prices. Countries such as West Germany and Japan had no local production of oil so they faced supply curve S_2. There were no price controls in the rest of the world so these countries were reacting to the price P_1. The high price of P_1 caused German and Japanese automakers to produce fuel-efficient cars in the 1970s, but the U.S. automakers did not do so because gas prices were at P*. The American gas guzzling cars of the 1970s were in jeopardy.

In 1973, the oil producing countries in the Middle East started to resent the U.S.'s interventionist policy. These countries expelled the U.S. from influencing Middle East oil production and formed a group referred to as OPEC. In 1973, the OPEC nations significantly reduced the production of oil. Gasoline prices in the U.S. skyrocketed within weeks. The U.S. was unable to target gasoline prices at P*, and gas prices rose substantially in the U.S.

Oil was the primary source of energy in the economy and because of its importance, a large increase in oil prices acted like a negative technology shock. This can be attributed to inputs, such as labor and capital, which required the use of energy to produce output. Due to rising oil costs, labor and capital became less efficient because it had to use more expensive energy to produce output. In a sense, labor and capital became less efficient in producing the same amount of output since much more expensive energy was required. The following aggregate supply and demand curve model describes these impacts in Figure 4.8.

Prior to the increase in oil prices in 1973, assume that the economy was operating at point E. The oil price shocks hit, and due to the significant reliance on oil related products, the

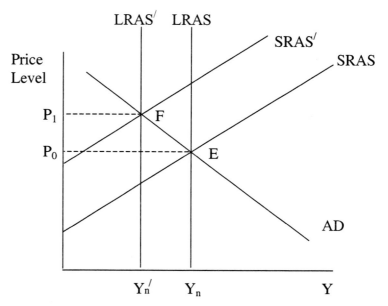

Figure 4.8   The 1973–75 Recession

LRAS shifted inward to LRAS'. The reason for this shift inward is that the increase in oil prices acted like a negative technology shock due to our large reliance on oil. A shift inward of the LRAS causes a reduction in the natural level of output from Y_n to Y_n'. At the same time, the costs of production have increased resulting in a shift upward in SRAS to SRAS'. The equilibrium solution is now at point F. The price level has increased from P_0 to P_1. When the oil prices increased, many economists viewed the potential for a recession to be very significant.

From our perspective, this can be viewed as a recession—one that has permanent impacts, because the natural level of output fell. This recession can also be viewed from the perspective of the labor market. Consider Figure 4.9.

The labor demand curve shifts inward, because, in a sense, there has been a reduction in technology. The rising energy costs have reduced the productivity of labor because it is more

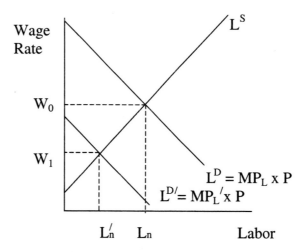

Figure 4.9   The Labor Market and the 1973–75 Recession

expensive for labor to produce the same amount of output. The shift inward in the labor demand curve reflects the idea that workers have become less productive. In terms of the mathematical representation of this idea, consider the following:

$$Y_n = f(L_n, K, T)$$
$$Y_n' = f(L_n', K, T)$$
$$Y_n > Y_n'$$

The natural level of output has fallen due to a reduction in the natural level of employment. Examining Figure 3.4, which displays real GDP over time, can reinforce this idea. As one looks at the 1973–75 period, it can be noted that there was a permanent fall in output. Looking at output right before the 1973 decline, output started to fall and never rose enough to get back to the level of output, that would have happened if the recession had not occurred.

The idea of looking at a recession from the perspective of the labor market got Robert thinking of the stories that Maria told him while she was working for IBM. In 1973, Maria was working in the department that was responsible for researching how to develop personal computers that could be used in homes and businesses. Apart from computer development, IBM also produced other electronic products, which were sold in the market as described below.

Looking at Figure 4.10, we can see that the equilibrium point prior to the increased oil prices was point E. When the price of oil rose, the supply curve for IBM shifted to S'. Why? Recall that the supply curve for a firm represents the firm's marginal cost curve. As the price of oil increased, so did the costs of inputs resulting in an increase in the firm's marginal costs. The shift of the supply curve decreased IBM's output from Q to Q' and the price of IBM's goods increased from P to P'. The decrease in output reduced the firm's demand for labor.

Maria and her coworkers began to worry that this situation may cause some of them to loose their jobs. In fact, though Maria survived, she did have to watch many of her close friends and coworkers get laid off. The experience was very painful for Maria, but was much harder for those who had lost their jobs. During this period, Maria said that the work environment was very and uncertain, and that life, in general, was much more difficult and expensive as prices for most goods and services increased.

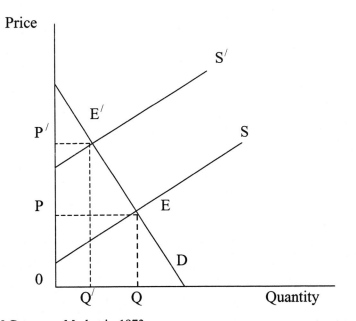

Figure 4.10 IBM Computer Market in 1973

Though Maria kept her job, she did not feel comfortable in her position. She knew that if another recession came, her job would again be in jeopardy. This got Maria into thinking about starting her own computer company. She thought about those coworkers that were laid off and decided they would be good candidates for her company because they already had training from IBM. The economy started to recover after 1975, and that was when Maria decided to quit her job at IBM and start her own computer business.

Robert had been hiking for about two hours and he was now above timberline. Hiking above tree line feels like you have entered a different world; it is both barren and beautiful. The scenery is spectacular because the only thing that blocks your view are other mountains. There is no protection against the elements, but that is exciting.

Robert decided to take a break from the hike. He took off his pack and started munching on some trail mix. When he had visited the grocery the store the day before as he prepared his hike up Quandry, he decided to be bad and buy the trail mix with chocolate chips. As he continued to eat, Robert thought about how the 1973–75 recession had impacted the attempt to target the federal funds rate.

As we discussed above, the Fed increased the money supply to hopefully minimize the impact of rising oil prices. An additional reason to increase the money supply was due to the interest rate targeting policy at the time. The increase in oil prices resulted in a higher inflation rate and upward pressure on all interest rates. To target interest rates, the response of the Fed was also to increase the money supply. The Fed thinking at the time was that an increase in the money supply would have dual benefit in the economy. It would stabilize interest rates and also stimulate economic growth, which would minimize the impact of the recession.

As Robert thought of this period, he smiled since this policy ended up being unsuccessful. The increase in the money supply only increased the price level, inflation and interest rates. We have learned that when the economy is at long-run equilibrium an increase in the money supply will only increase prices in the long-run and have no permanent impact on output. The only effect that the Fed policy had was to increase the inflation rate and drive up the federal funds rate above the target. The Fed eventually abandoned the idea of interest rate targeting.

THE FRIEDMAN RULE: RELATIONSHIP BETWEEN MONEY AND PRICES

A very prominent economist, Milton Friedman, was a professor at the University of Chicago in the 1970s. Friedman was one of the major critics of the Fed policy of targeting interest rate in the manner conducted by the Fed. While in graduate school and spending his time at the Fed, Robert was profoundly influenced by Friedman's writings. Friedman had a very different belief in how the Fed should conduct monetary policy. Friedman's views were growing in popularity and when he won the Nobel Prize in economics in 1976, Friedman became the man.

Robert was within 45 minutes of the summit as his thought wandered back to how Friedman arrived at his approach for monetary policy. It was accepted by most economists that there was a strong link between changes in the money supply and changes in the price level or the inflation rate. Consider Figures 4.11 and 4.12. First, Figure 4.11 displays the historical relationship between M1 and the overall price level, CPI. It is easy to see that there appears to be a very strong positive relationship between the levels of the two series. It is even more instructive to look at the growth rates of the money supply and the price level.

DM = the percentage growth rate of the money supply
DP = the percentage growth rate of the price level or the inflation rate

Figure 4.12 demonstrates that relationship between the money growth rate and inflation is also strongly positively correlated.

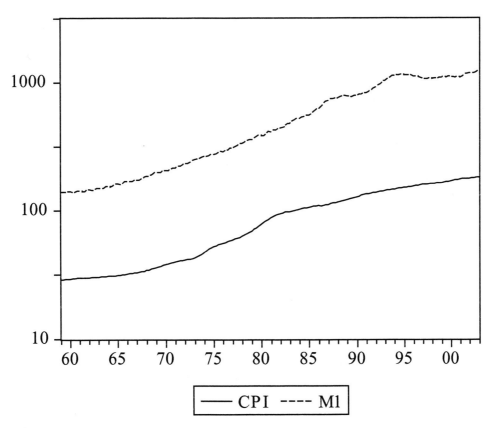

Figure 4.11   Historical Relationship between Price Level and Money Supply

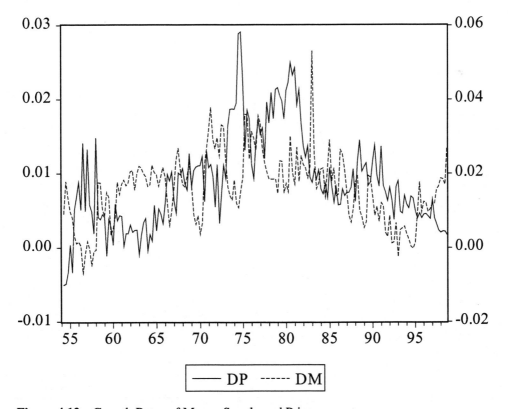

Figure 4.12   Growth Rates of Money Supply and Price

The **quantity theory** is a very simple model that can be used to explain Friedman's view of the world. The quantity theory is one of the oldest and most important theories in macroeconomics. It is written in the following manner:

$$MV = PY \tag{3.2}$$

The variable P is the price level for an economy. Recall that we computed the price level for Weena's village, the price level was a function of the prices for kiwi fruit and pineapples. With respect to the U.S., there are millions of goods so in the above equation P represents the average price of all goods in the economy. The variable Y represents real GDP, which we have also calculated before. The product of these two variables $P \times Y$, equals nominal GDP or total expenditures in the economy. In other words, all the households in the economy make purchases for the final goods and services that are produced in the economy. The expression PY represents those purchases.

It is assumed in this model that money is required to make or consummate all of these transactions. On the left-hand side of equation 3.2, M represents the total amount of money that circulates in the economy. Money is represented by currency such as a one-dollar bill, a five-dollar bill, etc. In addition, all the money that is contained in your checking account is another component of M. The variable V is referred to as **velocity** or the average turnover rate of a dollar bill. From another perspective, velocity represents the average number of times a dollar bill is spent to facilitate all the transactions in the economy.

As an example, suppose P = 10 and Y = 500. These numbers imply that the average price of all goods and services is $10 and that real GDP is $500. Therefore, nominal GDP is calculated to be $5000 or the total value of all transactions in the economy. Suppose there is $1000 in money in the economy that can be used to create the $5000 worth of transactions in the economy. On average, each dollar bill has to be spent five times to create $5000 worth of transactions.

$$MV = 1000 \times 5 = 10 \times 500 = PY$$

As an example, suppose person A purchases a glass of apple juice from person B for one dollar. Then person B takes that dollar and purchases a glass of grape juice from the grape stand down the block for one dollar. In this example, a single dollar bill has been used to create two dollars worth of transactions. In the real world, we can obtain very good data on M, P and Y but we cannot obtain data for velocity. Therefore, we solve out for velocity in the following way from equation 3.2:

$$V = PY/M$$

The quantity theory is actually written as an identity

$$MV \equiv PY$$

An identity requires that the right-hand side has to equal the left-hand side, but for our purposes, we will continue to use the equality sign.

Note that the quantity theory can be written in the following manner:

$$\%M + \%V = \%P + \%Y,$$

We have simply converted each of the variables to percentage growth rates.[1] The percentage growth rate of the money supply plus the percentage growth rate of velocity have to equal the percentage growth rate of the price level (inflation rate) plus the percentage growth rate of real GDP. From another perspective, if the right-hand side changes by 5% then the left-hand side has to change by 5% as well.

It is common to believe that spending patterns in the economy are relatively stable. Excluding teenagers and college students, most people who have full time jobs have fairly predictable spending patterns and therefore, we can assume that $\%\Delta V = 0$. To clarify, if the $\%\Delta V$ equaled a positive number that would mean that people are spending at a faster rate than they were before. There is no doubt that the average person can make a one time purchase that is atypical, but on average, it is reasonable to assume that velocity is relatively constant.

As we have presented above, the money supply is neutral in the long-run. An increase in the money supply can cause a temporary increase in output, but when prices and wages fully adjust to the increase in the money supply, output returns to the natural level of output. Friedman is a firm believer in this idea. Friedman believes that in the long run, growth in output is determined by changes in technology, population and accumulation of capital (factories, machinery, etc.). The money supply can influence output for a short period of time, but in the long run, changes in the money supply will have no impact on output. Economists have tested this theory for many years and there are many economists who believe this to be true. However, there are also a significant number of economists who believe that changes in the money supply can have a permanent impact on output.

Friedman's idea is straightforward. As an example, consider 1960–80 period in the U.S. where the average growth rate of real GDP was approximately 3% per year. Let's use the expression $\%Y^m$ to represent the mean or average growth rate of real GDP over time. The variable $\%Y$ will represent the actual value of the percentage growth rate in real GDP for a given year. In this context, there will be years when the actual growth rate in real GDP ($\%Y$) will be equal to the average growth rate in real GDP ($\%Y^m$). In other years, it will be the case that $\%Y^m > \%Y$, which would be consistent with a recession or slowdown in the economy. In other periods, the $\%Y^m < \%Y$, which is consistent with an expansion in the economy since it is growing at a faster rate than the average growth rate.

The **Friedman rule** states that monetary policy should be constructed in such a manner that the money growth rate, $\%M$, should be set equal to $\%Y^m$. In the case when $\%Y^m = 3\%$ per year, then the money supply should grow by 3% per year. As an example, suppose in a given year the actual growth rate of real GDP is equal to 3%. Then a 3% growth rate in the money supply will result in $\%P = 0$.

$$\%M + \%V = \%P + \%Y,$$

$$3\% + 0 = 0 + 3\%$$

Assuming that the $\%V = 0$ and setting $\%M = \%Y^m$ results in $\%P = 0$. In other words, the inflation rate would be zero for that year given this policy.

Of course there will be years when the growth rate of real GDP will differ from the average. During a recession, the value of $\%Y < \%Y^m$ and given a constant $\%M$, the inflation rate would rise. During an expansion when $\%Y > \%Y^m$ would cause a fall in the price level. Since we are examining the behavior of $\%Y$ over time, we would expect the expansions and contractions over time to offset one another. The inflation rate would rise during contractions and fall during expansions, but over time the average inflation would be zero.

---

[1] There is a mathematical proof to derive equation (3.3) from equation (3.2). That is beyond the scope of the class but if you are currently taking calculus, you may want to confer with your instructor on how to derive equation (3.3).

The Friedman rule says the changes in the money supply should be constant over time regardless of current economic conditions. Consider the following three years of economic activity.

$$\%M \ + \ \%V \ = \ \%P \ + \ \%Y$$

	%M + %V	=	%P + %Y
Year 1	3% + 0	=	0 + 3%
Year 2	3% + 0	=	1% + 2%
Year 3	3% + 0	=	−1% + 4%

In this example, we have three consecutive years where in year 1 the growth of real GDP is equal to the average of 3%. In year 2, the growth rate of real GDP is 2% while in year 3 the growth rate is 4%. The three values average to 3%. As you can see, the inflation rate will average out to zero. Friedman has argued that this policy over many years will result in an average inflation rate of zero. Thus, the zero inflation rate will result in stable interest rates since the expected inflation rate will be equal to zero. Recall the Fisher equation.

The Friedman rule became very controversial in economics for a number of reasons. One reason was that the policy was so simple that many economists did not believe it captured the complexities of the economy and therefore, would not be successful. Economists have been developing very complicated models of the economy, and using such a simple rule to guide monetary policy seemed counterintuitive. Another problem was that if such a policy were to be followed it would negate the need of the Fed in terms of regulating the economy. In terms of policy creation, there would be a diminished role of the Federal Reserve System. Robert always chuckled at that prospect. Most Fed economists were unsympathetic with the Freidman rule because it would put them out of a job.

One of Friedman's students, Robert Lucas, constructed an economic model to explain why the Friedman rule was potentially a very valuable policy rule. Lucas' theory revolved around the idea of relative prices, the prices of goods compared to other goods.

Consider the market for widgets in Figure 4.13. Let the price of widgets be represented by P^w. At point E, this market is in equilibrium and it is assumed that the firms who make up this market are producing at a level of output that maximizes profits. The issue that Lucas examined was the reaction of a firm to a change in demand. Lucas maintained that a demand curve would shift for two basic reasons. The first reason reflects decisions made by consumers, which are modeled to be unique to this particular market. Suppose this particular product has become more desirable to consumers and the the demand curve to shift from D to D'. The quantity supplied

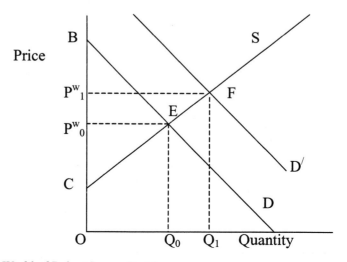

Figure 4.13   The World of Robert Lucas, Part I

increases and production rises to Q_1. This shift in demand is viewed as a market shift in demand due to reasons unique to that market.

Let P represent the price level for the entire economy. As the price of this good rises from P^w_0 to P^w_1, it is assumed that there is an increase in the relative price of this good. In other words,

$$P^w_1 / P > P^w_0 / P$$

It is assumed that the overall price level has not changed and, therefore, the relative price of this good has increased. We are assuming that this market is not large enough to affect the overall price level. An increase in the relative price of a good due to a shift in demand requires that the firm make some important decisions. Increasing production from Q_0 to Q_1 requires purchasing increasing amounts of labor and in some cases decisions about expanding the capital stock has to be considered. The decision to hire additional amounts of labor typically only requires a short-term commitment by the firm. It is not uncommon for a firm to attempt an expansion and hire more labor but only find out the demand was not sufficient. The new employees would be let go and the costs of making an incorrect decision to the firm are not large.

The decision to enlarge the capital stock for a firm requires a longer run decision by the firm. Expanding the size of a store or a factory or buying more machinery requires the firm to enter into a more substantial financial commitment that could last many years. The costs for the firms expanding the capital stock requires a longer run commitment for the firm and can have much more significant impacts when incorrect decisions are made. The purchase of capital typically requires borrowing money from the banking system. The firm will commit to paying back a loan over multiple years. The firm expects the proceeds attributed to the expansion of the business to at least pay back the loan and hopefully make a profit. For most firms, the revenue expected from the business is the only way to pay off the loan. If it turns out that the firm expanded and the shift in the demand curve to D' was only temporary then the firm could endure economic hardship.

In summary, the firm faces some very difficult decisions when faced with a shift outward in their market demand curve. If the demand curve facing the firm shifts outward for a reason unique to the firm or in other words, the relative position of the firm has improved. As discussed above, a decision about whether labor or capital should increase is an important decision that has to be made by the firm.

Unfortunately, there is another reason why the demand curve facing the firm can also shift outward. *An increase in the money supply will cause all demand curves to shift outward.* This

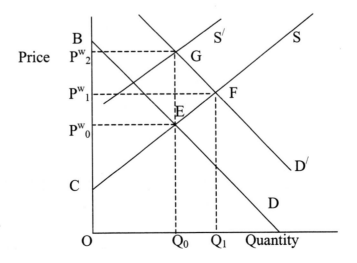

Figure 4.14 The World of Robert Lucas, Part II

is because the aggregate demand curve is made up of all the individual demand curves in the economy. The question is whether the average firm is better off when their demand curve shifts outward due to an increase in the money supply.

When there is an increase in the money supply, firms are temporarily better off as production increases from Q_0 to Q_1. However, as we have discussed previously, the overall price level increases faster than nominal wages for workers so workers are worse off as their real wage has declined. When workers are able to renegotiate their wage agreements, nominal wages will rise and costs of production will increase. In the case of our widget example, the supply curve will shift to S' and the production for this market returns to the original equilibrium quantity of production, Q_0.

This issue goes back to the idea underlying the production possibility frontier (PPF) as presented in Figure 4.15. With population and technology held constant and the economy operating on the PPF, the only way domestic production can increase is if resources are taken away from the production of national defense goods and reallocated to the production of domestic goods. However, for an increase in production of both goods, there has to be an increase in either population or technology.

In the case of an increase in the money supply, which causes all demand curves to shift outward, can all firms be made better off simultaneously? If the PPF does not shift outward, then all firms cannot be better off. The answer is no, an increase in the money supply will not cause the PPF to shift outward; therefore, all firms cannot be made better off. As we have discussed previously, an increase in the money supply can cause a *temporary* increase in output in the short-run but in the long run, an increase in the money supply has no impact on output.

The support for following the Friedman Rule comes from the above analysis. When the money supply increases, all demand curves will shift outward, but in the long run, no firms are made better off. When the firm sees that their demand curve has shifted outward, the problem is to determine whether the curve has shifted outward due to factors that are unique to this particular market or that the demand curve has shifted outward due to a change in the money supply. If the demand curve shifted outward due to market specific factors, then the firm can feel confident that at least hiring more labor is appropriate. Typically, when a firm believes that there has been an increase in demand and it is permanent, then they will hire more labor and possibly enlarge their capital stock. The important point is that the firm believes that the expansion in demand is permanent.

If the demand curve shifts outward and it is due to a change in the money supply, but the firm believes that the shift in demand is unique to their market, there can be a problem. The

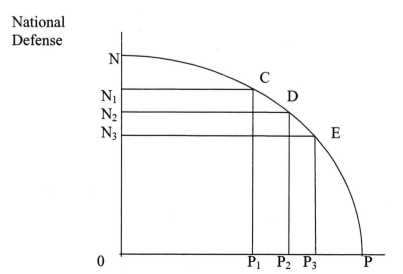

Figure 4.15   Production Possibilities Frontier

firm could hire more workers and enlarge the capital stock, which would be a mistake. Eventually, when all prices start to rise due to the increase in the money supply, the firm will realize that they are not better off and should not have expanded. It is possible that many firms may have been fooled and the performance of the overall economy could be hurt due to over-expansion. Firms that expanded their capital stock would have difficulty paying off the new loans since their production levels did not increase.

From the perspective of the Friedman Rule, if the money supply were to grow at an expected constant rate of say 3% per year and firms were aware of that then firms could anticipate what the impact of changes in the money supply would have on their demand curves. It would be less likely that they would be fooled and the chances of incorrectly increasing their productive capabilities would be reduced.

Robert was beginning to tire as both his mind and his legs were working hard. He decided to take a break and enjoy his surroundings. The scenery was surreal and he felt far removed from his daily routine even though his mind was not. As he rested, he thought that too many times during his climbs his excitement to reach the peak did not allow him to really enjoy the true beauty of nature. He vowed to change that, but as he sat, his eyes wandered over to the peak and he was soon on his way. Both his legs as well and his mind were back to work.

4.2.4. 1979 Recession

The recession in 1979 was a very short duration as it lasted less than one year. It was caused by another oil price increase emanating from the OPEC nations. However, since the U.S. economy had over six years to adjust to the first oil price shocks, the economy had since found a wide range of substitutes for oil related goods. The U.S. economy was much less dependent on oil related goods. As examples, many people had already purchased more fuel efficient cars, homes were being heated by electricity and natural gas, and people became accustomed to using mass transportation instead of driving their own automobiles to work. Nuclear power was also becoming more common in the U.S. Consider Figure 4.16, which presents the 1979 recession.

The increase in the price of oil caused a shift upward in the SRAS to SRAS'. Similar to the 1973–75 recession, the increase in oil prices caused an increase in the costs of production. The price level increased to P_1 and output fell from Y_n to Y_1. The LRAS did not shift during this recession as it did during the 1973–75 recession, thus the natural level of output did not change, only the *cyclical* component, Y_c, of output was negative.

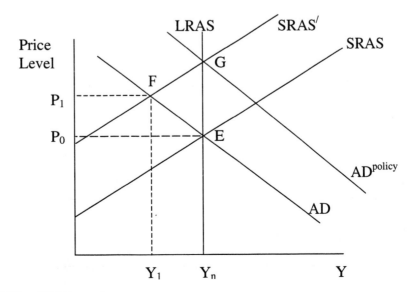

Figure 4.16 1979 Recession

This occurred for two reasons. The first is that the economy had already found substitutes for oil related products; therefore, the increase in oil prices had a smaller impact in the economy. The second reason was that since the U.S. was less dependent on oil, the OPEC nations did not benefit as much when they reduced oil production. By the end of 1979, the OPEC nations increased the production of oil and oil prices fell back to the early 1979 prices. The short-run aggregate supply curve shifted back to SRAS and the recession was over.

Robert again thought about Maria's experience with this recession. By this time, Maria's company, Knowledge Inc., was booming, as her company was building and selling personal computers to households and firms. Maria's company prospered because her computers were regarded as some of the highest quality computers made to date. In 1979, her company employed over 100 people, many of whom were her coworkers that had been laid off from IBM during 1973–1975 recessions. Maria felt good. Not only did she have her own company, she was able to help her coworkers improve their lives that would otherwise been hurt due to effects of unemployment.

When the 1979 recession hit, Maria panicked. She remembered what happened at IBM and dreaded having to lay off her friends and coworkers if the economic situation worsened. Fortunately, it did not. Since the recession was of short duration, Maria did not have to permanently lay off any of her workers. After a short period, the business of computers picked up and the few workers that she did lay off were quickly rehired; however, this short-term recession got Maria into thinking about her company. Building personal computers was getting to be extremely competitive and Maria could feel the pressure of trying to keep up.

4.2.5. 1981–82 Recession

Robert finally reached the summit of Mt. Quandry. He sat down, took out his lunch and started to eat. As he took in the sights of countless mountain tops his mind drifted to the 1981–82 recession. This recession was much more controversial since many economists blamed the Federal Reserve for causing this recession. The inflation rate in 1980 was close to 10%. This high rate was due to the general rise in oil prices during the 1970s and an aggressive monetary policy, which caused the aggregate demand curve to shift to far rightward during the 1973–75 and 1979 recessions. Figure 4.17 can explain the problem that occurred in early 1980.

Due to the oil price shocks of the 1970s as well as aggressive monetary policy, the economy was in long-run equilibrium; however, the economy was at point E. Since inflationary expecta-

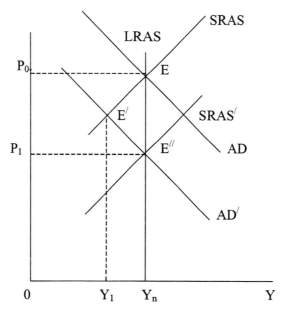

Figure 4.17 The 1981–82 Recession

tions were relatively high, the short-run aggregate supply curve was at SRAS and the price level was at P_0, which was very high relative to recent economic history. The Federal Reserve wanted to be at point E'', but that would require a significant reduction in inflationary expectations.

The chairman of the Federal Reserve, Paul Volcker, came to the conclusion that the only way to get to point E'' was to reduce the money supply, which should eventually cause a reduction in inflationary expectations, but there would be a temporary decrease in real GDP. As the story goes, the Federal Reserve started to reduce the growth rate of the money supply by open market operations. More specifically, the Federal Reserve sold bonds. The impact was a shift inward in the aggregate demand curve from AD to AD'. This caused a reduction in real GDP to Y_1 and the 1981–82 recession.

The reduction in output from Y_n to Y_1 caused the cyclical component of output, Y_c, to become negative. Output had fallen below the natural level of output, which implies that $Y_c < 0$. The natural level of output had not changed, but there has been a departure of output around the natural level of output. The distance $0Y_1 - 0Y_n = Y_c$, which is a negative value.

At point E', the economy has entered into a recession since output has fallen. Figure 4.18 displays the contemporaneous impact in the labor market. As the aggregate demand curve shifts inward, the labor demand curve shifts inward to $L^{D'}$. There is a reduction in employment to L_1. Since prices are more flexible than wages, it is the case that the price level falls more than the fall in the wage rate. At E' we have the following relationship:

$$W_0 / P_0 < W_1 / P_1.$$

The real wage has increased and the level of employment has fallen. When wage agreements can be renegotiated, workers will be willing to take a cut in their wages to get their jobs back. In the long-run, nominal wages are negotiated downward which results in a reduction in the costs of production. Simultaneously, the SRAS in Figure 4.16 shifts outward to SRAS' and the labor supply curve in Figure 4.18 shifts out to $L^{S'}$. When the economy returns to long-run equilibrium, we find that,

$$W_0 / P_0 < W_2 / P_2.$$

In the long-run workers are not worse off. They had to accept a lower nominal wage to keep their jobs, but since the price level had fallen by the same amount, the real wage stayed constant.

Robert was in full agreement with this approach to monetary policy. The Fed reduced the money supply which caused a recession, but the policy did reduce the high inflationary

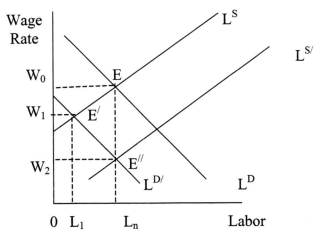

Figure 4.18 Labor Market

expectations that grew out of the unstable 1970s. This recession is viewed as temporary because the economy was able to return to the existing natural level of output.

After Robert finished lunch at the summit, he noticed some clouds below the peak and some bolts of lightening. This is the first time Robert ever remembers being above the lightening. He decided that he better get down soon because a headline reading, "Federal Reserve Economist Killed in a Lightening Storm: An Appropriate End", was not very appealing.

THE GREENSPAN YEARS

In the late 1980s, Alan Greenspan became the chairperson of the Federal Reserve. Greenspan realized that interest rate targeting was too difficult to implement and he was not a proponent of the Friedman Rule. Therefore, he needed to construct a monetary policy that did not have the potential pitfalls of the interest rate targeting. His objective was to create a policy that would result in the minimization of cyclical component of output. Recall the following relationship: $Y = Y_n + Y_c$, where the natural level of output (Y_n) is the optimal level of output. Any deviation away from Y_n was considered non-optimal. Greenspan's idea was to manage the position of the aggregate demand curve to minimize both inflation and deviations of output around the natural level of output.

Consider Figure 4.19. In the year 1997, the economy was very close to long-run equilibrium at point E. The logic of Greenspan's policy was to predict the positions of the LRAS, SRAS and AD curves for the following year, 1998. Greenspan had a number of econometricians on his staff. These are economists who examine the actual data for GDP, consumption, investment, interest rates and the money supply, and then use these data to construct economic models. The econometric models can then be used to predict the future in the sense of forecasting the positions of the LRAS, SRAS and AD curves.

In 1997, Greenspan's econometricians predicted that the aggregate demand curve would be at AD^{P98}. In other words, given the current direction of the economy, it was predicted that the aggregate demand curve would be too far rightward given the predicted positions of the LRAS

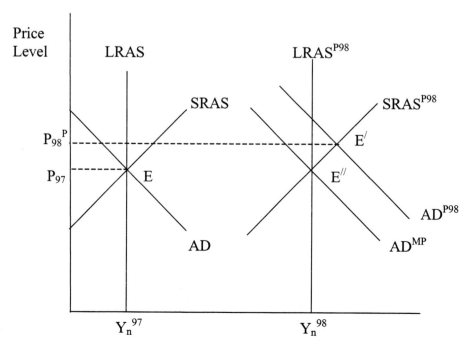

Figure 4.19   The Greenspan Approach to Monetary Policy

and SRAS curves. The predicted price level was $P_{98}{}^P$, indicating both an increase in the inflation rate and a departure away from long-run equilibrium. When Greenspan realized that his econometricians were predicting a short-run equilibrium in 1998 at E', the policy in 1997 was to reduce the growth rate of the money supply since it takes upward to a year for monetary policy to have an impact. He instructed the Federal Reserve to engage in open market sales of securities in 1997 in order to reduce the money supply. This would have the impact of shifting in the aggregate demand curve. Greenspan policy was very effective as the actual position of the aggregate demand curve in 1998 was at AD^{MP}. The policy caused there to be no increase in the price level and the economy operated at the natural level of output (E'') for 1998.

In fact, Greenspan had performed similar operations during most the 1990s that resulted in successful attempts of managing the position of the aggregate demand curve. However, in the summer of 1999, his econometricians predicted a similar scenario for the year 2000, as presented in Figure 4.20. In the summer of 1999, Greenspan's economists predicted that the AD would be at AD^{P00}, which again would result a large increase in the price level. The Federal Reserve engaged in open market sales of securities that reduced the money supply. Unfortunately, the predicted position of the aggregate demand curve was not correct since the actual demand curve would have been very close to long-run equilibrium (AD^A). When the Fed reduced the money supply in response to the expected position of AD^{P00}, it actually shifted the aggregated demand curve AD^A. The consequence was that the position of aggregate demand curve in 2000 was AD^{MP00}. This resulted in the beginning of the slowdown in the economy.

The reduction in money supply, though, was not the only factor that shifted the AD curve in 2000. Also during 2000, stock prices started a very slow two-year decline that was not predicted by the Federal Reserve. Falling stock prices resulted in decreasing wealth for households, and caused a further decline in the aggregate demand curve. In addition to the fall of stock prices, there was the terrorist attack on Septmeber 11, 2001, which caused a further decline in the aggregate demand curve. So in sense, the Greenspan monetary policy of 1999 was one of many factors in the recession that hit the U.S. economy. All of these factors resulted in AD curve being at AD^{mp00}. Output fell to $Y_1{}^{00}$ and the recession of 2001–03 started.

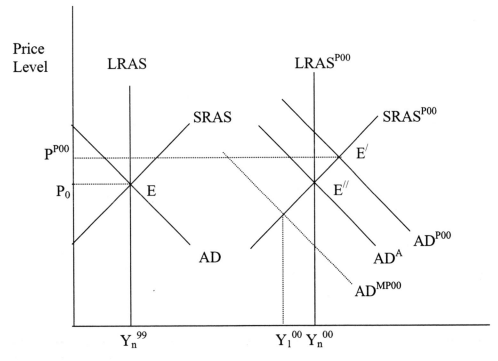

Figure 4.20 Illustration of 2001 Recession

Chapter 5

5.1. Government Sector

The role of federal, state and local governments has long been a controversial issue in our economy. Since this is a macroeconomics course, we will focus our discussion on federal government behavior. There are several levels that the government can influence the function of our economy. First, the government has imposed regulations in a variety of different markets such as the oil industry and the employment market for minimum wage workers. A second role of the government is to impose a wide range of taxes such as personal income taxes, corporate taxes and excise taxes. These taxes are used to finance government expenditures for national defense, domestic programs and for international aid.

The role of government expenditures in the economy is controversial. Early philosophers maintained that the role of the government should be to provide goods and services that the private sectors could not do profitably. As an example, consider how the private sector could provide national defense for the country. Private firms would have to run the army, air force and navy. They would have to charge a price to everyone for national security. How could private firms offer incentives for the average person to purchase a share of a naval submarine or jet fighter? Obviously, there would be problems in this market functioning at an acceptable level.

Instead, the federal government has imposed a series of laws that allows this institution to charge a wide range of taxes to households and firms that are used to finance a litany of government services that the private sector would be unable to supply profitably. The more high profile government services are:

- National defense
- Court system
- Police
- Highway system
- Domestic programs
- Space program

Our objective is to understand how expenditures for the above programs affect GDP and the price level. In addition, we need to understand how the imposition of taxes to pay for these expenditures also impacts the performance of the economy.

5.2. Government Expenditures and the Deficit

The federal government spends a vast amount of resources on many different programs that were briefly discussed above. Let us represent these expenditures as G. The government finances these expenditures by collecting taxes from private individuals and firms. There are many different types of taxes collected by all levels of government. There are income taxes, excise taxes, sales tax, import taxes, etc. To simplify our analysis, we can divide taxes into two parts; taxes on households and taxes on firms. Personal income taxes are an example of a tax on households. Taxes on firms could be corporate taxes, excise taxes or import taxes. Let the two tax rates be represented as the following:

t_1—tax rate on households

t_2—tax rate on firms

To keep our example simple, let's define tax revenue that is collected by the government as

$$(t_1 + t_2)\, Y = \text{tax revenue} = T.$$

Notice that tax revenue comes from payments made by firms and households but each component is a percentage of real GDP. In the real world, tax revenue is much more complicated but for our purpose this will do.

A major issue in our economy is the relative sizes of G and T. There have been periods of time when tax revenue exceeded government expenditures and the government ran a **surplus**. This occurred from approximately 1950–1969. From 1969–1998, the government expenditure exceeded tax revenue and this is referred to as a **deficit**. The government ran a surplus from 1999–2001 but after September 11, 2001 we moved into a deficit again.

The U.S. economy is currently experiencing a budget deficit, and this has been a major topic in the media. When there is a deficit, the government has to borrow money from the public. This loan is made through the use of bonds. The government will sell bonds to the public, offering a high enough rate of return to make it desirable for the public to invest in these bonds. From the standpoint of an individual, these bonds are viewed as a very safe investment because the government guarantees the stated rate of return. It is probably the safest form of investment that an individual can undertake. These bonds earn an interest rate that the individual receives several times a year. The process of the government borrowing from firms and households to help finance government expenditures is called *deficit financing*.

Adding up the deficits acquired each year sums to the value referred to as the *national debt*. The problem with the growing deficit is that the government has to borrow increasing amounts year after year. This implies that eventually the deficit could become larger than nominal GDP. In this case, it would be impossible for the government to borrow enough money from its citizens to finance the deficit. In early 2005, the national debt was about 65% of GDP. Obviously, the nation's leaders would not allow this to occur.

5.3. Impact of Government Expenditures on Aggregate Demand

The impact of an increase in government expenditures on aggregate demand is a controversial point. Recall the production possibility frontier (PPF), where the assumption of being on the PPF implies that an increase in government expenditures requires a decrease in private sector expenditures. As government expenditures increases by using more labor capital and land, it is the case that the private sector will use less of these inputs. There are three possible scenarios.

1 Some economists argue that since the private sector is more efficient at allocating resources, an increase in government expenditures will actually cause the aggregate demand curve to shift inward. As we have argued before, since the private sector is motivated by the maximization of profits, any behavior that does not lead to this maximization will be discontinued. Inefficient use of resources will be stopped in favor of a more efficient use of resources. Since the government does not maximize profits, their incentive to be efficient is quite lower, which leads to a more inefficient use of resources. The most obvious example is all the pork barrel spending that the congress and president authorizes each year. In summary, as the government increases expenditures, resources are allocated away from efficient uses towards inefficient uses. The result is that an increase in government expenditures leads to a decrease in aggregate demand.

2 Other economists argue that the government has a better understanding of the needs of the economy and the decision to allocate more resources to national defense, domestic programs, the judiciary and transportation needs is optimal for the long-run stability of the country. In this way, taking resources away from the private sector will make the economy stronger and contribute to greater growth in aggregate demand.

3 The third case is where (1) and (2) exactly offset each other and an increase in government expenditures has no effect on the position of the aggregate demand curve.

In summary, it is difficult to model in an aggregate supply and demand curve, the impact of an increase in government expenditures. It is more common to view government expenditures from the perspective of the specific purposes of the expenditures. As an example, the current discussion about the expenditures on the Iraq War emphasizes the impact on national security and not on the impact on aggregate demand.

5.4. Aggregate Supply

Another avenue where government expenditures can impact the economy is the research and development that arises from government expenditures. As an example, government expenditures in the space program led to much thinner and stronger plastic products that has been used by the private sector in making thinner and more attractive glasses. The increase in technology would be modeled as a simultaneous shift outward in the SRAS and LRAS curves.

5.4.1. Changes in Taxes

The government can also change tax rates, which can have significant impacts in the economy. As we have discussed above, there are income taxes on households, t_1 and taxes on firms, t_2, which can be changed in our model. A decrease in t_1 will result in households having a greater amount of their income to spend on goods and services, and thus the aggregate demand curve would shift outward. A decrease in the tax rate for firms, t_2, will result in a decrease in the costs of production. In addition, we model the reduction in this tax rate as also increasing the natural level of output. So a decrease in t_2 will cause the SRAS and LRAS curves to shift outward.

The history of tax rate changes in the U.S. has been interesting. The Republican Party has had the reputation of wanting lower taxes which they argue should lead to greater economic growth. The Democratic Party has argued that there are important government expenditures that need to be financed so that taxes for some groups should be higher than they currently are. There is no consensus in the economics profession regarding what the optimal set of taxes are so it is difficult to determine whether the Republicans or Democrats are correct.

Another important issue is the impact on the deficit of a change in tax rates. Consider a decrease in t_1 and t_2, which at the first level of effects should increase the deficit. Falling tax rates will initially cause a decrease in tax revenue and thus, an increase in the deficit. This can be seen by inspecting the following equation

$$(t_1 + t_2)\, Y = \text{tax revenue} = T.$$

A reduction in t_1 and t_2 will initially cause a reduction in tax revenue. However, over time it is argued by some economists that real GDP (Y) will increase enough such it will offset the fall in t_1 and t_2 and tax revenue will rise. A decrease in tax rates will cause the SRAS and LRAS schedules to shift outward and if the increase in output is large enough, tax revenue could eventually increase. The Reagan administration in the early 1980s made this argument as a reason to lower tax rates. Theoretically, this scenario is possible but it is difficult to determine whether this has ever happened.

Exams

Midterm 1A: Fall 2002

1. In 1953, President Eisenhower said:

   "Every gun that is made, every warship launched, every rocket fired signifies, in the final sense, a theft from those who hunger and are not fed, those who are cols and are not clothed. This world in arms is not spending money alone. It is spending the sweat of its laborers, the genius of its scientists, the hopes of its children."

   The President's statement most clearly expresses the concept of:
   a. Marginal Benefit
   b. Comparative advantage
   c. The law of demand
   d. Opportunity cost.

2. Specialization is important to trade because:
   a. increases the opportunity cost of producing output
   b. allows a country to purchase goods for a lower price from another country than they could purchase the good locally
   c. consume a combination of goods that could be produced without trade
   d. all of the above.

3. As country moves along the production possibility frontier:
   a. As the production of one good increases, the production of the other good increases
   b. As more of one good is produced, the cost of producing that good increases
   c. The more of one good that is produced, the resources used to produce that good become more and more efficient
   d. All of the resources or factors of production are not being used.

4. An example of rational behavior is:
   a. Arthur decides to get a job to purchase the guitar because the cost of buying the guitar is greater than the benefit he will get from buying it
   b. Rachel chooses to vacation in Aspen instead of the Bahamas because she enjoys the Bahamas more

c. Robert chooses to work as the manager of the apartment house because there are better jobs at the university

d. Maria decides to sell Chocolate Chip Cookies instead of running the retail store because she considers the Chocolate Chip Cookie business more profitable than the retail store.

Use the following information to answer the following four questions.

The U.S. and Argentina both produce wheat and beef. The production possibility frontiers for those countries are as follows:

United States		Argentina	
Beef	Wheat	Beef	Wheat
75	3	50	0
60	4	40	1
45	5	30	2
30	6	20	3

5. What should the U.S. do?
   a. Trade wheat for beef
   b. Not trade at all because they have an absolute advantage
   c. Trade beef for wheat
   d. Take the goods it needs by force.

6. Assume that the U.S. is consuming 45 pounds of beef and 6 bushels of wheat. What is true about the U.S. economy?
   a. It is impossible for the the U.S. to be in this situation
   b. The U.S. economy is at the optimum level of production for both beef and wheat
   c. The U.S. must be trading wheat for beef with Argentina to achieve this combination
   d. The U.S. must be trading beef for wheat with Argentina to achieve this combination.

7. Suppose the U.S. is producing 45 units of beef and 5 units of wheat and Argentina is producing 40 units of beef and one 1 of wheat. Assume that 1 bushel of wheat is traded for 13 pounds of beef. After trading, what is the combination of beef and wheat for both countries?
   a. U.S. 50 pounds of beef & 5 bushels of wheat; Argentina 43 pounds of beef & 2 bushels of wheat
   b. U.S. 17 pounds of beef & 5 bushels of wheat; Argentina 33 pounds of beef & 4 bushels of wheat
   c. U.S. 32 pounds of beef & 6 bushels of wheat; Argentina 53 pounds of beef & 0 bushels of wheat
   d. U.S. 62 pounds of beef & 4 bushels of wheat; Argentina 23 pounds of beef & 5 bushels of wheat.

8. Which of the following prices is the most favorable price for Argentina to trade at
   a. 1 bushel of wheat for 10 pound of beef
   b. 1 bushel of wheat for 1/10 pounds of beef
   c. 1 bushel of wheat for 1/15 pounds of beef
   d. 1 bushel of wheat for 15 pounds of beef.

Use the graph below in order to answer questions 9–10.

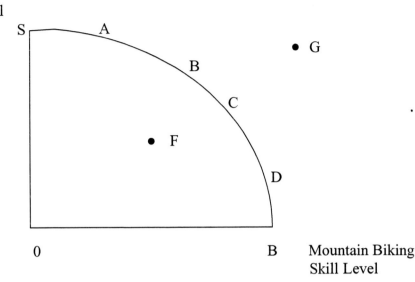

Rock Climbing Skill Level

S   A

B

C

G

F

D

0   B   Mountain Biking Skill Level

9. Given the above production possibility frontier, which of the following statements is true?
   a. The resources that are least suited to mountain biking are being reallocated as one moves from A to B
   b. A comparable reduction in time rock climbing results in a relatively larger improvement in mountain biking when comparing movements from A to B as opposed to C to D
   c. It is never a good idea to move from A to B
   d. Resource allocation efficiency is being reduced.

10. Which statement is accurate concerning the above graph?
    a. Point F is never attainable
    b. Point G is attainable
    c. Point A is unattainable
    d. Point G is attainable but it requires an improvement in technology.

11. The law of diminishing marginal returns (or product) implies:
    a. there will be an increase in wages and therefore an increase in labor demand
    b. eventually, there is a decline in the amount an additional variable input contributes to output
    c. output will increase indefinitely
    d. usually, output is inversely related to the amount of inputs.

The next two questions are based on the notion that the technology to produce personal computers has increased and as a result, the demand curve for typewriters has shifted inward.

12. Based on this information, which of the following is true?
    a. Computers and typewriters are compliments
    b. There has been a decrease in the quantity demanded for typewriters
    c. Computers and typewriters are substitutes
    d. There is no relationship between computers and typewriters.

13. Which is true?
    a. The quantity supplied for computers has decreased
    b. The supply of computers must increase
    c. The quantity demanded for computers decreased
    d. The demand for computers has increased.

14. An increase in the quantity demanded of baseball bats will likely result from:
    a. an increase in demand
    b. an increase in the quantity supplied
    c. an increase in the price of bats
    d. a decrease in cost of producing bats.

15. If the price of T-shirts in the market decreases, then it is likely that:
    a. supply has increased and the quantity demanded has increased
    b. the quantity demanded has increased and supply has decreased
    c. the quantity supplied has decreased and demand has increased
    d. supply has decreased and quantity demanded has decreased.

16. In order to protect local breweries, the government of Fort Collins has declared that "no 12 oz. bottle of apple juice shall be sold for under $1.25." The equilibrium price of a 12 oz. bottle of apple juice is $1.00. The result will likely be:
    a. an excess supply of apple juice on the market, driving the price further up
    b. an excess demand of apple juice on the market, driving the price down
    c. an excess demand of apple juice on the market at the price floor
    d. an excess supply of apple juices.

17. A change in the price of a good may
    a. shift the demand curve and cause a movement along it
    b. shift the demand curve but does not cause a movement along it
    c. not shift the demand curve but causes a movement along it
    d. neither shifts the demand curve nor causes a movement along it.

18. Which of the following **would** shift the demand curve for tacos?
    a. an increase in the number of taco bells
    b. A decrease in cheese and ground beef costs
    c. the surgeon general states that tacos will cause cancer
    d. A technological advance.

19. If the price of a good changes but everything affecting the demand curve remains constant, then there is a
    a. new demand curve
    b. movement along the demand curve
    c. movement along the supply curve
    d. rotation of the old demand curve around the old price.

20. If **Good X** is used to produce **Good Y**, then a rise in the cost of **X** will cause
    a. the supply of **Good Y** to increase
    b. the demand for **Good X** to increase

c. the supply of **Good Y** to decrease

d. the demand for **Good Y** to increase.

21. Consider the market for TV's and suppose there is a decrease in the costs of production. Which statement is false?

   a. consumer surplus increases

   b. the equilibrium price of TV's decreases

   c. the marginal value of the last unit consumed increases

   d. producer surplus or profits will increase.

22. Suppose there is an increase in income and an increase in the costs of production. What will be the effect on the equilibrium price and quantity?

   a. Both the price and the quantity will increase

   b. The quantity will increase but the change in price is ambiguous

   c. The price will rise but the change in quantity is ambiguous

   d. The price will fall and the change in quantity will increase.

23. In 1973, the price of oil rose dramatically as the OPEC nations reduced the production of oil which caused the supply curve of oil to shift inward. Why did economists predict that the price of oil would eventually decrease?

   a. the quantity demanded for oil should increase

   b. there is an increase in supply

   c. consumers will find substitutes for oil and substitute out of oil related goods

   d. the demand curve for oil becomes steeper.

24. Given the Second Law of Demand, which of the following is accurate?

   a. after price decreases, quantity demanded decreases over time

   b. given some price change, the demand curve shifts out over time

   c. given a decrease in price, quantity demanded increases over time

   d. none of the above.

25. What will happen to producer and consumer surplus when there is a decrease in demand?

   a. both producer and consumer surplus will increase

   b. both producer and consumer surplus will decrease

   c. producer surplus will increase and consumer surplus will decrease

   d. producer surplus will decrease and consumer surplus will increase.

ANSWERS

1. D	8. D	15. A	22. C
2. B	9. B	16. D	23. C
3. B	10. D	17. C	24. C
4. D	11. B	18. C	25. B
5. C	12. C	19. B	
6. D	13. B	20. C	
7. C	14. D	21. C	

Midterm 1B: Fall 2003

Use the following model to answer the next four questions. Assume the economy specializes in the production of only two goods, pineapples and kiwi fruit. This production possibility frontier is influenced by the law of increasing costs.

1. With respect to our model described above, the Production Possibilities Frontier
   a. could be drawn as a downward sloping straight line intercepting the vertical axis at some positive level of pineapples and the horizontal axis at some positive level of kiwi fruit.
   b. could be drawn as an upward sloping straight line intercepting the vertical axis at some positive level of pineapples and the horizontal axis at some negative level of kiwi fruit.
   c. could be drawn as an outward-bowing arc intercepting the vertical axis at some positive level of kiwi fruit and the horizontal axis at some positive level of pineapples
   d. cannot be drawn because no specific information regarding exact numerical amounts of production of either pineapples or kiwi fruit is presented in the model.

2. The Production Possibilities Frontier
   a. describes combinations of total output at which the economy is operating inefficiently.
   b. describes combinations of total output at which the economy is operating at less than full employment
   c. describes combinations of total output at which the economy is operating beyond its capacity and that is why it is referred to as a frontier
   d. illustrates the economic principle that for an economy to produce more of one good it must give up increasing amounts of the other good.

3. A parallel shift of the Production Possibilities Frontier inward or toward the origin
   a. could accurately be interpreted as an illustration of the concept that the capacity of the economy to produce both kinds of goods, pineapples and kiwi fruit, has improved or expanded over time
   b. could accurately be interpreted as a contraction in the capacity of the economy to produce both pineapples and kiwi fruit
   c. could accurately be interpreted as an illustration of the economic concept of opportunity cost
   d. could accurately be interpreted as an illustration of the economic concept of increasing costs of production.

4. The economic principle of scarcity is demonstrated in the Production Possibilities Frontier (PPF) model
   a. by the fact that society faces tradeoffs when it makes decisions regarding the relative quantities of goods to produce
   b. by the fact that points outside the PPF curve are unattainable for the economy in the given time period
   c. by the fact that the position of the PPF curve for any given time period is constrained by the limited quantity and productivity of the total factors of production
   d. all of the above are accurate representations of the economic principle of scarcity.

5. If **Good X** is used to produce **Good Y**, then a rise in the cost of **X** will cause
   a. the supply of **Good Y** to increase
   b. the demand for **Good X** to increase
   c. the supply of **Good Y** remains the same
   d. the quantity demanded for **Good Y** decreases.

The following four questions relate to the table below. Julia and Margaret both operate pie and cake stores. Below are their respective production table:

Julia		Margaret	
Cakes	Pies	Cakes	Pies
16	35	8	12
14	49	6	18
12	63	4	24
10	77	2	30

6. The tables above represent:
   a. The demand schedules for Julia and Margaret
   b. The supply schedules for Julia and Margaret
   c. The production possibilities frontiers for Julia and Margaret
   d. The gains from trade for Julia and Margaret.

7. A price of 1 cake for 7 Pies offered by Margaret to Julia:
   a. Offers gains from trade for Julia but not for Margaret
   b. Offers gains from trade for Margaret but not for Julia
   c. Offers gains from trade for both Margaret and Julia
   d. Does not offer gains for trade for either Margaret or Julia.

8. Using a price of 1 cake for 5 pies. Assume that Julia initially produced 14 cakes and 49 pies and Margaret initially produces 4 cakes and 24 pies. Assume that 2 cakes are traded for 10 pies. Which of the following is true.
   a. Margaret has 6 cakes after the trade
   b. Julia has 14 cakes after the trade
   c. Margaret has 34 pies after the trade
   d. Julia has 15 cakes after the trade.

9. The price range of pies to cakes that would interest Julia and Margaret to trade:
   a. Lies between 7 Pies and 4 Pies for 1 Cake
   b. Lies between 1/3 Cake and 1/7 Cake for 1 Pie
   c. Always lies somewhere within a range described by the opportunity costs of the person with the absolute advantage in production
   d. There is no price where both parties can benefit from trade.

U.S. companies like Nike and Brooks have located factories in Thailand to produce footware since production costs are much lower in Thailand than in the U.S.

10. The reason why U.S. citizens purchase footware made in Thailand is because
    a. profits will be lower for U.S. companies locating in Thailand
    b. consumer surplus is greater than if the footware purchased was produced in the U.S.
    c. prices for footware produced in Thailand are higher than if it was produced in the U.S.
    d. the costs of production in Thailand are higher than the U.S.

11. The relative position of the supply curve for footware in the U.S. and Thailand is best described by which of the following?
    a. The supply curve for footware in the U.S. should be further to the right than in Thailand due to higher costs of production in the U.S.
    b. The supply curve for footware in the U.S. should be further to the right than in Thailand due to lower costs of production in the U.S.
    c. The supply curve for footware in the U.S. should be further to the left than in Thailand due to lower costs of production in the U.S.
    d. The supply curve for footware in the U.S. should be further to the left than in Thailand due to higher costs of production in the U.S.

12. A reason why Thailand specializes in the production of footware is that
    a. profits will be greater if the footware is produced in Thailand
    b. profits will be smaller if the footware is produced in Thailand
    c. Consumer surplus will be smaller if the footware is produced in Thailand
    d. The costs of production would be lower in the U.S.

Consider the market for computers and suppose there is a substantial increase in technology in producing computers. Answer the following two questions.

13. Which of the following is true?
    a. the demand for computers should increase
    b. costs of producing computers should increase per unit
    c. consumer surplus should increase
    d. the quantity supplied should increase.

14. After the technological change has fully impacted this market, the second law of demand tells us that over time, we should expect to see
    a. the price of computers fall as consumers substitute out of computers
    b. no change in the price of computers
    c. the price of computers increase as consumers further substitute into computers
    d. a fall in technology.

In the 1970s, the federal government imposed a price floor for airline tickets. In other words, they would not allow airline tickets to fall below a certain level, which was above the equilibrium price. Answer the following two questions.

15. Relative to the equilibrium solution, this policy should
    a. cause the quantity demanded to increase
    b. cause an increase in the amount of unused airline seats

c. cause the price of airline tickets to fall

d. cause an increase in the number of airline tickets sold.

16. This policy should cause

    a. consumers to be made better off

    b. airline travel by consumers to increase

    c. consumer surplus to decrease

    d. the level of travel by consumers to be equal to the equilibrium solution.

17. If the price of T-shirts in the market decreases, then it is likely that:

    a. supply has increased and the quantity demanded has increased

    b. the quantity demanded has increased and supply has decreased

    c. the quantity supplied has decreased and demand has increased

    d. supply has decreased and quantity demanded has decreased.

18. The law of diminishing marginal returns implies:

    a. that costs rise per unit as production increases

    b. average output per worker is reduced as more workers are hired

    c. output increases but at a decreasing rate as production increases

    d. all of the above.

19. If supply increases then:

    a. There is an increase in consumer surplus

    b. There is an increase in quantity demanded

    c. There is an increase in quantity sold and a decrease in the price

    d. All of the above.

Use the Demand and Supply diagram below to answer the following four questions. Let the diagram represent a hypothetical national market for automobiles in which the only differentiating characteristic among automobiles is price.

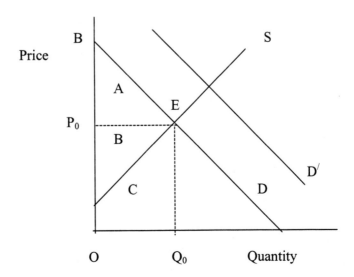

20. The area marked by the letter C, represents
    a. consumer surplus gained by buyers of automobiles at the market price P_0
    b. profits gained by buyers of automobiles at the market price P_0
    c. profits to sellers at the market price P_0
    d. cost to sellers for producing quantity OQ_0 at the market price P_0.

21. The area marked by the letter B represents
    a. Cost to sellers to supply output OQ_0
    b. Surplus gained by buyers of automobiles at the market price P_0
    c. The profit to sellers at the market price P_0
    d. total revenue.

22. The area A + B + C is best described by which of the following
    a. consumer surplus
    b. the minimum amount that consumers are willing to pay for OQ_0 units
    c. the total value to the consumer of consuming OQ_0 units
    d. Total revenue earned by sellers producing output OQ_0 units.

23. Which of the following will cause the demand curve to shift to D'?
    a. an increase in the cost of producing a complement
    b. a decrease in the cost of producing a substitute
    c. a decrease in income
    d. none of the above.

24. Total revenue increases
    a. because a shift outward in demand causes an increase in supply
    b. because an increase in supply leads to an increase in price
    c. when there is an increase in demand
    d. when consumer surplus remains unchanged.

25. If bicycles are a substitute good for automobiles and the cost of producing bicycles rises then:
    a. there is a decrease in total revenue for automobiles
    b. there is a decrease in the demand lines for bicycles
    c. there is a decrease in consumer surplus for automobiles
    d. there is a decrease in the quantity demanded for bicycles.

ANSWERS

1. C	9. B	17. A	25. D
2. D	10. B	18. D	
3. B	11. D	19. D	
4. D	12. A	20. D	
5. D	13. C	21. C	
6. C	14. C	22. C	
7. B	15. B	23. D	
8. C	16. C	24. C	

Midterm 1B: Fall 2004

Use the diagram below to answer the next three questions.

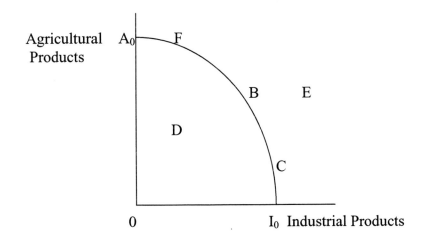

1. If an economy is operating at point D, this could be explained by
   a. many of the country's factories being destroyed in a war
   b. the country experiencing high unemployment during a recession
   c. choices that any country must make due to limited resources
   d. the law of diminishing returns.

2. Which of the following is true?
   a. The Law of Increasing Costs is demonstrated when we see that a movement from B to C will bring a smaller increase in industrial products than a move from F to B
   b. A move from C to B will cause the resources best suited to produce industrial products to shift to the production of agricultural products
   c. Point E is unattainable due to opportunity costs
   d. Point C is the most desirable on the curve because it is furthest to the right.

3. Consider the following production functions.

   Industrial Products = f(K,L,T)   Agricultural Products = f(K,L,T,X)
   where an increase in X results in an increase in Agricultural Products An increase in the input X will cause which of the following?
   a. The PPF to intersect the Y axis at a lower point
   b. The PPF to intersect the X axis at a point further to the right
   c. The PPF to intersect the Y axis at a point higher than A_0
   d. The maximum amount of industrial products that can be produced increases.

4. The economic principle of scarcity is demonstrated in the Production Possibilities Frontier (PPF) model
   a. by the fact that the PPF curve is hard to attain for most economies
   b. by the fact that the position of the PPF curve can never change over time

    c. by the fact that society faces tradeoffs when it makes decisions regarding the relative quantities of goods to produce

    d. by the fact that the PPF should always be a straight line.

5. If **Good X** is used to produce **Good Y**, then a decrease in the cost of producing **X** will cause

    a. the demand of **Good Y** to decrease

    b. the supply of **Good X** to increase

    c. the supply of **Good Y** to remain the same

    d. the quantity demanded for **Good X** to decrease.

The following four questions relate to the tables below. Jeremiah, Buck and Tex all produce corn and beef. Assume in the following 4 questions that the low cost producer of a good trades that good to the other two people in this system. Their production possibility frontiers (PPF) are the following:

Jeremiah		Buck		Tex	
Corn	Beef	Corn	Beef	Corn	Beef
10	0	18	0	4	0
8	2	14	2	3	2
6	4	10	4	2	4

6. The table above represents:

    a. the impact of the law of increasing costs in a PPF

    b. the law of diminishing marginal returns

    c. the maximum combinations of beef and corn that can be produced by Jeremiah, Buck and Tex

    d. both (a) and (b).

7. The low cost producer of beef is

    a. Tex

    b. Buck

    c. Jeremiah

    d. Jeremiah and Buck.

8. Which of the following statements is correct?

    a. Buck is willing to trade at a price of one corn for 1/4 beef

    b. For Tex, a price of one beef for 3/4 corn is a better price than one beef for 13/4 corn

    c. With a price of one beef for 11/4 corn, all three people can benefit from trade

    d. There is no single acceptable price that all three people can benefit from.

9. Suppose Buck trades corn, Tex trades beef and for Jeremiah to obtain corn he must trade with Buck and to obtain beef he must trade with Tex. The price is one corn for 3/4 beef. Which of the following is correct?

    a. No one can benefit from this price

    b. Jeremiah will trade with Tex to obtain beef

    c. Jeremiah will not trade with anyone

    d. Jeremiah will trade with Buck to obtain corn.

U.S. companies like Nike and Brooks have located factories in Thailand to produce footwear since production costs are much lower in Thailand than in the U.S. Answer the next 3 questions.

10. The reason why U.S. companies produce footwear in Thailand is because
    a. prices for footwear produced in the U.S. are lower than if it was produced in the Thailand
    b. consumer surplus is greater in the U.S. if the footwear was produced in the U.S.
    c. profits will be higher for U.S. companies locating in Thailand
    d. the marginal benefit to the consumer is lower when footwear is produced in U.S. rather than Thailand.

11. The relative position of the supply curve for footwear in the U.S. and Thailand is best described by which of the following?
    a. The supply curve for footwear produced in the U.S. should be further to the right than in Thailand due to higher costs of production in the U.S.
    b. The supply curve for footwear in the U.S. should be further to the right than in Thailand due to lower costs of production in the U.S.
    c. The supply curve for footwear in Thailand should be further to the left than in the U.S. due to lower costs of production in the Thailand
    d. The supply curve for footwear in Thailand should be further to the right than in the U.S. due to lower costs of production in the Thailand.

12. Consumer surplus may be greater if the footwear is produced in Thailand because
    a. profits will be lower if the footwear is produced in U.S.
    b. profits will be greater if the footwear is produced in Thailand.
    c. prices for footwear may be lower due to lower production costs
    d. All of the above are reasons consumer surplus may be greater

Consider the market for computers and suppose there is an improvement in technology in producing computers. Answer the following two questions.

13. Which of the following is true?
    a. the quantity demanded for computers should increase
    b. costs of producing computers should increase per unit
    c. consumer surplus should decrease
    d. the quantity supplied should increase.

14. After the technological change has fully impacted this market, the second law of demand tells us that over time, we should expect to see
    a. the price of computers fall as consumers substitute out of computers
    b. the demand curve flatten, causing the price of computers to fall as consumers substitute into computers
    c. the demand curve flatten, causing the price of computers to rise as consumers further substitute into computers
    d. a decline in technology.

In the 1970s, the federal government imposed a price floor for airline tickets. In other words, they would not allow airline tickets to fall below a certain level, which was above the equilibrium price. Answer the following two questions.

15. Relative to the free market solution, this policy should
    a. shift the consumer demand curve to the left
    b. create an excess demand of airline seats
    c. cause a fall in the welfare or consumer surplus for consumers
    d. cause an increase in the number of airline tickets sold.

16. If prices were allowed to fall to the equilibrium level
    a. consumers would be worse off
    b. airline travel by consumers would increase
    c. the consumer surplus would decrease
    d. the level of travel by consumers to would not change.

17. If the price of T-shirts in the market decreases, then it is likely that:
    a. technology increased and income decreased
    b. the costs of production increased and income increased
    c. the quantity supplied has decreased and demand has increased
    d. demand has decreased and the quantity supplied has increased.

18. The law of diminishing marginal returns implies:
    a. that costs per unit will always fall as production increases because of increased efficiency
    b. average output per worker is increased as more workers are hired
    c. a consumer gets satisfaction from the second unit of a product that is consumed, but not quite as much as from the first.
    d. average output per worker is reduced as more workers are hired.

19. If supply increases then:
    a. There is also an increase in quantity supplied
    b. There is an increase in quantity demanded
    c. There is a decrease in quantity sold and a decrease in the price
    d. Both price and quantity sold will increase.

Use the following Demand and Supply diagram for automobiles to answer the following 3 questions.

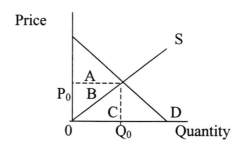

20. The area marked by the letter A, represents
    a. consumer surplus gained by buyers of automobiles at the market price P_0
    b. profits gained by buyers of automobiles at the market price P_0
    c. profits to sellers at the market price P_0
    d. cost to sellers for producing quantity OQ_0 at the market price P_0.

21. The seller's cost to produce output OQ_0 is shown by the area marked by

    a. B b. C c. B + C d. A

22. Which of the following will cause the demand curve to shift outward?

    a. an increase in the cost of producing a complement
    b. an increase in the cost of producing a substitute
    c. an increase in technology
    d. all of the above.

23. If peanut butter and jelly are complements, which of the following would cause a decrease in the demand for jelly?

    a. An increase in the demand for peanut butter
    b. A decrease in the costs of producing peanut butter
    c. A decrease in the costs of producing jelly
    d. An increase in the costs of producing peanut butter.

24. If bicycles are a substitute for automobiles and the cost of producing bicycles rises then:

    a. there is an increase in total cost for producing automobiles
    b. there is an increase in the supply for bicycles
    c. there is an increase in consumer surplus for bicycles
    d. there is a decrease in the quantity demanded for automobiles.

25. Which of the following would shift the demand curve for tacos?

    a. an increase in the number of taco bells
    b. A decrease in cheese and ground beef costs
    c. the surgeon general states that tacos will cause cancer
    d. A technological advance.

ANSWERS

1. B	13. A	25. C
2. A	14. C	
3. C	15. C	
4. C	16. B	
5. B	17. A	
6. C	18. D	
7. A	19. B	
8. C	20. A	
9. D	21. B	
10. C	22. B	
11. D	23. D	
12. C	24. A	

Midterm 2B: Fall 2002

1. Which of the following would cause a decrease in demand for SUV cars?
   a. a rise in the price of SUVs
   b. a rise in the price of a substitute
   c. a fall in the price of the steel that is used to make SUVs
   d. a rise in the price of gasoline.

2. If oranges and apples are substitutes in consumption but are grown in different parts of the country, then bad weather in orange-growing territory will cause:
   a. the price of apples to rise
   b. the price of apples to fall
   c. the demand for apples decreases
   d. the supply of apples decreases.

3. Suppose the surgeon general announces that apple juice is good for the heart and will help people live longer. Which of the following is most likely to occur?
   a. the supply of apple juice will decrease
   b. the price of apple juice will fall
   c. the equilibrium quantity of apple juice will fall
   d. the price of a substitute for apple juice should fall.

4. An editorial in the Coloradoan on Sunday, Oct. 6 2002 argues:
   "Water taps for new homes come out of existing [quantities] of water. This means that there is no increase in demand on our water … by these homes or taps." Given that water taps are a homes access to the city water supply, determine if this argument is true or false, and for what reason.
   a. true, because supply will change
   b. true, because demand will change
   c. false, because demand would increase
   d. false, because supply will change.

5. Orthodontists put braces on teeth. Suppose the proportion of the population that need braces falls but orthodontists decide not to lower the price for braces. The initial impact would be
   a. a shortage in the braces market
   b. an excess supply in the braces market
   c. an excess demand in the braces market
   d. a quality decrease.

6. Professional baseball teams in the United States use only wooden bats. If aluminum bats were permitted, the likely result would be
   a. A shift in the supply curve for aluminum bats.
   b. A shift in the supply curve for wooden bats.
   c. A change in the quantity supplied of aluminum bats
   d. A persistent shortage of aluminum bats.

7. An increase in the price of steel used to manufacture bicycles will lead to
    a. Higher prices for bicycles
    b. Lower prices for bicycles
    c. A shift in the demand curve for bicycles
    d. Larger output of bicycles.

8. The recession of 1973–75 is viewed as a permanent recession since there was a permanent loss in output. The 1981–82 recession is viewed as a temporary recession since there was no permanent loss in output. Given these facts, which of the following statements is correct?
    a. The level of consumption should have increased due to the 1973–75 recession
    b. The level of consumption should have decreased due to the 1981–82 recession
    c. The level of consumption should have decreased due to the 1973–75 recession
    d. The level of consumption should have increased due to the 1981–82 recession.

9. We have assumed in class that the percentage change in velocity is zero. Which of the following supports this assumption?
    a. The money supply will increase due to an open market purchase of securities
    b. Consumption is viewed as a function of expected income and therefore the behavior of consumption is relatively stable
    c. Spending patterns in the economy are relatively volatile
    d. The percentage change in output over time is about 3%.

10. Economists believe that there is a strong positive relationship between changes in the money supply and the price level. Concerning these two variables, which of the following statements is **false?**
    a. An increase in the money supply will cause all demand curves to shift inward in the economy and cause all market prices to rise
    b. A decrease in the money supply extracts money from the economy and reduces the ability of people to spend money
    c. The quantity theory states that all expenditures have to be consummated with the use of money
    d. An increase in the money growth rate will increase the inflation rate.

The following three questions are related to the Friedman Rule. Assume that the average growth rate of real GDP is 3% per year, the percentage change in velocity is zero and the Federal Reserve is following the Friedman rule.

11. Suppose for 1999, the percentage growth in real GDP was 4% and for 2000 the percentage change in real GDP was 1%. Which of the following is true?
    a. The average inflation rate over the two years should be 5.0%
    b. The average inflation rate over the two years should be 3.0%
    c. The average inflation rate over the two years should be –2.0%
    d. The average inflation rate over the two years should be 0.5%.

12. The primary advantage of the Friedman Rule is that
    a. over the long-run, the inflation rate should average out to equal the average long-run growth rate in real GDP
    b. over the long-run, positive inflations rates should average out with negative inflation rates to equal zero

c. the velocity rate should always be maximized

d. For a given year, the inflation rate should always be equal to zero.

13. Regarding the growth rate in output, Friedman assumed that

    a. the inflation rate is directly related to the growth rate in real GDP

    b. the growth rate in output is primarily influenced by changes in the money growth rate

    c. the growth rate in real GDP is primarily influenced by changes in population, technology and the capital stock

    d. the percentage change in velocity is always changing.

14. Suppose you lend $100 to a friend for a year and during that year the price level decreased by 3 percent. Which of the following is correct?

    a. The purchasing power of your $100 has risen over the year regardless of the interest rate at which you lent it out at

    b. The purchasing power of your $100 has remained constant over the year regardless of the interest rate at which you lent it

    a. You must have earned a nominal interest rate of 10 percent to maintain the purchasing power of your $100

    b. You must have earned a real interest rate of 10 percent to maintain the purchasing power of your $100.

15. Suppose the inflation rate is 3% and the nominal interest rate is 8%. What is the present benefit of the income stream of $100 today, $300 a year from now and $500 two years from now.

    a. $862.56

    b. $806.45

    c. $839.23

    d. $900.00.

16. Suppose you expect to receive $5000 three years from now. Suppose the inflation rate is 10% and the nominal interest rate is 10%. Which of the following statements is true?

    a. The present benefit of the $5000 is $3757

    b. The present benefit of the $5000 is $4319

    c. If the payment was shifted to the second year then the present benefit should increase

    d. Receiving the money today or three years from now results in the same present value.

17. Suppose you lend money out a three-year period of time and during the length of the loan there is an unexpected increase in the inflation rate. Which of the following is true?

    a. The lender would be better off

    b. The lender would be worse off

    c. The borrower would be worse off

    d. Neither the borrower or lender would be impacted.

18. A(n) _____ in the discount rate will _____ the money multiplier

    a. increase; have no effect on

    b. increase; decrease

    c. decrease; decrease

    d. increase; increase.

19. The money creation process (money multiplier effect) continues until
    a. required reserves are eliminated
    b. the Federal Reserve eliminates required reserves
    c. excess reserves are positive
    d. banks are fully loaned out.

20. Suppose the required reserve ratio is 0.05 or five percent and banks hold no excess reserves. If the money supply decreases by $5 million then the Federal Reserve must have sold how much in bonds?
    a. $1 million
    b. $0.25 million
    c. $10 million
    d. $0.5 million.

21. An open market purchase of securities should
    a. decrease the availability of excess reserves that could be loaned out
    b. decrease the money supply
    c. have no impact on the money supply
    d. increase the availability of excess reserves that could be loaned out.

The following four questions are based on this table of information:

		Price	Quantity
2000	Tacos	1	300
	Hamburgers	2	100
2001	Tacos	2	350
	Hamburgers	2.50	250
2002	Tacos	3	350
	Hamburgers	3	300

Assume for the next three questions, 2000 is the base year.

22. What is real GDP in 2001 and 2002?
    a. 850 (2001), 950 (2002)
    b. 1395 (2001), 1950 (2002)
    c. 1200 (2001), 1300 (2002)
    d. 850 (2001), 1575 (2002).

23. What is the inflation rate from 2001 to 2002?
    a. 57%
    b. 114%
    c. 27%
    d. 36%.

24. What is the price level in 2001?
    a. 1.4
    b. 2.2
    c. 2.7
    d. 3.

25. What would happen to real GDP in 2000 if we changed the base year to 2002?
    a. increase
    b. decrease
    c. stay the same
    d. cannot determine past GDP.

ANSWERS

1. D	9. B	17. B	25. A
2. A	10. A	18. A	
3. D	11. D	19. D	
4. C	12. B	20. B	
5. B	13. C	21. D	
6. C	14. A	22. A	
7. A	15. C	23. D	
8. C	16. D	24. B	

2nd Midterm A: Fall 2003

1. If the marginal productivity of capital increases then all of the following are true **except**:
    a. The MP_k schedule has shifted to the right
    b. Total investment at equilibrium has increased
    c. The MP_k schedule has rotated around its old investment point for a flatter slope
    d. The government bond market has become less appealing.

2. A(n) _____ in the discount rate will _____ the money multiplier
    a. increase; have no effect on
    b. increase; decrease
    c. decrease; decrease
    d. increase; increase.

3. The money creation process (money multiplier effect) continues until
    a. required reserves are eliminated
    b. the Fed eliminates required reserves
    c. excess reserves are positive
    d. none of the above.

4. Suppose the required reserve ratio is 0.15 or fifteen percent and banks hold no excess reserves. If the money supply increases by $10 million then the FED must have purchased how much in bonds?
    a. $1 million
    b. $1.5 million
    c. $10 million
    d. $0.5 million.

5. An open market purchase of securities should

   a. decrease the availability of excess reserves that could be loaned out

   b. decrease the money supply

   c. have no impact on the money supply

   d. increase the availability of excess reserves that could be loaned out.

6. The real interest rate is used to calculate present value problems because

   a. the nominal interest rate controls for inflation

   b. including the inflation rate in the present value analysis increases the present value of a future sum

   c. it does not eliminate the impact of inflation

   d. it removes the impact of inflation.

7. Ron has an option for two contracts with the Chicago Bulls. Option 1 is getting paid $300,000 for today, $400,000 one year from now and $600,000 two years from now. Option 2 is getting paid $400,000 today, $500,000 one year from now and $525,000 two years from now. With a real interest rate of 12%, which contract should he accept?

   a. Option 1 because he will make more in year two

   b. Option 2 because the present value of option 2 is $129,496 more than the present value of option 1

   c. Option 2 because the total value for option 1 is $1,300,000 (300,000 + 400,000 + 600,000) and the total value for option 2 is $1,425,000 (400,000 + 500,000 + 525,000)

   d. Option 2 because the present value of option 2 is $139,496 more than the present value of option 1.

8. Jimmy has just accepted a new contract that pays him once in two years from today's date and then one more time in five years from today's date. He has calculated his present value earnings at $198,030 and he also knows that he will earn $100,000 on his first payment. With a real interest rate of 8%, what is his last payment going to be?

   a. $166,469

   b. $186,233

   c. $164,999

   d. $178,987.

9. Rachael is just out of college and has gotten two job offers from George's Banners. Offer 1 pays her $30,000 dollars today, $45,000 one year from now and $50,000 two years from now. Offer 2 pays her $40,000 dollars today, $40,000 a year from now and $40,000 two years from now. However for the second option, the company allows her to put half her income today in an account that will earn 30% for one year. The real interest rate is 6%. Which offer should she accept?

   a. Offer 2 because the company bank has a higher interest rate

   b. Offer 1 because over the life times of both contracts she will be paid $3,617 more for offer 1 than for offer 2

   c. Offer 2 because its present value is higher than offer 1

   d. Offer 1 because its present value is higher than offer 2.

10. Sara knows she will receive 20,000 dollars when she graduates from college, which will be in 2 years. She has been wanting a car for some time now and is wondering if she should buy the car now or if she should wait and buy the car when she graduates. Knowing that car prices on average rise 5% per year and that the interest rate is 3%, when should she buy the car?

    a. She should buy it now because it would cost her more as a fraction of her income in the future
    b. She should buy it in the future because car prices are rising faster than interest rates
    c. She should buy it now because her present value of income is higher now than in the future
    d. She should buy it in the future because interest rates are growing slower than car rates.

11. Real GDP per person in both Alpha and Omega equals $2,000. Over the next 100 years real GDP per person grows at 10 percent annual rate in Alpha and at a 20 percent annual rate in Omega. After three years real GDP person in Alpha is approximately _____ smaller than real GDP per person in Omega.

    a. $300
    b. $680
    c. $720
    d. $790.

12. If technological improvement in the production of a good takes place at the same time the cost of producing a substitutes rises, then

    a. the equilibrium quantity sold will decrease
    b. the equilibrium price will increase
    c. the equilibrium quantity sold will increase
    d. the equilibrium price will decrease.

Answer the following five questions using the information in the table below.

Assume this economy produces two goods, pineapples and kiwi fruit. Use the year 2001 as the base year.

	Price	**Quantity**	**Total Revenue**
2000			
Pineapples	$10	500	$5,000
Kiwi Fruit	$15	300	$4,500
2001			
Pineapples	$14	550	7700
Kiwi Fruit	$18	350	6300
2002			
Pineapples	$17	600	10200
Kiwi Fruit	$16	450	7200

13. Which of the following is correct about real GDP?
    a. The percentage change in real GDP from the year 2000 to 2001 is equal to the percentage change from the year 2001 to 2002
    b. Real GDP is equal to nominal GDP in 2002
    c. The percentage change in real GDP is smaller from the year 2000 to 2001 than from the year 2001 to 2002
    d. Real GDP can never be less than real GDP.

14. Which of the following can explain what has happened to the price and quantity of kiwi fruit from 2001 to 2002?
    a. Nominal GDP had to rise in 2002
    b. The demand for kiwi fruit increased in 2002
    c. A technological improvement in producing kiwi fruit occurred in 2002
    d. The demand for kiwi fruit decreased in 2002.

15. Pineapples are more important in determining the price level because
    a. their contribution to nominal GDP in 2002 is greater than the contribution of Kiwi fruit
    b. their contribution to nominal GDP in 2000 is greater than the contribution of Kiwi fruit
    c. their contribution to real GDP in 2001 is greater than the contribution of Kiwi fruit
    d. they sold more pineapples than kiwi fruit.

16. Which of the following best explains the differences in the inflation rate from 2000 to 2001 and from 2001 to 2002?
    a. the base year weights give too much importance to pineapples
    b. The inflation rate for 2002 is greater than that for 2001 because individual prices increased by larger percentage amounts in 2002 than 2001
    c. There are no differences in the inflation rates
    d. The inflation rate for 2002 is less than that for 2001 because individual prices increased by smaller percentage amounts in 2002 than 2001.

17. Suppose the base year changed to 2002. Which of the following should occur?
    a. More weight should be assigned to kiwi fruit when determining the inflation rate
    b. More weight should be assigned to kiwi fruit when determining only real GDP
    c. A greater emphasis should be placed on the importance of pineapples when calculating the price level for any year
    d. Nominal GDP will be different than real GDP in 2002.

18. Holding other factors constant, a technological improvement that increases the marginal product of capital will
    a. cause aggregate demand to decrease
    b. cause the equilibrium level of investment to increase
    c. not have any impact on aggregate demand
    d. cause the price level to remain unchanged.

19. The minimum value of the ratio of bank reserves to bank deposits that the Federal Reserve allows commercial banks to hold is called:
    a. open-market purchases
    b. open-market sales

    c. the discount rate
    d. reserve requirements.

20. In Macroland there is $2,000,000 in currency. The public holds half of the currency their pockets and the other half is deposited in checking accounts. If banks' required reserve ratio is 5%, deposits in Macroland equal _____ and the money supply equals _____.

    a. 2,000,000; 2,100,000
    b. 20,000,000; 21,000,000
    c. 20,000,000: 22,000,000
    d. 20,000,000; 20,000,000.

21. Investment is a(n) _____ that changes the _____ of capital.
    a. flow; stock
    b. stock; flow
    c. asset; liability
    d. liability; asset.

22. We have assumed in class that the percentage change in velocity of money is zero. Which of the following supports this assumption?
    a. The money supply will increase due to an open market purchase of securities
    b. Consumption is viewed as a function of expected income and therefore the behavior of consumption is relatively unstable
    c. Spending patterns in the economy are relatively stable
    d. The percentage change in output over time is about 3%.

23. Economists believe that there is a strong positive relationship between changes in the money supply and the price level. Which of the following statements supports this idea.
    a. An increase in the money supply will cause all demand curves to shift inward in the economy and cause all market prices to rise
    b. A decrease in the money supply extracts money from the economy and reduces the ability of people to spend money
    c. The quantity theory states that all expenditures have to be consummated with the use of money
    d. An increase in the money growth rate will not affect the inflation rate.

24. If an increase in taste on the part of buyers of a good occurs at the same time the number of sellers of the good increases
    a. the equilibrium quantity sold of the good will fall
    b. the equilibrium price of the good will fall
    c. the equilibrium price of the good will rise
    d. the equilibrium quantity sold of the good will rise.

25. If trade negotiated market expansion leads to an increase in the number of buyers of a good at the same time costs of producing that good rise
    a. the equilibrium quantity sold will increase
    b. the equilibrium price will fall

c. the equilibrium quantity sold will decrease

d. the equilibrium price will rise

ANSWERS

1. C	9. C	17. C	25. D
2. A	10. A	18. B	
3. D	11. D	19. D	
4. B	12. C	20. B	
5. D	13. C	21. A	
6. D	14. C	22. C	
7. B	15. C	23. B	
8. C	16. D	24. D	

2nd Midterm A: Fall 2004

1. Ron has two options for a contract with the Minnesota Twins. Option 1 is getting paid $150,000 today, $150,000 one year from now and $150,000 two years from now. Option 2 is getting paid $100,000 today, $150,000 one year from now and $210,000 two years from now. With a real interest rate of 10%, which contract should he accept?

    a. Option 2 because the total value is $10,000 more than option 1

    b. Option 1 because the present value of option 1 is $1400 more than the present value of option 2

    c. Option 2 because his salary would increase sharply every year

    d. Option 1 because the present value of option 1 is about $413 more than the present value of option 2.

2. Jimmy has just accepted a new contract that pays him once in one year from today's date and then one more time in three years from today's date. He has calculated his present value earnings at $340,000 and he also knows that he will earn $100,000 on his first payment. With a real interest rate of 8%, what is his last payment going to be?

    a. $342,541

    b. $311,662

    c. $364,999

    d. $378,987.

$$v = .8 \qquad PV = \frac{340000}{(1.8)^1} + \frac{100,000}{(1.8)^3}$$

3. Rachael is just out of college and has gotten two job offers from George's Banners. Offer 1 pays her $30,000 dollars today, $45,000 one year from now and $50,000 two years from now. Offer 2 pays her $40,000 dollars today, $40,000 a year from now and $40,000 two years from now. The nominal interest rate of 8% and the inflation rate of 3% are expected to remain the same for the next three years. Which offer should she accept?

    a. Offer 1 because its present value is $3832 more than offer 2

    b. Offer 1 because its present value is $3203 more than offer 2

    c. Offer 2 because its present value is $4062 more than offer 1

    d. Offer 2 because its present value is $4321 more than offer 1.

4. Sara just received a 20,000 dollar college graduation gift from her rich uncle. If she saves the money for four years, what is the future value of the gift? She is offered a 6% interest rate and expects inflation to be stable at 3% annually.

   c. 22,510

   d. 25,250.

5. Real GDP per person is $2,000 in both of the neighboring countries of Collins and Greelia. However, real GDP is growing at an annual rate of 4% in Collins, but only 1% in Greelia. After five years what is the difference between the two countries in real GDP per person?

   a. $234

   b. $286

   c. $303

   d. $331.

Answer the following five questions using the information in the table below.

Assume this economy produces two goods, mangoes and bananas. **Use the year 2001 as the base year.**

6. Which of the following is correct?

   a. Real GDP increased in each year

   b. Both nominal and real GDP increased in each year

   c. Nominal GDP increased in each year

   d. Both nominal and real GDP declined in at least one year.

7. Which of the following can explain what has happened to the price and quantity of Mangoes from 2001 to 2002?

   a. Nominal GDP pushed up the price of mangoes in 2002

   b. The demand for mangoes increased in 2002

	Price	**Quantity**	**Total Revenue**
2000			
Mangoes	$10	500	$5,000
Bananas	$15	300	$4,500
2001			
Mangoes	$12	500	$6000
Bananas	$18	300	$5400
2002			
Mangoes	$14	600	$8400
Bananas	$20	450	$9000

    c. A technological improvement occurred in producing kiwi fruit, a substitute

    d. The supply for mangoes increased in 2002.

8. What is the percentage change in real GDP from the year 2001 to 2002?

    a. 25%

    b. 29%

    c. 34%

    d. 53%.

9. Is the rate of inflation larger between 2000 and 2001 or between 2001 and 2002?

    a. Between 2000 and 2001 (about 20%); inflation between 2001 and 2002 is less at about 13%

    b. The inflation rate for 2002 is greater than that for 2001 because individual prices increased by larger percentage amounts in 2002 than 2001

    c. There are no differences in the inflation rates

    d. The inflation rate between 2001 and 2002 is greater at about 25%; it is less that 15% between 2000 and 2001.

10. If the base year changed to 2000, to determine the price level

    a. bananas should be given the most weight.

    b. mangoes would be given the most weight in 2000, but bananas would be given the most weight in 2001

    c. mangoes would be given the most weight in 2001, but bananas would be given the most weight in 2002

    d. mangoes should be given the same weight as before.

11. Holding other factors constant, investment will increase

    a. if the price level rises

    b. if the marginal product of capital declines

    c. if the real interest rate decreases

    d. to counteract a decline in consumption.

12. If the Federal Reserve decides to raise the reserve requirement for banks

    a. banks will make more loans and money creation will accelerate

    b. investment will increase

    c. the discount rate will be pushed down

    d. less money will be created.

13. Suppose a bank receives a new demand deposit of $100,000. With a required reserve ratio of 10%, by how much can this bank increase its lending? As a result, how much is the additional increase in demand deposits in the banking system?

    a. 10,000; 100,000

    b. 900,000; 4,500,000

    c. 90,000; 900,000

    d. 1,000,000; 5,000,000.

14. Which of the following is true about real GDP and the price level?
    a. Changes in real GDP are determined by base year prices and not current prices
    b. Changes in real GDP will be proportionate to changes in the price level
    c. Changes in real GDP are inversely (same as negative) related to the price level
    d. No prices are used to calculate real GDP.

15. An increase in demand deposits will result in:
    a. An increase in the required reserves
    b. A decrease in the bank's liabilities
    c. no change in the loans of a bank
    d. A decrease in the loans of a bank.

16. There is a _____ relationship between the rate on government bonds and _____.
    a. inverse; the marginal productivity of capital
    b. positive; investment
    c. negative: opportunity cost
    d. inverse: rate of return on investment.

17. If a decrease in the demand on part of buyers of a good occurs at the same time that technology of producing that good increases, then
    a. the equilibrium quantity sold of the good will fall
    b. the equilibrium price of the good will fall
    c. the equilibrium price of the good will rise
    d. the equilibrium quantity sold of the good will rise.

18. If trade negotiated market expansion leads to an increase in the number of buyers of a good and at the same time, costs of producing that good falls
    a. the equilibrium quantity sold will increase
    b. the equilibrium price will fall
    c. the equilibrium quantity sold will decrease
    d. the equilibrium price will rise.

19. If technological improvement in the production of a good takes place at the same time that the cost of producing a complement falls, then
    a. the equilibrium quantity sold will decrease
    b. the equilibrium price will increase
    c. the equilibrium quantity sold will increase
    d. the equilibrium price will decrease.

20. If the marginal productivity of capital increases then:
    a. The MP_k schedule has shifted to the left
    b. The total cost of investment has not changed
    c. The return on government bonds has decreased
    d. The government bond market has become less appealing.

21. A(n) _____ in the required reserve ratio will _____ the money multiplier.
    a. decrease; have no effect on
    b. increase; decrease
    c. decrease; decrease
    d. increase; increase.

22. The money creation process (money multiplier effect) continues until
    a. required reserves are met
    b. the discount rate is higher than the market rate of interest
    c. loan possibilities are exhausted
    d. demand deposits are eliminated.

23. Suppose the Fed wants to increase the money supply by $20 million and the Fed purchased $4 million in bonds, what must the required reserve ratio be?
    a. 10 percent
    b. 15 percent
    c. 20 percent
    d. 25 percent.

24. In a given year, suppose the prices of all goods and services increase and the production possibility frontier has remained the same. One can be sure that:
    a. Inflation has occurred
    b. Real GDP has risen
    c. The Base Year has changed
    d. The price level has decreased.

25. A decrease in the money supply should:
    a. cause prices to increase due to a shifts outward in market demand curves
    b. cause prices to decrease due to a shifts outward in market demand curves
    c. cause prices to decrease due to a shifts inward in market demand curves
    d. cause prices to remain the same even though market demand curves shift inward.

ANSWERS

1. D	9. A	17. B	25. C
2. B	10. D	18. A	
3. A	11. C	19. C	
4. C	12. D	20. D	
5. D	13. C	21. B	
6. C	14. A	22. C	
7. B	15. A	23. C	
8. C	16. D	24. A	

Midterm 3: Fall 2002

Country Cutlerland is dominated by long-term wage contracts and country Econland is dominated by short-term wage contracts. Suppose there is an identical open market purchase of securities by the central bank (Federal Reserve) in both countries. These two countries are identical in all other respects. The next two questions are related to this occurrence.

1. In the short-run
   a. output in Cutlerland will rise by less than in Econland
   b. the price level will fall less in Econland than Cutlerland
   c. there will be an increase in output in Cutlerland
   d. the labor supply curve will shift in both countries.

2. In the long-run:
   a. The labor supply curve will shift outward for both countries
   b. The labor supply curve will shift outward for only Cutlerland
   c. The countries will reach different solutions for output
   d. None of the above.

Suppose Bill Gates dies suddenly and every computer that uses any Microsoft program explodes. The data can never be recovered and the technological level of the country decreases. Answer the following 4 questions based on this information.

3. Which is correct concerning the labor and output markets?
   a. the wage rate will decrease and output will increase
   b. there is a permanent decrease in output and a decrease in the nominal wage rate
   c. the increase in the supply of labor will cause an increase in the price level
   d. the natural level of employment decreases while the natural level of output will remain unchanged.

4. Which of the following is true concerning the nominal and real wage in the short-run?
   a. the nominal wage will rise
   b. the real wage will fall
   c. the real wage will rise
   d. none of the above.

5. Because of this decrease in technology, we should expect to see:
   a. Output increase
   b. The marginal productivity of labor decreases
   c. The price level falls
   d. The nominal wage increases.

6. What is the value of the cyclical component of output in the long-run?
   a. positive
   b. negative
   c. zero
   d. cannot determine.

7. Long term effects associated with the OPEC countries decision to reduce the world supply of oil in the mid 1970s resulted in
    a. a temporary loss in output
    b. a low rate of inflation during the late 1970's
    c. a permanent increase in employment
    d. households and firms finding substitutes for oil related products.

Suppose there are two countries, Cutlerland and Econland where the only difference is that Cutlerland is dominated by long-run contracts and Econland is dominated by short-run contracts. The next four questions relate to this scenario.

8. Which of the following is correct in the long-run?
    a. Consumer surplus should be larger in Cutlerland than in Econland
    b. Producer surplus should be larger in Econland than in Cutlerland
    c. Gains from trade should be the same in both countries
    d. You cannot compare the sizes of the gains from trade in both countries.

9. Suppose both countries raise the required reserve ratio from ten percent to twenty percent. We should expect to see which of the following:
    a. the cyclical component of output will be positive for a longer period of time in Econland
    b. the cyclical component of output will be positive for a shorter period of time in Cutlerland
    c. the price level will be the same in both countries in the long-run
    d. none of the above.

10. Suppose there is a temporary negative supply shock in both countries. Which of the following is correct?
    a. the SRAS will shift inward sooner in Cutlerland
    b. the SRAS will shift inward sooner in Econland
    c. the SRAS will shift inward at the same time for both countries
    d. the SRAS will not shift at all for either country.

11. Suppose the central bank in each country decides to engage in an open market purchase of bonds. Which of the following will occur?
    a. the price level in both countries will increase
    b. the price level in both countries will stay the same
    c. output will increase in both countries in the long-run
    d. the price level will fall in both countries.

12. Suppose the fast food labor market is in equilibrium and then the government establishes a minimum wage that is above the equilibrium wage in this market. Which of the following is correct?
    a. the number of workers employed in this industry should rise
    b. the number of workers employed in this industry should fall
    c. there will be an increase in the quantity demanded of labor in this market
    d. the wage rate will decrease.

13. An increase in the demand for a good will cause
    a. an increase in consumer surplus
    b. an increase in producer surplus

    c. an increase in gains from trade

    d. all of the above.

14. A fall in the discount rate and a fall in required reserve ratio will cause the money supply to

    a. rise

    b. fall

    c. stay the same

    d. unable to tell.

15. A decrease in technology will

    a. cause the SRAS to shift outward and the supply of labor to increase

    b. cause the SRAS to shift inward and the demand for labor to decrease

    c. cause the SRAS to shift outward and the demand for labor to increase

    d. cause the SRAS to shift inward and the LRAS to shift outward.

16. An increase in the money supply will result in

    a. an increase in the nominal wage in the short-run

    b. an increase in the real wage in the short-run

    c. a higher real wage in the long-run

    d. a lower real wage in the long-run.

17. The concept of long-run equilibrium is useful because:

    a. It reflects all the uncertainties in the economy

    b. It provides a reference point to evaluate the impact of economic policies in both c0 the short-run and long-run

    c. It demonstrates that monetary policy only has short-run impacts on the price level

    d. It demonstrates that monetary policy only has an impact on the price level in the long-run.

18. If the public expects the price level to decrease due to a decrease in the money supply, one can be sure that:

    a. the labor supply curve will shift inward and the SRAS will decrease

    c. the labor supply curve will shift inward and the SRAS shift outward

    b. the labor supply curve will shift outward and the LRAS will decrease

    d. the labor supply curve will shift outward in the long-run.

19. In the long-run, an increase in technology will:

    a. decrease employment and increase the nominal wage

    b. increase employment and increase the nominal wage

    c. have no effect on employment and decrease the nominal wage

    d. have no effect on employment and increase the nominal wage.

20. Suppose the average worker decided to spend more time working and less time pursuing leisure interests. We should expect to see:

    a. increase in the nominal wage, an increase in the price level, and a decrease in the LRAS

    b. a decrease in the nominal wage, a decrease in the price level, and an increase in the natural level of output

    c. a decrease in the price level and an increase in the nominal wage

    d. not enough information to predict outcomes.

21. The Federal Reserve decides that the economy needs a temporary slow down in the growth of output in order to avoid inflation. What policy should it implement to affect output in the short-run?
    a. Federal Reserve should engage in an open market sale that will, in turn, decrease the money supply
    b. Federal Reserve should not do anything at all since, in the long run, the output will be at its natural level
    c. Federal Reserve should engage in open market purchase that will, in turn, reduce the money supply
    d. Federal Reserve should engage in open market purchase that will, in turn, increase the money supply.

22. Suppose the Federal Reserve decides to boost the economy. What are the short run effects of an increase in the money supply?
    a. Output will stay the same and so will the prices
    b. Output will decrease and so will the prices since the SRAS is upward sloping
    c. Output will increase but the prices will stay the same
    d. Output will increase and the price level will rise.

23. Support for the Friedman Rule is obtained from the result that
    a. The money supply is neutral in the short-run
    b. An open market purchase of securities will have no impact on output in the long-run
    c. A decrease in the Federal funds rate will cause output to increase in the long-run
    d. None of the above.

24. Suppose a market chooses to produce output above the equilibrium quantity but sells the goods at the equilibrium price. We should expect to see a(n)
    a. Increase in producer surplus
    b. Increase in technology
    c. Decrease in the gains from trade
    d. Increase in consumer surplus.

25. Consumer and producer surplus describe
    a. Why people trade
    b. The gains that consumers obtain when trading
    c. The gains that producers obtain when trading
    d. All of the above.

ANSWERS

1. C	9. C	17. B	25. D
2. D	10. C	18. D	
3. B	11. A	19. B	
4. B	12. B	20. B	
5. B	13. D	21. A	
6. C	14. A	22. D	
7. D	15. B	23. B	
8. C	16. A	24. C	

Midterm 3B: Fall 2003

1. The money supply formula is $M^S = mm \times B$, where M^S represents the money supply, mm is the money multiplier, and B is the monetary base. Suppose the monetary base increases by 5%, then the money supply should increase by
   a. 2%
   b. 5%
   c. an amount determined by the value of the money multiplier
   d. 3%.

2. The foundation of the Friedman Rule $(\%)M = (\%) Y$ is based on the concept that
   a. in the long-run, an increase in the money supply increases the price level
   b. in the long-run, an increase in the money supply increases output
   c. in the long-run, an increase in the money supply has no effect on output
   d. in the short-run, an increase in the money supply increases output.

Assume for the next two questions that monetary policy follows the Friedman rule based on an average growth rate of real GDP = 5%.

3. Suppose for a given year that the $(\%) Y$ is 2%. According to the Friedman rule, the rate of inflation would be
   a. 2%
   b. 3%
   c. 5%
   d. –3%.

4. Continuing to implement the Friedman rule, now suppose over a three-year period the economy experienced an average 3% growth rate for real GDP. We should expect monetary policy to result in
   a. higher prices
   b. lower prices
   c. no change in prices
   d. a decrease in interest rates.

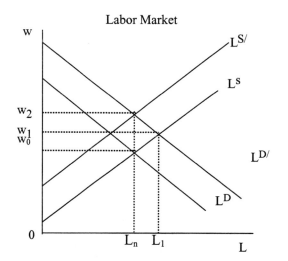

Labor Market

5. If expansionary monetary policy were to increase employment to $0L_1$, then in the long-run
   a. the real wage should increase
   b. the real wage should decrease
   c. the real wage should not change
   d. employment should increase.

6. An open market sale of US Treasury bonds by the Federal Reserve would
   a. increase the federal funds rate
   b. shift the demand curve for reserves inward
   c. shift the supply curve for reserves outward
   d. increase the equilibrium quantity of reserves.

7. Which of the following **best** explains why an open market purchase of securities (bonds) by the Federal Reserve leads to an increase in expected prices?
   a. more people are expected to borrow money but the aggregate demand curve should remain unchanged
   b. excess reserves will rise which should lead to an expected increase in loans and also an increase in the demand for goods and services
   c. the money supply should fall and prices should eventually fall
   d. excess reserves should rise but loans will not increase.

Country A is dominated by long-term wage contracts and Country B is dominated by short-term wage contracts. Suppose there is an identical open market purchase of securities by the central bank (Federal Reserve) in both countries. These two countries are identical in all other respects. The next two questions are related to this occurrence.

8. In the short-run
   a. real wages should remain unchanged in both countries
   b. real wages should increase for both countries
   c. real wages should be lower for a shorter period of time for Country B
   d. it is not possible to tell what will happen to real wages in the short run.

9. In the long-run:
   a. the solution for output will not be influenced by short-run or long-run labor contracts
   b. the solution for the price level will not be influenced by short-run or long-run labor contracts
   c. real wages will be the same in both countries
   d. all of the above.

The following three questions deal with interest rate targeting by the Federal Reserve in the 1960–75 period.

10. The logic of pursuing a policy of targeting the federal funds rate is best described by which of the following?
    a. Increasing the money supply every time commercial banks need to borrow from other banks will offset economic growth that is undesirable
    b. Stable interest rates should make it more difficult to estimate the discounted present value of expected income

c. It should allow consumers to make more informed consumption decisions as they view the future

d. It should minimize the inflation rate.

11. Suppose a number of commercial banks run short of excess reserves and find it necessary to increase their borrowing in the federal funds market. If the Federal Reserve wants to maintain the federal funds rate it will

a. engage in an open market purchase of securities (bonds) which should decrease excess reserves

b. engage in an open market sale of securities (bonds) which should increase excess reserves

c. engage in an open market purchase of securities (bonds) which should put downward pressure on the federal funds rate

d. raise the discount rate.

12. By the late 1960's, the ultimate problem for the Federal Reserve with targeting the federal funds rate was

a. increases in the money supply caused interest rates to fall

b. increases in the money supply caused the supply of reserves to increase

c. increases in the money supply resulted in stable interest rates

d. increases in the money supply caused an increase in the expected price level.

The next three questions relate to the 1973–75 recession.

13. This recession can be characterized by which of the following:

a. oil price shocks that caused the SRAS curve to become steeper

b. oil price shocks that caused the real wage to decline

c. oil price shocks that caused the SRAS to shift outward and the LRAS curves to shift inward

d. oil price shocks that caused the SRAS to remain unchanged.

14. Which of the following statements is true concerning this recession?

a. The U.S. reliance on oil-related products at that time increased the severity of this recession

b. Real wages increased during this recession

c. Changes in the money supply caused this recession

d. There was a shift outward in the labor demand curve.

15. The monetary policy of interest rate targeting had what effect during this recession?

a. Since prices were rising the Federal Reserve would decrease the money supply

b. Since prices and interest rates were rising, the Federal Reserve engaged in open market sale of bonds

c. Since prices and interest rates were rising, the Federal Reserve did nothing

d. Since prices were rising the Federal Reserve would increase the money supply.

16. The concept of long-run equilibrium is useful because:

a. it reflects all the uncertainties in the economy

b. it provides a reference point to evaluate the impact of economic policies in the short-run but not in the long-run

c. it demonstrates that monetary policy only impacts the price level in the short run

d. it demonstrates that monetary policy only impacts the price level in the long-run.

The next two questions are related to the 1979 recession.

17. This recession was less severe than the 1973–75 recession because
    a. oil prices rose permanently
    b. of the impact of the second law of demand
    c. the LRAS curve permanently decreased
    d. the money supply decreased.

18. This recession is viewed as temporary because
    a. oil price shocks had a permanent impact
    b. the long-run trend of output was never affected
    c. the long-run trend of output was reduced
    d. the cyclical component of output was never affected.

19. Assume Coke and Pepsi are substitutes. If the cost of producing Pepsi increases then
    a. the price of Coke would decrease and the price of Pepsi would increase
    b. the quantity supplied of Coke would increase and the quantity demanded for Pepsi would increase
    c. the quantity supplied of Coke would increase and the supply of Pepsi would decrease
    d. the price of Pepsi would decrease and the price of Coke would decrease.

20. In Harman country, some of the workers can renegotiate their contracts after one year, while others can only renegotiate their contracts after two years. If Harman experiences a ten percent increase in prices then:
    a. Overall workers are better off
    b. After one year all workers are equally well off
    c. After two years all workers are earning a lower real wage
    d. After one and a half years the real wage is lower than before the price increase.

21. If real wages have increased in the short run then:
    a. The SRAS has shifted inward
    b. The Federal Reserve Bank has sold securities in the market
    c. The natural level of output shifted inward
    d. Consumption has increased, while investment has fallen by the same amount.

22. If LRAS were to increase an average of three percent per year due to technological growth then real wages would:
    a. increase
    b. remain constant
    c. decrease
    d. be indeterminant.

23. If the natural rate of unemployment falls then:
    a. SRAS has shifted to the right
    b. AD has increased

c. The natural level of output has increased
d. The price level has increased.

24. If the natural level of output has decreased and the labor supply has remained constant then in the long run:
   a. Nominal wages have decreased
   b. Real wages have increased
   c. Price level has decreased
   d. Price level has remained constant.

25. In the spring of every year, people working in the ski industry in Colorado are laid off. This is an example of
   a. structural unemployment
   b. cyclical unemployment
   c. an increase in the natural level of unemployment
   d. a decrease in the natural level of unemployment.

ANSWERS

1. B	9. D	17. B	25. A
2. C	10. C	18. B	
3. B	11. C	19. C	
4. A	12. D	20. D	
5. C	13. B	21. B	
6. A	14. A	22. A	
7. B	15. D	23. C	
8. C	16. D	24. A	

Midterm 3B: Fall 2004

1. The money supply formula is $M^S = mm \times B$, where M^S represents the money supply, mm is the money multiplier, and B is the monetary base. Suppose the monetary base increases by 2%, then the money supply should increase by
   a. 2%
   b. 20%
   c. an amount determined by the value of the required reserve ratio
   d. an amount determined by the value of the real interest rate.

Assume for the next two questions that monetary policy follows the Friedman rule based on an average growth rate of real GDP = 3%.

2. Suppose for a given year that the (%) Y is 4%. According to the Friedman rule, the rate of inflation would be
   a. −1%
   b. 7%

    c. 1%

    d. −4%.

3. Continuing to implement the Friedman rule, now suppose over a three-year period the economy experienced an average 3% growth rate for real GDP. We should expect monetary policy to result in

    a. higher prices

    b. lower prices

    c. no change in prices

    d. an increase in inflationary expectations.

The following three questions is related to the labor market graph below.

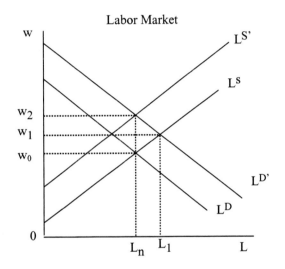

4. The increase in employment from L_n to L_1 is _____ if it is due to an _____.

    a. temporary; increase in the money supply

    b. temporary; increase in technology

    c. permanent; decrease in technology

    d. permanent; increase in the money supply.

5. Due to an increase in the money supply, the Labor supply schedule will shift from Ls to Ls′ in the long run due to _____, which will cause the SRAS curve to shift _____ .

    a. higher expected prices; inward;

    b. workers being better off; inward;

    c. worker's demanding higher wages;

    d. higher expected inflation; outward;

6. In the short-run a(n) _____ in the money supply will lead to a _____ real wage.

    a. increase; higher;

    b. decrease; lower;

c. increase; no change in the;

d. decrease; higher;

7. How will an increase in the money supply affect the country's Production Possibility Frontier (PPF)?

   a. It will permanently shift it out due to increases in all demand curves

   b. It will permanently shift it in due to higher inflation

   c. It will have no effect in the long run

   d. It will temporarily shift it in due to lower real wages.

Country A is dominated by long-term wage contracts and Country B is dominated by short-term wage contracts. Suppose there is an identical open market purchase of securities by the central bank (Federal Reserve) in both countries. These two countries are identical in all other respects. The next two questions are related to this occurrence.

8. Which of the following statements is **true** about price flexibility in each country?

   a. Prices should more flexible in Country A

   b. Prices should be more flexible in Country B

   c. Price flexibility should be the same in both countries

   d. It is not possible to tell which country has more flexible wages.

9. Which of the following statements is **true** about the Production Possibility Frontiers (PPF) in each country in the long-run?

   a. The PPF should be further out in Country A

   b. The PPF should be further out in Country B

   c. The PPF is the same in both countries

   d. There is not enough information to answer the question.

The following three questions deal with interest rate targeting by the Federal Reserve in the 1960–75 period.

10. The logic of pursuing a policy of targeting the federal funds rate is best described by which of the following?

    a. Increasing the money supply every time commercial banks need to borrow from other banks will offset economic growth that increases the federal funds rate

    b. A fixed inflation rate should make it easier to estimate present value analysis

    c. It should stabilize prices

    d. Controlling the nominal interest rate will reduce uncertainty in consumption decisions.

11. In the federal funds market for bank reserves, demand is characterized by:

    a. commercial banks that need to meet the required reserve ratio

    b. large commercial banks that desired to lower the discount rate

    c. commercial banks that want to increase their excess reserves in order to make more loans

    d. commercial banks that must buy securities(bonds) from the federal reserve.

12. Milton Friedman's criticism of the Fed's interest rate targeting was that:

    a. increases in the money supply would lead to a recession because of lower real wages

    b. increases in the money supply would result in an increase in inflationary expectations

    c. increases in the money supply would cause unemployment due to higher nominal wages

    d. increases in the money supply would make workers worse off in the short run.

The next three questions relate to the 1973–75 recession.

13. In this recession real wages declined because:

    c. LRAS shifted inward and the L_d also shifted inward

    d. SRAS shifted inward, causing labor supply to shift outward

    c. AD shifted left and labor supply shifted right

    d. The premise is false; only the nominal wage changed.

14. Which of the following statements is **false** concerning this recession?

    a. The U.S. reliance on oil-related products at that time increased the severity of this recession

    b. Real wages decreased during this recession

    c. As with most recessions, the price level fell

    d. There was a shift inward in the labor demand curve.

15. With a monetary policy of interest rate targeting, which of the following was implemented by the Fed?

    a. Since prices were rising the Federal Reserve would decrease the money supply

    b. To maintain constant interest rates, the Federal Reserve engaged in open market purchases of bonds

    c. Since prices and interest rates were rising, the Federal Reserve did nothing

    d. Since prices were rising the Federal Reserve rapidly increased the federal funds rate to slow down the growth of AD.

The next two questions are related to the 1979 recession.

16. This recession was less severe than the 1973–75 recession because

    a. oil prices were not involved

    b. of the second law of demand which suggests that with time consumers found lower cost sources of oil

    c. the LRAS curve permanently decreased

    d. By 1979, consumers had found substitutes for oil related products.

17. This recession is viewed as temporary because

    a. output returned to its previous level

    b. output returned to its long-run trend

    c. it was shorter than the 1973–1975 recession

    d. it was less severe than the 1973–1975 recession.

The next three questions relate to the 1981–82 recession. Prior to 1981, inflationary expectations were high due to the supply shocks of the 1970s.

18. During this recession

    a. Employment decreased temporarily due to supply shocks

    b. Employment decreased temporarily due to the Federal Reserve attempting to reduce inflationary expectations by increasing the money supply

c. Employment decreased temporarily due to the Federal Reserve attempting to reduce inflationary expectations by decreasing the money supply

d. Employment decreased temporarily due to the Federal Reserve attempting to increase inflationary expectations by increasing the money supply.

19. Which of the following statements is true?

a. output fell in the short-run due to the Fed buying bonds

b. output fell in the long-run due to the Fed buying bonds

c. output fell in the short-run due to the Fed selling bonds

d. the natural level of output was constant during this recession.

20. This recession is viewed as temporary because

a. the money supply increased

b. the long-run trend of output was never affected

c. the natural level of output decreased

d. the cyclical component of output was never affected.

Alan Greenspan, the Chairman of the Federal Reserve, has pursued a policy of predicting the future positions of the aggregate demand and supply curves and then using monetary policy to insure that the $Y = Y_n$ and the inflation rate should be minimized. This relates to the following two questions.

21. Suppose that Greenspan predicts that the future aggregate demand curve will cause the inflation rate to increase. This suggests that

a. it is predicted that the cyclical component of output will be positive in the future

b. Greenspan should increase the money supply today

c. Greenspan should lower the federal funds rate today

d. Greenspan should engage in an open market purchase of bonds.

22. Suppose that Greenspan predicts that the future aggregate demand curve will cause the inflation rate to be negative. Greenspan should

a. lower the federal funds rate today

b. engage in an open market sale of bonds

c. raise the required reserve ratio today

d. do nothing.

ANSWERS

1. A	9. bad question	17. B
2. A	10. D	18. C
3. C	11. A	19. C
4. A	12. B	20. B
5. A	13. A	21. A
6. D	14. C	22. A
7. C	15. B	
8. B	16. D	

Final Exam B: Fall 2002

1. If Good X is used to produce Good Y, then a decrease in the price of Good X would cause:
   a. Demand for Good Y to increase
   b. Supply for Good Y to increase
   c. Supply for Good Y to decrease
   d. Demand for Good X to increase.

2. If the demand for a good decreases while at the same time the costs of production increase, the likely result will be:
   a. Quantity will decrease and the price change is ambiguous
   b. Quantity will increase and price will decrease
   c. Quantity change is ambiguous and price will decrease
   d. Quantity change is ambiguous and price will increase.

3. Assume Coke and Pepsi are substitutes. If the cost of producing Pepsi increases then
   a. The price of Coke would decrease and the price of Pepsi would increase
   b. The quantity supplied of Coke would increase and the quantity demanded for Pepsi would increase
   c. The quantity supplied of Coke would increase and the supply of Pepsi would decrease
   d. The price of Pepsi would decrease and the price of Coke would decrease.

4. If peanut butter and jelly are complements, which of the following would cause a decrease in the demand for jelly?
   a. An increase in the demand for peanut butter
   b. A decrease in the costs of producing peanut butter
   c. A decrease in the price of jelly
   d. An increase in the costs of producing peanut butter.

5. A decrease in the price of plastic used to produce computer equipment will lead to:
   a. Higher prices for computers
   b. Lower prices for computers
   c. Output of computers to decrease
   d. Quantity demanded for computers to decrease.

Suppose there is a terrible storm in Florida and many of the orange trees die. The next two questions are related to this situation.

6. In the orange market:
   a. Supply decreases causing higher prices
   b. Demand decreases causing lower prices
   c. There is a decrease in quantity supplied and prices increased
   d. There is an increase in quantity demanded and prices decreased.

7. In the apple market (assume apples and oranges are substitutes):
    a. Supply decreases causing higher prices
    b. Demand increases causing higher prices
    c. Quantity supplied decreases
    d. Quantity demanded increases.

8. Suppose the government enacts a policy that stated that the maximum you can charge for apple juice is $1 per bottle. The price in equilibrium is $2. What is true?
    a. There is an excess supply and prices will not return to equilibrium
    b. There is an excess demand and prices will not return to equilibrium
    c. Producer surplus decreases
    d. Supply decreases.

9. Supply curve slopes upward because of the fact that as more units of a good are produced there are:
    a. increasing marginal costs
    b. increasing marginal benefits
    c. decreasing marginal costs
    d. decreasing marginal benefits.

10. What would have to happen in the labor market to have higher nominal wages?
    a. the expected price level will fall
    b. the marginal productivity of labor will have to increase
    c. the price of the good produced will fall
    d. money supply has to decrease.

The next three questions relate to the 1981–82 recession. Prior to 1981, inflationary expectations were high and due to the supply shocks of the 1970s.

11. During this recession
    a. Employment decreased temporarily due to supply shocks
    b. Employment decreased temporarily due to the Federal Reserve attempting to reduce inflationary expectations by increasing the money supply
    c. Employment decreased temporarily due to the Federal Reserve attempting to reduce inflationary expectations by decreasing the money supply
    d. Employment decreased temporarily due to the Federal Reserve attempting to increase inflationary expectations by increasing the money supply.

12. Which of the following statements is true
    a. the cyclical component of output was positive during this recession
    b. the natural level of output grew during this recession
    c. the natural level of output fell during this recession
    d. the natural level of output was constant during this recession.

13. This recession is viewed as temporary because
    a. the money supply increased
    b. the long-run trend of output was never affected
    c. the natural level of output decreased
    d. the cyclical component of output was never affected.

The next three questions relate to the 1973–75 recession.

14. This recession was caused by
    a. oil price shocks that caused the SRAS curve to shift outward
    b. a decrease in the money
    c. oil price shocks that caused the SRAS and LRAS curves to shift inward
    d. oil price shocks that caused the SRAS to remain unchanged.

15. Which of the following statements is true concerning this recession
    a. The U.S. reliance on oil related products at that time increased the severity of this recession
    b. Real wages increased during this recession
    c. Changes in the money supply caused this recession
    d. There was a shift outward in the labor demand curve.

16. This recession is viewed as permanent because
    a. the LRAS never shifted
    b. the long-run trend of output was never affected
    c. the long-run trend of output was reduced
    d. the cyclical component of output was never affected.

The next two questions are related to the 1979 recession.

17. This recession was less severe than the 1973–75 recession because
    a. Oil prices rose permanently
    b. The second law of demand
    c. LRAS permanently decreased
    d. The money supply decreased.

18. This recession is viewed as temporary because
    a. oil price shocks had a permanent impact
    b. the long-run trend of output was never affected
    c. the long-run trend was reduced
    d. the cyclical component of output was never affected.

19. A firm will increase production because
    a. a shift outward in a demand curve implies that the firms' relative price has fallen
    b. a shift outward in a demand curve implies that the firms' relative price has risen
    c. a shift outward in a demand curve implies that the firms' absolute price has fallen
    d. a shift outward in a demand curve implies that the firms' absolute price has remain the same

Suppose there is an unexpected increase in the money supply. Answer the following four questions.

20. An unexpected increase in the money supply can
    a. cause the firm to believe that their relative price has fallen
    b. cause the firm to believe that their absolute price is rising slower than the price level
    c. cause the firm to believe that their absolute price is rising faster than the price level
    d. cause the expected price level to rise.

21. The demand curves facing all firms will shift outward and
    a. output will rise in the short-run and the gains from trade will increase
    b. output will rise in the short-run and the gains from trade will remain the same
    c. output will rise in the short-run and the gains from trade will decrease
    d. output will rise permanently in the short-run.

22. The short-run impact of the unexpected increase in the money supply will
    a. cause output to increase because relative prices have increased
    b. cause output to increase because firms believe that there relative position has improved
    c. cause output to increase because relative prices have decreased
    d. cause output to decrease because relative prices have increased.

23. In the long-run
    a. gains from trade will increase relative to the short-run solution for the gains from trade
    b. gains from trade will decrease relative to the short-run solution for the gains from trade
    c. gains from trade will remain the same relative to the short-run solution for the gains from trade
    d. it is not possible to say anything about the gains from trade when comparing short-run and long-run solutions.

24. The role of the Federal government is to provide services such as national defense and domestic programs because
    a. the private sector is more efficient than the government in providing these services
    b. there is not enough employment in the private sector to provided these services
    c. the private sector cannot provide these services profitably
    d. the government is inefficient.

25. From the 1969–1999, the Federal government ran a budget deficit. The government was able to do this because
    a. they borrowed money from the private sector to make up the difference between tax revenue and expenditures
    b. they borrowed from the Federal Reserve to make up the difference between tax revenue and expenditures
    c. they borrowed from themselves to make up the difference between tax revenue and expenditures
    d. it is not possible to run a deficit.

26. Under the current Bush administration, the tax rate has been reduced for the private sector. This should have which of the following impacts
    a. increase the LRAS curve
    b. increase the SRAS curve
    c. increase the AD curve
    d. all of the above.

Over the period 1999–02, it is viewed that the economy is operating below the natural level of output.

Answer the following two questions in this context.

27. The economy is below the natural level of output because
    a. the LRAS has shifted inward
    b. the AD curve has shifted inward and inflationary expectations have not adjusted
    c. the SRAS has shifted outward
    d. the SRAS is unstable.

28. Greenspan has pursued a policy of expansionary monetary policy as a remedy to stimulate the economy because
    a. aggregate demand is viewed as too high
    b. aggregate demand is exactly where we want it to be
    c. aggregate demand is viewed as too low
    d. aggregate demand is stable.

The next two questions relate to the 1946–72 period in the U.S. economy. This is a period when the inflation was low and the wage rate was growing at a faster rate than inflation due to technological growth.

29. An increase in the money supply had a more permanent impact on output than in later periods because
    a. inflationary expectations were very sensitive to changes in the money supply
    b. an increase in the money supply resulted in a quick response of the SRAS
    c. an increase in the money supply did not lead to a higher expected price level
    d. an increase in the money supply was neutral.

30. A reason why changes in inflationary expectations were not sensitive to changes in the money is that
    a. the real wage was always falling
    b. the nominal wage remained the same
    c. the nominal wage continually fell
    d. technological changes out paced the inflation rate.

Alan Greenspan, the Chairman of the Federal Reserve, has pursued a policy of predicting the position of the future aggregate demand curve and then using monetary policy to insure that the aggregate demand is at a place such that the inflation rate should be equal to zero. This relates to the following two questions.

31. Suppose that Greenspan predicts that the future aggregate demand curve will cause the inflation rate to increase. This suggests that
    a. it is predicted that the cyclical component of output will be positive in the future
    b. Greenspan should increase the money supply today
    c. Greenspan should lower the federal funds rate today
    d. Greenspan should engage in an open market purchase of bonds.

32. Suppose that Greenspan predicts that the future aggregate demand curve will cause the inflation rate to be negative. Greenspan should
    a. lower the federal funds rate today
    b. engage in a open market sale of bonds
    c. raise the required reserve ratio today
    d. do nothing.

Jeremiah owns a farm that produces corn and beef. His neighbor Buck also owns a farm of similar size producing corn and beef. To the north of Buck, is another farmer named Tex. Tex also raises corn and beef. Their production possibility frontiers are the following:

Jeremiah		Buck		Tex	
Corn	Beef	Corn	Beef	Corn	Beef
10	0	14	0	4	0
8	1	12	2	3	2
6	2	10	4	2	4
4	3	8	6	1	6
2	4	6	8	0	8
0	5	4	10		

33. If all three farmers want to produce collectively 10 bushels of corn and as much beef as possible, you should have
   a. Buck grow all 10 bushels of corn
   b. Jeremiah grow all 10 bushels of corn
   c. Tex grow 4 bushels of corn and Buck grows the remaining 6 bushels of corn
   d. Tex grow 4 bushels of corn and Jeremiah the other 6 bushels of corn.

34. The maximum amount of corn that can be raised given that exactly 8 pounds of beef must be raised is:
   a. 17   b. 22   c. 24   d. 16

35. The least efficient corn grower is
   a. Buck
   b. Tex
   c. Jeremiah
   d. Jeremiah and Buck are equally inefficient.

36. A(n) _____ in the required reserve ratio will _____ the money multiplier
   a. increase; have no effect on
   b. increase; increase
   c. decrease; decrease
   d. increase; decrease.

37. The money creation process (money multiplier effect) continues until
   a. required reserves are eliminated
   b. the Federal Reserve eliminates require reserves
   c. excess reserves are eliminated
   d. the discount rate is lower than the market rate of interest.

38. Suppose the required reserve ratio is 0.10 or ten percent and banks hold no excess reserves. If the money supply increases by $10 million then the Federal Reserve must have purchased how much in bonds?
   a. $1 million
   b. $2 million

  c. $10 million

  d. $0.5 million.

39. The movements along a production possibility frontier is best described

  a. As the production of one good increases, the production of the other good increases

  b. As the price of a good increases, quantity demanded of that good decreases

  c. The more of one good is produced, the resources used to produce that good become less and less efficient

  d. All of the resources or factors of production are not being used.

40. Countries specialize in production in order to

  a. reduce the opportunity cost of producing output

  b. benefit from trading with other countries

  c. consume a combination of goods that could not be produced without trade

  d. all of the above.

ANSWERS

1. B	9. A	17. B	25. A	33. B
2. A	10. B	18. B	26. D	34. C
3. C	11. C	19. B	27. B	35. B
4. D	12. B	20. C	28. C	36. D
5. B	13. B	21. C	29. C	37. C
6. A	14. C	22. B	30. D	38. A
7. B	15. A	23. A	31. A	39. C
8. C	16. C	24. C	32. A	40. D

Final Exam B: Fall 2003

Use the Demand and Supply diagram below to answer the following four questions. Let the diagram represent a hypothetical national market for automobiles.

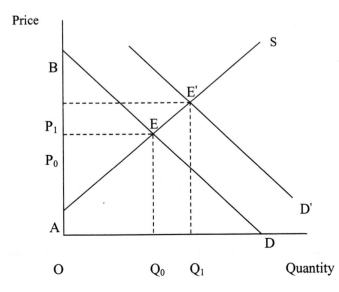

1. Given demand for automobiles, D, and supply of automobiles, S, the area BEP_0, represents
   a. producer surplus for sellers of automobiles at the quantity sold Q_0
   b. consumer surplus for buyers of automobiles at the market price P_1
   c. consumer surplus for buyers of automobiles at the quantity sold Q_0
   d. cost to sellers for producing quantity OQ_0 at the market price P_0.

2. Given demand for automobiles, D, and supply of automobiles, S, the area P_0EA represents
   a. cost to sellers to supply output OQ_0
   b. consumer surplus for buyers of automobiles at the market price P_0
   c. profit to sellers at the market price P_0
   d. total revenue for sellers at output Q_0.

3. If demand for automobiles increases to D′
   a. the area $P_1E′A$ is total cost for producers at output Q_1
   b. the area $P_1E′Q_10$ is total cost for producers at output Q_1
   c. the area AEQ_00 is the surplus for sellers after the increase in demand
   d. the area BEA is total market surplus from trade prior to the increase in demand.

4. Which of the following might cause the demand curve to shift to D′?
   a. An increase in the cost of producing a complement
   b. A decrease in the cost of producing a substitute
   c. An increase in the number of buyers of automobiles
   d. A decrease in the cost of producing automobiles.

5. If bicycles are a substitute good for automobiles and the cost of producing bicycles falls then
   a. the cost of producing automobiles will fall
   b. the demand for bicycles will increase
   c. the quantity demanded of automobiles will fall
   d. the price of automobiles will fall.

6. If Good Y is used to produce Good X, then a fall in the cost of producing Y will cause
   a. the demand for Good X to increase
   b. the supply of Good Y to increase
   c. the quantity supplied of Good Y to increase
   d. the quantity demanded of Good X to decrease.

7. Total revenue for a good increases
   a. because an increase in demand causes an increase in supply
   b. because an increase in supply leads to an increase in price
   c. because an increase in consumer income increases market sales
   d. because an increase in demand generates a fall in producer cost.

8. During a period of sustained technological improvement in the design and production of personal computers which of the following is true?
   a. Consumer surplus and producer surplus cannot rise simultaneously
   b. Consumer surplus would fall as producer surplus rose

   c. Consumer surplus should rise

   d. Producer surplus would rise as consumer surplus falls.

9. After technological progress has a total impact in the market, the second law of demand tells us that over time, we should expect to see

   a. the demand curve for the good should becomes flatter

   b. the quantity of the good sold should fall as consumers lose interest in the novelty of the good

   c. the demand curve for the good should become steeper

   d. the price of the good should fall as consumers substitute into the good.

10. A student of economics would expect that a government imposed price ceiling for airline tickets below the market equilibrium price of tickets would

   a. create an excess supply of airline tickets

   b. create an excess demand for airline tickets

   c. have no impact on the market for airline tickets

   d. make it easier for airlines to compete for customers.

11. A parallel shift of the Production Possibilities Frontier outward or away from the origin

   a. would indicate an economy is undergoing economic contraction

   b. is similar to a shift to the left of the economy's LRAS curve

   c. shows the opportunity costs of production have changed within the economy

   d. is similar to a shift to the right of the economy's LRAS curve.

12. The Production Possibilities Frontier

   a. shows combinations of total output at which the economy is operating efficiently

   b. shows combinations of total output where the economy is operating beyond its full capacity

   c. shows how much the economy is able to produce as demand falls

   d. shows what an economy could produce if it experienced technological improvement.

The following two questions relate to the tables below. Julia and Margaret both operate pie and cake stores. Below are their respective production tables:

Julia		Margaret	
Cakes	Pies	Cakes	Pies
14	32	7	12
11	44	5	16
8	56	3	20
5	68	1	24

13. Julia:

   a. must give up 2/5 of a cake to make 1 pie.

   b. is more efficient at making cake than is Margaret.

c. would be interested in trading 1 pie for 1/3 of a cake

d. and Margaret cannot increase their consumption through trade.

14. A price of 1 pie for 2/5 of a cake:

a. would be tempting to Margaret but not to Julia

b. falls inside the range of prospective prices of pie in terms of cake

c. would be tempting to Julia but not to Margaret

d. falls outside the range of prospective prices of cake in terms of pie.

15. If the LRAS were to decrease due to an increase in oil prices then real wages would?

a. Increase

b. Decrease

c. Remain constant

d. Indeterminate.

16. If real wages were to increase in the short run then:

a. aggregate demand has decreased

b. aggregate demand has remain constant

c. aggregate demand has increased

d. aggregate demand has shifted to the right.

17. If aggregate demand has decreased due to a change in the money supply then in the short-run, cyclical output is:

a. Unchanged

b. Zero because LRAS has shifted inward

c. Positive

d. Negative.

18. If the cyclical component of labor has decreased, then in the long run real wages will:

a. increase

b. decrease

c. not change

d. be indeterminate.

19. If the money supply increases spending then:

a. The natural level of output will increase

b. the natural level of employment will increase

c. The cyclical level of output will increase

d. The cyclical level of employment will decrease.

20. If the natural rate of unemployment increases then:

a. SRAS has shifted to the right

b. AD has increased

c. The natural level of output has decreased

d. The price level has remained unchanged.

21. If the natural level of output has increased and the labor supply has remained constant then in the long run:
    a. Nominal wages have decreased
    b. Real wages have increased
    c. Price level has increased
    d. Price level has remained constant.

22. If the discount rate were to increase, then in the long run output would:
    a. decrease
    b. increase
    c. remain constant
    d. be undetermined.

23. If the expected price level increases, then nominal wages will:
    a. decrease
    b. increase
    c. remain constant
    d. be undetermined.

24. If money supply has increased, then in the short-run the:
    a. price level has increased
    b. price level has decreased
    c. real wages have remained constant
    d. real wages have increased.

25. If the required reserve ratio is 20 percent and the Federal Reserve buy $2,000,000 worth of bonds then money supply has:
    a. decreased by $10 million
    b. increased by $10 million
    c. remained unchanged
    d. decreased by $2 million.

26. An open market purchase of US Treasury bonds by the Federal Reserve would:
    a. increase the federal funds rate
    b. shift the demand curve for reserves inward
    c. shift the supply curve for reserves outward
    d. decrease the equilibrium quantity of reserves.

27. Suppose a number of commercial banks have excess reserves and find it necessary to decrease their borrowing in the federal funds market. If the Federal Reserve wants to keep the federal funds constant, it will
    a. engage in an open market purchase of securities (bonds) which should decrease excess reserves
    b. engage in an open market sale of securities (bonds) which should increase excess reserves

c. engage in an open market sale of securities (bonds) which should put upward pressure on the federal funds rate

d. increase the money supply.

28. In Macroland there is $6,000,000 in currency. The public holds half of the currency their pockets and the other half is deposited in checking accounts. If banks' required reserves ratio is 10%, deposits in Macroland equal _____ and the money supply equals _____.

 a. 3,000,000; 3,300,000

 b. 30,000,000; 33,000,000

 c. 30,000,000: 36,000,000

 d. 30,000,000; 30,000,000.

29. Matt has to choose between two contracts, contract A pays $10,000 dollars today and $30,000 dollars one year from now. Contract B pays $20,000 today and $20,000 dollars one year from now. If the real interest rate increases then

 a. the present value of contract B should rise

 b. the present value of contract B should fall but the present value of contract A should rise

 c. the present value of contract B should fall more than for contract A

 d. the present value of contract A should fall more than for contract B.

30. Investment is a(n) _____ that changes the _____ of capital.

 a. flow; stock

 b. stock; flow

 c. asset; liability

 d. liability; asset.

31. The role of the federal government is to provide services such as national defense and domestic programs because

 a. the private sector is more efficient than the government in providing these services

 b. there is not enough employment in the private sector to provided these services

 c. the private sector cannot provide these services profitably

 d. the government is inefficient.

32. From the 1969–1999, the federal government ran a budget deficit. The government was able to do this because

 a. they borrowed money from the private sector to make up the difference between tax revenue and expenditures

 b. they borrowed from the Fed to make up the difference between tax revenue and expenditures

 c. they borrowed from themselves to make up the difference between tax revenue and expenditures

 d. it is not possible to run a deficit.

33. Under the current Bush administration, the tax rate has been reduced for the private sector. This should have which of the following impacts

 a. increase the LRAS curve

 b. increase the SRAS curve

    c. increase the AD curve

    d. all of the above.

Over the period 1999–02, it is viewed that the economy is operating below the natural level of output.

Answer the following two questions in this context.

34. The economy is below the natural level of output because

    a. the LRAS has shifted inward

    b. the AD curve has shifted inward and inflationary expectations have not adjusted

    c. the SRAS has shifted outward

    d. the SRAS is unstable.

35. Greenspan has pursued a policy of expansionary monetary policy as a remedy to stimulate the economy because

    a. aggregate demand is viewed as too high

    b. aggregate demand is exactly where we want it to be

    c. aggregate demand is viewed as too low

    d. aggregate demand is stable.

Alan Greenspan, the Chairman of the Federal Reserve, has pursued a policy of predicting the position of the future aggregate demand curve and then using monetary policy to insure that the aggregate demand is at a place such that the inflation rate should be equal to zero. This relates to the following two questions.

36. Suppose that Greenspan predicts that the future aggregate demand curve will cause the inflation rate to increase. This suggests that

    a. it is predicted that the cyclical component of output will be positive in the future

    b. Greenspan should increase the money supply today

    c. Greenspan should lower the federal funds rate today

    d. Greenspan should engage in an open market purchase of bonds.

37. Suppose that Greenspan predicts that the future aggregate demand curve will cause the inflation rate to be negative. Greenspan should

    a. lower the federal funds rate today

    b. engage in a open market sale of bonds

    c. raise the required reserve ratio today

    d. do nothing.

The next three questions relate to the 1981–82 recession. Prior to 1981, inflationary expectations were high due to the supply shocks of the 1970s.

38. During this recession

    a. Employment decreased temporarily due to supply shocks

    b. Employment decreased temporarily due to the Fed attempting to reduce inflationary expectations by increasing the money supply

    c. Employment decreased temporarily due to the Fed attempting to reduce inflationary expectations by decreasing the money supply

    d. Employment decreased temporarily due to the Fed attempting to increase inflationary expectations by increasing the money supply.

39. Which of the following statements is true
    a. the cyclical component of output was positive during this recession
    b. the natural level of output grew during this recession
    c. the cyclical component of output was negative during this recession
    d. the price level rose during this recession.

40. This recession is viewed as temporary because
    a. the money supply increased
    b. the long-run trend of output was never affected
    c. the natural level of output decreased
    d. the cyclical component of output was never affected.

ANSWERS

1. C	9. A	17. D	25. B	33. D
2. C	10. B	18. C	26. C	34. B
3. D	11. D	19. C	27. C	35. C
4. C	12. A	20. C	28. B	36. A
5. D	13. C	21. B	29. D	37. A
6. B	14. B	22. C	30. A	38. C
7. C	15. B	23. B	31. C	39. C
8. C	16. A	24. A	32. A	40. B

Final Exam A: Fall 2004

The following two questions relate to the table below. Julia and Margaret both operate pie and cake stores. Below are their respective production table:

Julia		Margaret	
Cakes	Pies	Cakes	Pies
14	32	7	12
11	44	5	16
8	56	3	20
5	68	1	24
3	12	2	4

1. Julia:
    a. must give up 1/3 of a cake to make 1 pie
    b. would be willing to trade 3 pies for one cake
    c. is more efficient at making cake than is Margaret
    d. and Margaret cannot increase their consumption through trade.

2. With respect to trade, a price of 1 pie for 2/3 of a cake:
    a. would be tempting to Margaret but not to Julia
    b. falls inside the range of prospective prices of pie in terms of cake

c. would be acceptable to Julia but not to Margaret

d. falls outside the range of prospective prices of cake in terms of pie for both parties.

3. If the LRAS were to decrease due to an increase in oil prices then

   a. demand for labor would decline

   b. labor supply would decline

   c. the natural rate of employment would increase

   d. the wage rate would increase.

4. Which of the following will cause the real wage rate to increase in the long run?.

   a. Technology has improved

   b. Aggregate demand has remained constant

   c. LRAS has shifted left

   d. Aggregate demand has shifted to the right.

5. If aggregate demand has increased due to a change in the money supply then in the short-run, cyclical output is

   a. unchanged

   b. zero because LRAS has shifted inward

   c. positive

   d. negative.

6. If the cyclical component of the employment level is positive,

   a. wages are rising faster than prices

   b. prices are rising faster than wages

   c. AD shifted inward

   d. It will cause SRAS to shift right.

7. If the money supply decreases then

   a. the natural level of output will increase

   b. the natural level of employment will increase

   c. the cyclical level of output will decrease

   d. the cyclical level of employment will increase.

8. If the discount rate was to decrease, then in the short run, output would:

   a. decrease

   b. increase

   c. remain constant

   d. be undetermined.

9. If the required reserve ratio is 10 percent and the Federal Reserve sells $1,000,000 worth of bonds then money supply has:

   a. decreased by $10 million

   b. increased by $10 million

   c. remained unchanged

   d. decreased by $1 million.

Use the Demand and Supply diagram below to answer the following four questions. Let the diagram represent a hypothetical national market for automobiles.

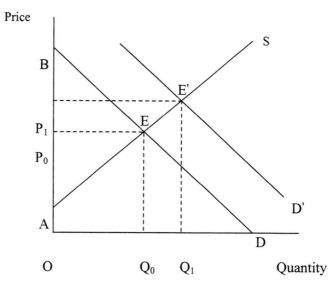

10. Given demand for automobiles, D, and supply of automobiles, S, the area AEQ_00, represents
    a. producer surplus for sellers of automobiles at the quantity sold Q_0
    b. consumer surplus for buyers of automobiles at the market price P_1
    c. consumer surplus for buyers of automobiles at the quantity sold Q_0
    d. cost to sellers for producing quantity OQ_0 at the market price P_0.

11. Given demand for automobiles, D, and supply of automobiles, S, the area BEP_0 represents
    a. cost to sellers to supply output OQ_0
    b. consumer surplus for buyers of automobiles at the market price P_0
    c. profit to sellers at the market price P_0
    d. total revenue for sellers at output Q_0.

12. If demand for automobiles increases to D'
    a. the seller's profit will increase
    b. the sellers cost will decrease
    c. the area $AE'Q_10$ is the surplus for sellers after the increase in demand
    d. the area $P_1 E'Q_10$ is total market surplus from trade after the increase in demand.

13. Which of the following might cause the demand curve to shift to D'?
    a. An increase in the cost of producing a complement
    b. A decrease in the cost of producing a substitute
    c. An increase in the cost of public transportation
    d. A decrease in the cost of producing automobiles.

14. If bicycles are a substitute good for automobiles and the cost of producing bicycles increases then
    a. the cost of producing automobiles will fall
    b. the demand for bicycles will increase

c. the quantity supplied of automobiles will increase

d. the price of automobiles will fall.

15. Suppose you receive $1000, and want to save it for three years. If the nominal interest rate (R) increases, the future value will

    a. decrease

    b. increase

    c. remain unchanged

    d. will be undetermined regarding an increase or decrease.

16. Suppose you expect to receive $1000 in three years and the real rate of interest declines. Your present value in real terms will be

    a. higher

    b. lower

    c. unchanged

    d. dependent on fiscal policy.

The next two questions are related.

17. During a period of sustained technological improvement in the design and production of personal computers which of the following is true?

    a. Both the consumer surplus and producer surplus can rise

    b. Both consumer and producer surpluses would fall

    c. Cost of production increases as consumer surplus rises

    d. Producer surplus would rise as consumer surplus falls.

18. After technological progress has a total impact in the market, the second law of demand tells us that over time, we should expect to see

    a. the price of the good fall as consumers substitute into the good

    b. the quantity of the good sold falls as new substitutes are invented

    c. consumers substituting into the good, causing the demand curve for the good should become steeper

    d. consumers substituting into the good, causing the demand curve for the good to becomes flatter.

19. In the past, government regulation created a price floor above the market price for airline tickets. Students of economics would expect the price floor to

    a. create an excess supply of airline tickets

    b. create an excess demand for airline tickets

    c. have no impact on the market for airline tickets

    d. make it easier for airlines to compete for customers.

20. Which of the following are compatible with a rightward shift of the long-run aggregate supply curve (LRAS)?

    a. An inward shift of the Production Possibilities Frontier

    b. A movement along the Production Possibilities Frontier

    c. An outward shift of the Production Possibilities Frontier

    d. A decline in technology.

21. On a Production Possibilities Frontier a country can
    a. increase production of both goods
    b. show what an economy could produce if worker skills improve
    c. show how much the economy is able to produce as demand falls
    d. increase production of one good only by decreasing production of another.

22. An open market sale of US Treasury bonds by the Federal Reserve would:
    a. increase the federal funds rate
    b. shift the demand curve for reserves inward
    c. shift the supply curve for reserves outward
    d. increase the equilibrium quantity of reserves.

23. Suppose a number of commercial banks lack required reserves and find it necessary to increase their borrowing in the federal funds market. If the Federal Reserve wants to keep the federal funds rate constant, it will
    a. engage in an open market purchase of securities (bonds) which should decrease reserves
    b. engage in an open market sale of securities (bonds) which should increase excess reserves
    c. engage in an open market sale of securities (bonds) which should put upward pressure on the federal funds rate
    d. engage in an open market purchase of securities (bonds) which should put downward pressure on the federal funds rate.

24. Matt has to choose between two contracts, contract A pays $20,000 dollars today and $40,000 dollars one year from now. Contract B pays $40,000 today and $20,000 dollars one year from now. If the real interest rate decreases then
    a. the present value of contract B should fall
    b. the present value of contract B should rise but the present value of contract A should fall
    c. the present value of contract B should rise more than for contract A
    d. the present value of contract A should rise more than for contract B.

25. For the present value to remain constant given an increase in the real interest rate, the future value must:
    a. increase
    b. decrease
    c. remain the same
    d. There is not enough information.

Suppose that over the next few years the economy operates above the natural level of output. Answer the following two questions in this context.

26. The economy is above the natural level of output because
    a. the LRAS has shifted outward
    b. the AD curve has shifted outward and wages are slow to adjust
    c. the SRAS has shifted outward
    d. the SRAS is unstable.

27. Suppose the Fed pursues a policy of expansionary monetary policy
    a. inflation will be minimal
    b. inflation will increase
    c. inflation will be negative
    d. unable to tell what will happen to inflation.

Alan Greenspan, the Chairman of the Federal Reserve, has pursued a policy of predicting the position of the aggregate supply and demand curves and then using monetary policy to insure that the aggregate demand is at a place such that the inflation rate should be equal to zero. This relates to the following two questions.

28. Suppose that Greenspan predicts that the future aggregate demand curve will cause prices to fall. This suggests that
    a. it is predicted that the cyclical component of output will be positive in the future
    b. Greenspan should increase the money supply today
    c. Greenspan should raise the federal funds rate today
    d. Greenspan should engage in an open market sale of bonds.

29. Suppose that Greenspan predicts that the future aggregate demand curve will cause the cyclical component of output to be positive. Greenspan should
    a. lower the federal funds rate today
    b. engage in an open market purchase of bonds
    c. engage in an open market sale of bonds
    d. do nothing.

30. During the 1981–82 recession
    a. Output decreased temporarily due to supply shocks
    b. Output decreased temporarily due to the Fed attempting to reduce inflationary expectations by increasing the money supply
    c. Output decreased temporarily due to the Fed attempting to reduce inflationary expectations by decreasing the money supply
    d. Output decreased temporarily due to the Fed attempting to increase inflationary expectations by increasing the money supply.

31. It was feared that the 2001–02 recession could have long-run impacts. Which of the following best explains why this concern was unwarranted?
    a. After 2002, output returned to its long-run trend
    b. After 2002, output was continued to fall
    c. After 2002, the money supply fell
    d. After 2002, interest rates decline.

The following two questions relate to the concept of shipping the good apples out. However, in this example we shall consider the market for expensive and inexpensive homes. We typically observe that expensive homes are built on expensive land and inexpensive homes are built on inexpensive land.

32. If all land prices increase by $1,000, then we should expect to see the relative price of expensive homes to
    a. increase
    b. decrease

    c. remain the same

    d. unable to tell.

33. If all land prices fall by the same amount, we should expect to see

    a. more inexpensive homes are built on inexpensive land

    b. more expensive homes are built on expensive land

    c. more expensive homes built

    d. less inexpensive homes built.

34. When the federal government is running a surplus, an increase in government expenditures will cause the aggregate demand curve to shift outward because

    a. the government has to borrow to finance this expenditure

    b. the government is injecting additional resources into the economy even though they have to borrow to do so

    c. Interest rates are rising

    d. additional resources are injected in the economy.

35. It is generally believed that the federal government is _____ than the private sector in producing national defense.

    a. more efficient

    b. less efficient

    c. just as efficient

    d. more technologically advanced.

36. An increase in business taxes should have which of the following impacts

    a. shift the LRAS curve inward and cause prices to rise

    b. shift the SRAS curve outward and cause prices to fall

    c. shift the AD curve inward

    d. it should not have an effect in the output market.

37. A decrease in the personal income tax rate should

    a. cause the aggregate demand curve to shift inward

    b. cause the price level to increase

    c. cause tax revenue to increase

    d. cause tax revenue to decrease.

The Bush Administration decreased both the personal income tax rate as well as business taxes. The next three questions relate to this policy.

38. Which of the following will definitely be a result of such a policy?

    a. the deficit will decline

    b. the price level will rise

    c. output will increase

    d. output will fall.

39. It is difficult to predict the impact on the deficit/surplus because

    a. a fall in tax rates will cause tax revenue to rise and the impact on output will cause tax revenue to fall

    b. a fall in tax rates will cause tax revenue to fall and the impact on output will cause tax revenue to fall

c. a fall in tax rates will cause tax revenue to fall and the impact on output will cause tax revenue to rise

d. a fall in tax rates will cause tax revenue to rise and the impact on output will cause tax revenue to rise.

40. Suppose the deficit rises as result of this policy. The reason why this deficit may be a larger problem than the deficit during the 1969–00 period is that

a. the number of people employed in the future will be a greater percentage of the total population

b. The government will always borrow enough money to finance the deficit

c. The number of retired people in the future will be a smaller percentage of the total population

d. The number of retired people in the future will be a greater percentage of the total population

ANSWERS

1. B	9. A	17. A	25. A	33. A
2. C	10. D	18. D	26. C	34. D
3. A	11. B	19. A	27. B	35. A
4. A	12. A	20. C	28. B	36. A
5. C	13. C	21. D	29. C	37. B
6. B	14. C	22. A	30. C	38. C
7. C	15. D	23. D	31. A	39. C
8. B	16. A	24. D	32. B	40. D

Exams

Midterm I: Fall 2005

Use the following illustration to answer the following four questions.

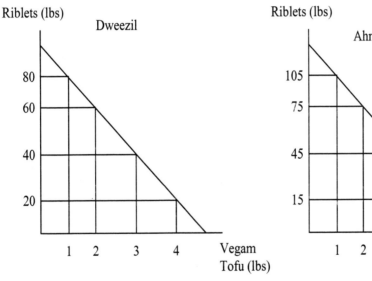

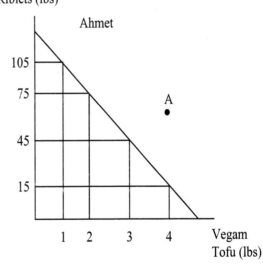

1. Consider the above graphs for Dweezil and Ahmet. Who is the low cost producer of vegan tofu?

    a. Dweezil

    b. Ahmet

    c. Both Dweezil and Ahmet can produce vegan tofu at the same price

    d. Not enough information to answer this question.

2. What is the best price for Dweezil to trade at?

    a. 25 lbs of riblets for 1 lb of tofu

    b. 29 lbs of riblets for 1 lb of tofu

    c. 20 lbs of riblets for 1 lb of tofu

    d. 1/20 lb of riblets for 1 lb of tofu.

3. Is it possible for Ahmet to obtain the combination of the two goods at point A?

    a. No because no point outside of the PPF is attainable

    b. Yes, if Ahmet trades tofu for riblets

    c. Yes, if Ahmet trades riblets for tofu

    d. Ahmet cannot reach point A even with trade.

4. Dweezil and Ahmet's dad, Frank, sets the price of 1 lb.   of vegan tofu at 20 lbs. of riblets. Dweezil and Ahmet trade 2 lbs. of tofu and 40 lbs. of riblets. Who gains from this trade?

    a. Dweezil

    b. Ahmet

    c. Ahmet and Dweezil

    d. No one.

5. If the quantity of T-Shirts sold in the market increases, then it is likely that:

    a. Technology has increased and income has decreased

    b. Income increased and costs of production decreased

    c. Demand has increased and t-shirt labor costs have increased

    d. Income has not changed and t-shirt labor costs have increased.

6. If bicycles are a substitute for automobiles and the cost of producing bicycles rises then:

    a. there is an increase in total cost for producing automobiles

    b. there is an increase in the supply for bicycles

    c. there is an increase in consumer surplus for bicycles

    d. there is a decrease in the quantity demanded for automobiles.

Moon Unit		Diva Muffin	
Fish (lb)	**Gravy (gallons)**	**Fish (lb)**	**Gravy (gallons)**
20	8	30	7
40	6	40	6
60	4	50	5
80	2	60	4

7. Consider the above tables for Moon Unit and Diva Muffin. Who has the comparative advantage in the production of gravy?

    a. Moon Unit

    b. Diva Muffin

    c. Both Moon Unit and Diva Muffin can produce gravy at the same price

    d. Not enough information to answer this question.

8. Germany is currently in a recession and is experiencing an unemployment rate of 18%. Germany also desires to be at point B, on the PPF. Currently, at which point is Germany *most likely* at?

    a. B only

    b. D only

Use the diagram below to answer the next three questions.

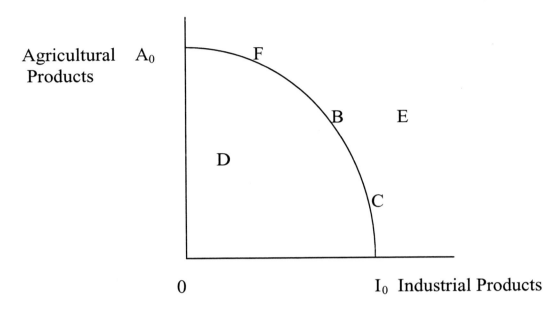

Agricultural Products A_0

F

B   E

D

C

0   I_0 Industrial Products

    c. F, B, or C

    d. none of the above.

9. Which of the following is true?

    a. The Law of Increasing Costs is demonstrated when we see that a movement from B to C will bring a smaller increase in industrial products than a move from F to B.

    b. A move from C to B will cause the resources best suited to produce industrial products to shift to the production of agricultural products.

    c. Point E is unattainable due to idle factors of production.

    d. Point C is the most desirable on the curve because it is furthest to the right.

10. Given the above graph, resource allocation efficiency along the Production Possibility Frontier:

    a. is decreasing due to diminishing marginal returns

    b. is increasing due to increasing costs

    c. is increasing due to diminishing marginal returns

    d. is as efficient as possible.

11. The town of Springfield just instituted a mass transportation system that reduces bus passes to $30. According to the second law of demand, we should expect:

    a. The price of a bus pass will remain at $30, and the demand curve will become steeper

    b. The price of a bus pass will increase as more people buy bus passes because demand shifts out.

    c. The price of a bus pass will decrease as Springfield increases supply

    d. More bus passes will be purchased over time.

12. Cheesy Poofs and Cheetos are substitutes. An increase in the quantity of Cheesy Poofs demanded could mean that:

    a. The price of Cheetos has increased

    b. Quantity demanded of Cheetos has increased

c. Cheetos are a low quality good

d. The cost of producing Cheesy Poofs has decreased.

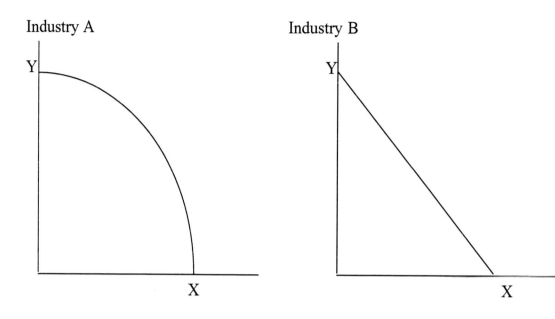

13. Industry A and B both produce goods X and Y. Their respective tradeoffs are described above. Which industry has factors of production that are contrary to the law of increasing costs?

a. Industry A

b. Industry B

c. Both industries

d. Neither industry.

The following relates to the next two questions. *U.S. companies like Nike and Brooks have located factories in Thailand to produce footwear because of lower production costs.*

14. In terms of profits or producer surplus, is Nike better off?

a. Yes, Nike is better off when production was in the US

b. No

c. Producer surplus for Nike is identical regardless of where footware is produced.

d. Yes, Nike is better off when production was in Thailand.

15. The majority of Nike's factories are simultaneously destroyed in a series of freakish asteroid strikes, causing the price of Brooks shoes to go up. Which of the following is **false**?

a. Nike and Brooks shoes are substitutes

b. Higher prices caused Brooks to increase supply

c. The supply of Nike shoes has decreased

d. Demand for Brooks shoes has increased.

16. Consumer surplus may be greater if the footwear is produced in Thailand because:
    a. Profits will be lower if footwear is produced in the US
    b. Profits will be higher if footwear is produced in the US
    c. Prices for footwear will be lower if footwear is produced in the US
    d. Costs of production are lower in Thailand.

A rumor widely circulates that the price of tacos will increase next month due to an expected labor strike. The next two questions are related to this rumor.

17. What happens to the taco market now?
    a. Nothing happens until next month when the price changes
    b. Demand for tacos increases
    c. Taco corporations increase the taco supply
    d. The quantity demanded of tacos increases.

18. A month passes and the supply of Tacos is reduced due to the strike. The government responds by fixing the price of tacos before there was any mention of a strike. What do you predict will happen?
    a. The supply curve will shift outward
    b. An increase in consumer surplus
    c. Non market mechanisms will allocate tacos
    d. The market should remain in equilibrium.

Use the following Supply & Demand curve to answer the next three questions.

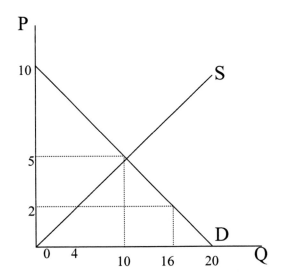

19. Producer surplus is:
    a. 50
    b. equal to consumer surplus
    c. 10
    d. less than consumer surplus.

20. Total revenue is:
    a. 10
    b. less than cost
    c. 50
    d. none of the above.

21. Suppose there is an increase in the cost of production. Which of the following is true?
    a. Total revenue will increase
    b. Gains from trade will decrease
    c. The price of the good will decrease
    d. Quantity sold will increase.

22. If the price of frisbees in the market decreases, then it is likely that:
    a. technology increased and income decreased
    b. the costs of production increased and income increased
    c. the quantity supplied has decreased and demand has increased
    d. demand has decreased and the quantity supplied has increased.

23. In 1973, the price of oil rose dramatically as the OPEC nations reduced the production of oil which caused the supply curve of oil to shift inward. Why did economists predict that the price of oil would eventually decrease?
    a. the quantity demanded for oil should increase
    b. there should be an increase in supply
    c. the demand curve for oil will shift outward
    d. the demand curve for substitutes for oil will shift outward.

24. Given the Second Law of Demand, which of the following is accurate?
    a. after price decreases, quantity demanded decreases over time
    b. given some price change, the demand curve shifts out over time
    c. given an increase in price, quantity demanded increases over time
    d. none of the above.

25. In order to protect local apple juice breweries, the government of Fort Collins has declared that "no 12 oz. bottle of apple juice shall be sold for under $1.25." The market price of a 12 oz. bottle of apple juice is $1.00. The result will likely be:
    a. an excess supply of apple juice on the market, driving the price further up
    b. an excess demand of apple juice on the market, driving the price down
    c. an excess supply of apple juice on the market at the price floor
    d. an increase in the sale of apple juices, driving the price up.

KEY:

1. A	2. B	3. C
4. B	5. B	6. A
7. C	8. B	9. A
10. D	11. D	12. D
13. B	14. D	15. B

16. D   17. B   18. C
19. B   20. C   21. B
22. A   23. D   24. D
25. C

Midterm 2A: Fall 2005

1. Frank expects his income over the next three years from his comeback album to be:
   End of year 1 – $150 mil, End of year 2 – $170 mil and End of year 3 – $40 mil.
   If inflation is 3% and the nominal interest rate is R = 7%, what is the present value of
   Frank's income today?
   a. $346 mil
   b. $320 mil
   c. $342 mil
   d. $336 mil.

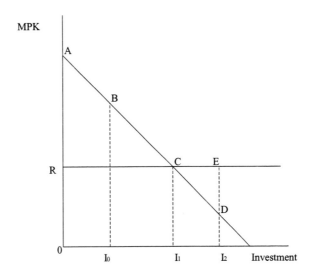

2. Given: a Future Value = 110 (one year from now), Present Value = 100 and Inflation
   = 2%, What is the nominal interest rate?
   a. 14%
   b. 12%
   c. 10%
   d. 8%.
   Use the following graph to answer the next two questions.

3. At point B,
   a. MB = MC and firms should not increase or decrease investment
   b. MB < MC and firms should increase investment
   c. MB > MC and firms should increase investment
   d. MB > MC and firms should reduce investment.

4. Which statement is **false**?

   a. The marginal product of capital is decreasing

   b. At point I_1, the marginal benefit equals the opportunity cost

   c. The marginal benefit of investing in another unit of capital is decreasing

   d. Area CDE represents the amount by which the opportunity cost of the investment is less than the marginal benefit.

Consider the economy of Elbonia which has only two goods:

	Q	P
Mud	5000	$1.00
Frisbees	10000	$2.00

5. There is $12,500 in currency in Elbonia's economy. What is the velocity of money?

   a. 0.5

   b. 1.6

   c. 2.0

   d. 0.6.

6. The head of Elbonia's central bank, which runs exactly the same as the US Federal Reserve, engaged in Open Market Purchases. What happened to Elbonia's economy as a result?

   a. The number of loans decreased

   b. The money supply decreased

   c. Velocity decreased

   d. The money supply increased.

The next three question relate to the table below. Assume that 1996 is the base year.

	Price	Quantity	Total Revenue
1996			
Soda	$1.00/case	100 cases	
Crackers	$3.00/case	200 cases	
1997			
Soda	$2.00/case	150 cases	
Crackers	$5.00/case	300 cases	

7. In 1997 nominal GDP exceeds real GDP in 1997 by:

   a. 0

   b. 550

   c. 350

   d. 750.

8. What is the inflation rate from 1996 to 1997?

   a. 68%

   b. 45%

   c. 35%

   d. 29%.

9. A friend approached you in 1996 to borrow $100, which she will pay back in 1 year. She says that she wants you to make 2% profit on the loan. Now that you have the data from 1996 and 1997 (above) at what interest rate should you have loaned out the $100?

   a. 41%

   b. 70%

   c. 39%

   d. 29%.

10. Suppose political pressure caused the base year to be changed from 1996 to 1997. How will the price level for 1997 be impacted when the base year changes from 1996 to 1997?

    a. the price level for 1997 will decrease

    b. the price level for 1997 will increase

    c. the price level in 1996 increases

    d. it is not possible to answer this question with the information given.

11. Lou turned on the TV and heard a reporter say that from last year to this year inflation went up while production in the US has not changed. What was the reporter describing?

    a. An increase in real GDP

    b. A decrease in real GDP

    c. An increase in nominal GDP

    d. A decrease in nominal GDP.

12. An economy's velocity of money is constant at 3. You know the value of real GDP for that year. What one additional piece of information do you need to know to determine the price level?

    a. The federal funds rate

    b. Money supply

    c. Changes in the discount rate

    d. The required reserve rate.

13. Fred has deposited $50,000 in the bank and the bank has loaned out all of its excess reserves. Fred just bought a used Mercedes for $15,000 and withdrew the money from his account. What will the bank do?

    a. Borrow $15,000 from another depositor

    b. Borrow $15,000 from another commercial bank at the federal funds rate

    c. Borrow $15,000 from the Federal Reserve at the federal funds rate

    d. Borrow $15,000 from the Federal Reserve at the discount rate.

14. A(n) _____ in the discount rate will _____ the money multiplier.

    a. increase; increase

    b. decrease; decrease

    c. increase; decrease

    d. increase; have no effect on.

15. Nominal GDP has been more stable over time than real GDP because:

    a. the continual rise in the price level typically overwhelms changes in real GDP

    b. Velocity is constant GDP

    c. inflation is built into real GDP

    d. none of the above

16. A person whose paycheck increases by 10% annually:

    a. experiences a loss in real income when inflation is 3%

    b. experiences an increase in nominal and real income when inflation is 7%

    c. experiences a decrease in nominal income and an increase in real income when inflation is 12%

    d. experiences a decrease in real and nominal income.

17. If the Fed engages in an Open Market purchase, Federal Funds Rate will:

    a. increase because the money multiplier will be reduced

    b. increase because the supply of excess reserves will be reduced

    c. not change

    d. decrease because the supply of excess reserves will be increased.

18. Robert buys both lobster and caviar, paying $10 per pound for lobster and $10 per pound for caviar. What can we conclude about the value that he places on the two goods if he purchases the same amount of both goods?

    a. He places a higher marginal value on lobster

    b. He places a higher marginal value on caviar

    c. He places an equal marginal value on both

    d. None of the above.

Peanut butter and jelly are complements and the cost of producing peanut butter increases. Answer the following two questions.

19. Which statement is correct?

    a. consumer surplus in the jelly market increases

    b. consumer surplus in the peanut butter market increases

    c. consumer surplus in both markets decrease

    d the change in consumer surplus is indeterminate

20. Which statement is correct concerning the Jelly market?

    a. there is an increase in the quantity supplied

    b. there is a decrease in demand

    c. there is a decrease in the quantity supplied

    d. both (b) and (c).

21. The foundation of the Friedman Rule $(\%)M$ = average $\%(Y)$ is based on the concept that

    a. in the long-run, an increase in the money supply increases the price level

    b. in the long-run, an increase in the money supply increases output

c. in the long-run, an increase in the money supply has no effect on output

d. in the short-run, an increase in the money supply increases output.

Assume for the next two questions that monetary policy follows the Friedman rule based on an average growth rate of real GDP = 5%.

22. Suppose for a given year that the (%)Y is 4%. According to the Friedman rule, the rate of inflation would be

a. 2%

b. 3%

c. 1%

d. –3%.

23. Continuing to implement the Friedman rule, now suppose over a three-year period the economy experienced an average 3% growth rate for real GDP. We should expect

a. higher prices

b. lower prices

c. no change in prices

d. a decrease in interest rates.

Country A is dominated by long-term wage contracts and Country B is dominated by short-term wage contracts. Suppose there is an identical open market purchase of securities by the central bank (Federal Reserve) in both countries. These two countries are identical in all other respects. The next two questions are related to this occurrence.

24. In the short-run

a. real wages should remain unchanged in both countries

b. real wages should increase for both countries

c. real wages should be lower for a shorter period of time for Country B

d. it is not possible to tell what will happen to real wages in the short run.

25. In the long-run:

a. the solution for output will not be influenced by short-run or long-run labor contracts

b. the solution for the price level will not be influenced by short-run or long-run labor contracts

c. real wages will be the same in both countries

d. all of the above.

KEY A:

1. D	2. B	3. C	4. D	5. C
6. D	7. D	8. A	9. B	10. A
11. C	12. B	13. B	14. D	15. A
16. B	17. D	18. C	19. C	20. D
21. C	22. C	23. A	24. C	25. D

Midterm 3A: Fall 2005

The following three questions deal with interest rate targeting by the Federal Reserve in the 1960–75 period.

1. The logic of pursuing a policy of targeting the federal funds rate is best described by which of the following?
   a. Increasing the money supply every time commercial banks need to borrow from other banks will offset economic growth
   b. A fixed inflation rate should make it easier to estimate present value analysis
   c. It should stabilize prices
   d. Controlling interest rates will reduce uncertainty in consumption decisions.

2. In the federal funds market for bank reserves, demand is characterized by:
   a. commercial banks that have unexpected withdrawls by depositors that results in the bank falling below their required reserve amount
   b. large commercial banks that desired to lower the discount rate
   c. commercial banks that want to increase their excess reserves in order to make more loans.
   d. commercial banks that must buy securities(bonds) from the federal reserve.

3. Milton Friedman's criticism of the Fed's interest rate targeting was that:
   a. increases in the money supply would lead to a recession because of lower real wages
   b. increases in the money supply would result in an increase in inflationary expectations, which would result in a reduction in the interest rate target
   c. increases in the money supply would result in an increase in inflationary expectations, which would result in an increase in the interest rate target
   d. increases in the money supply would make workers better off in the long-run.

4. If the required reserve ratio is 20 percent and the Federal Reserve buy $2,000,000 worth of bonds then money supply has:
   a. decreased by $10 million
   b. increased by $10 million
   c. remained unchanged
   d. decreased by $2 million.

5. An open market sale of bonds/securities by the Federal Reserve would:
   a. increase the federal funds rate
   b. shift the demand curve for reserves inward
   c. shift the supply curve for reserves outward
   d. increase the equilibrium quantity of reserves.

6. Suppose a number of commercial banks have excess reserves and decrease their borrowing in the federal funds market. If the Federal Reserve wants to keep the federal funds rate constant, it will
   a. engage in an open market purchase of securities (bonds) which should decrease excess reserves

b. engage in an open market sale of securities (bonds) which should increase excess reserves

c. engage in an open market sale of securities (bonds) which should put upward pressure on the federal funds rate

d. increase the money supply.

7. The Fed conducts open market sales. What happens in the labor market in the short run?

a. Nominal wages rise

b. Real wages rise

c. Real wages fall

d. Real wages remain the same.

8. Congress passes the Frisbee worker solidarity bill of 2005 requiring Frisbee manufacturers to increase the wages of all Frisbee workers above the equilibrium wage. This will cause:

a. A decrease in the nominal wage

b. An increase in labor demand

c. A shift outward in labor supply

d. A decrease in labor hired.

As a result of the Frisbee bill, Frisbees, Inc. is considering moving Frisbee production offshore. A U.S. Frisbee worker makes $20 an hour and has a MP_L of 4 and a foreign Frisbee worker makes $8 an hour and a MP_L = 2. Using this information, answer the following 2 questions:

9. Which country pays a higher nominal wage to Frisbee workers?

a. U.S.

b. The foreign country

c. Both countries pay the same

d. Not enough information to answer this question.

10. Which of the following is correct regarding the relative position of supply curves for Frisbees in the U.S. and the foreign country?

a. The supply curve in the U.S. should be further inward

b. The supply curve in the U.S. should be flatter

c. The supply curve in the foreign country should be further inward

d. The supply curve in the foreign country should be steeper.

11. Why did the level of employment decrease during the 1981–82 recession?

a. Compensation for positive cyclical changes in labor hired

b. The price level decreased

c. The Fed made open market purchases to reduce the money supply

d. Real wages decreased so not as many people were willing to work.

12. An increase in technology will

a. shift the labor supply curve inward

b. shift the labor supply curve outward

c. increase the nominal wage

d. increase the price level.

13. When population increases:
    a. wages and prices will change proportionately in the long-run
    b. the MP_L will decrease
    c. wages will increase slowly in the short-run
    d. the price level will rise.

14. Suppose the US, Canada, and Mexico decide to open their borders to unlimited immigration between the three countries. As a result, Tuktoyaktuk, Canada, expects to its population to triple. What do you expect will happen to the economy of Tuktoyaktuk?
    a. There will be a temporary increase in output, but eventually prices will increase and output will return to its previous level
    b. There will be a temporary decrease in output, but eventually prices will decrease and output will return to its previous level
    c. Output will increase permanently because Tuktoyaktuk's productive capacity has increased
    d. Output will increase permanently because Tuktoyaktuk's new workers are willing to accept a higher nominal wage.

The next three questions relate to the 1973–75 recession.

15. In this recession real the natural level of output fell because
    a. The increase in oil prices acted like a negative technology shock
    b. nominal wages decreased
    c. LRAS shifted outward
    d. all of the above.

16. Which statement is true?
    a. In 1973, workers marginal productivity increased
    b. The oil supply shock acted like a technology increase
    c. The price of oil decreased
    d. The price level in the economy increased.

17. In response to this recession, the Fed
    a. increased the money supply to slow down the output growth
    b. decreased the money supply
    c. increased the money supply to offset the impact of rising oil prices
    d. did nothing.

The next two questions relate to the 1979 recession.

18. After OPEC decreased the supply of oil in 1979
    a. The reduction in the quantity demanded for oil was less than the reduction in the quantity demanded for oil in 1973
    b. The impact of the second law of demand during the 1970s reduced the impact of the 1979 oil price shock
    c. The two shocks had the same effect in the economy
    d. The price level fell in 1979.

19. The supply shock of 1979 was not permanent because:

    a. Technology did not change

    b. The Federal Reserve followed the Friedman rule after their experience in the 1973 recession

    c. Output returned to its previous long-run trend

    d. The Fed was able to eliminate the recession by increasing the money supply.

20. Jimmy Carter's "Misery Index" was a combination of inflation and the unemployment rate

    a. the index increased in 1974 because oil prices increased

    b. The index increased in 1979 because of a shift inward in the SRAS

    c. The index increased in 1974 because the LRAS shifted inward

    d. All of the above.

The next three questions relate to the 1981–82 recession.

21. Regarding this recession, the Fed

    a. is often cited as creating the recession

    b. temporarily decreased employment

    c. was attempting to reduce inflation

    d. all of the above.

22. Observed output

    a. decreased as a result of the Fed selling bonds

    b. decreased as a result of a negative oil supply shock

    c. decreased as a result of the Fed increasing the money supply

    d. Stayed the same because there were no changes to population or technology.

23. This recession was

    a. temporary because output never returned to its natural level

    b. permanent because output never returned to its natural level

    c. in response to the events of the 1970's

    d. all of the above.

24. If peanut butter and jelly are complements, which of the following would cause a decrease in the demand for jelly?

    a. An increase in the demand for peanut butter

    b. A decrease in the costs of producing peanut butter

    c. A decrease in the price of jelly

    d. An increase in the costs of producing peanut butter.

KEY:

1. D	2. A	3. C	4. B	5. A
6. C	7. B	8. D	9. A	10. A
11. B	12. C	13. A	14. C	15. A
16. D	17. C	18. B	19. C	20. D
21. D	22. A	23. C	24. D	

Final Exam A: Fall 2005

1. Given: a Future Value = 1050 (one year from now), Present Value = 1000 and Inflation = 2%, What is the nominal interest rate?
   a. 7%
   b. 6%
   c. 5%
   d. 4%.

2. Given the following graph, which statement is *true*?

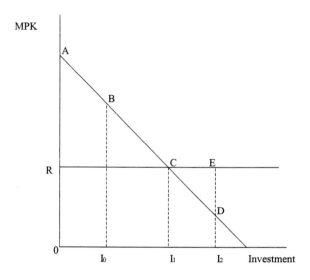

   a. The marginal product of capital is constant
   b. Area CDE represents the amount by which the opportunity cost of investment is greater than the marginal benefit
   c. The optimal level of investment is where the marginal product of capital is greatest
   d. At point B, the marginal benefit is less than the marginal cost of investment.

The next two questions relate to the table below. Assume that 1996 is the base year.

	Price	Quantity	Total Revenue
1996			
Soda	$2.00/case	300 cases	
Crackers	$3.00/case	100 cases	
1997			
Soda	$7.00/case	200 cases	
Crackers	$3.00/case	400 cases	

3. In 1997 nominal GDP exceeds real GDP in 1997 by:

    a. 0

    b. 700

    ⓒ 1000

    d. 1700.

4. What is the inflation rate from 1996 to 1997?

    a. 189%

    ⓑ 143%

    ⓧ 121%

    d. 0%.

5. A(n) _____ in the required reserve ratio will _____ the money multiplier.

    a. increase; will have no effect on

    b. increase; increase

    c. decrease; decrease

    ⓓ decrease; increase.

6. A person whose paycheck increases by 8% annually:

    a. experiences a loss in real income when inflation is 4%

    b. experiences a decrease in nominal income and an increase in real income when inflation is 10%

    c. experiences a decrease in nominal and real income

    ⓓ experiences an increase in nominal income and real income when inflation is anything under 8%.

7. The foundation of the Friedman Rule is based on the concept that:

    a. in the long-run, and increase in the money supply increases output

    ⓑ in the long-run, an increase in the money supply has no effect on output

    c. in long-run, an increase in the money supply increases the price level

    d. in the short-run, an increase in the money supply increases output.

8. We have assumed in class that the percentage change in velocity is zero. Which of the following supports this assumption?

    a. The money supply will increase due to an open market purchase of securities.

    ⓑ Consumption is viewed as a function of expected income and therefore the behavior of consumption is relatively stable

    c. Spending patterns in the economy are relatively volatile

    d. The percentage change in output over time is about 3.

9. Assume monetary policy follows the Friedman Rule. If the average growth rate of real GDP=6%, inflation will be:

    a. 1% if this years output growth is 4%

    b. 1% if this years output growth is 1%

    ⓒ 2% if this years output growth is 4%

    d. 2% if this years output growth is 1%.

10. Country A is dominated by short-term wage contracts and Country B is dominated by long-term wage contracts. Suppose there is an identical open market purchase of securities by the central bank (Federal Reserve) in both countries. These two countries are identical in all other respects. In the short-run

    a. real wages should remain unchanged in both countries

    b. real wages should increase for both countries

    c. real wages should be lower for a shorter period of time for Country A

    d. it is not possible to tell what will happen to real wages in the short run.

11. An open market purchase of bonds/securities by the Federal Reserve would:

    a. increase the federal funds rate

    b. increase the supply of excess reserves of banks

    c. increase the demand for reserves

    d. decrease the equilibrium quantity of reserves.

12. The 1981–1982 recession was

    a. caused by the Fed increasing the money supply in response to the oil price shocks of the 1970s

    b. temporary because output never returned to its natural level

    c. permanent because output never returned to its natural level

    d. temporary because the money supply decreased to counter the high inflation of the 1970s.

13. The 1979 recession was different from the 1973–75 recession because

    a. the price level fell in 1979

    b. the 1979 recession was permanent

    c. the impact of the second law of demand resulting from the 1973–75 recession caused the 1979 recession to be less severe

    d. the 1979 recession was caused by an inward shift of the aggregate demand curve.

14. The federal funds rate is different from the discount rate in that:

    a. the federal funds rate is the rate of interest charged by the Fed to loan money to banks

    b. the federal funds rate is the rate of interest charged by banks to lend money to other banks

    c. the discount rate is always equal to the market rate of interest

    d. the federal funds rate is for short-term loans to individuals.

15. If the required reserve ratio is 20% and the Federal Reserve sells $2 million worth of bonds, then the money supply has:

    a. decreased by $10 million

    b. increased by $2 million

    c. decreased by $2 million

    d. remained unchanged.

16. Peanut butter and jelly are complements. There is an increase in the quantity of peanut butter demanded, so we can infer:

    a. The price of jelly has increased

    b. Quantity demanded of jelly has increased

c. Jelly is a low quality good

b. The cost of producing peanut butter has increased.

17. Fort Collins city counsel just passed legislation instituting a price floor in the market for apple juice, effective in one month. This will most likely immediately cause:

a. An increase in quantity demanded

b. Excess demand

c. Excess supply

d. An increase in consumer surplus.

Use the following supply and demand diagram of the taco market to answer the next two questions:

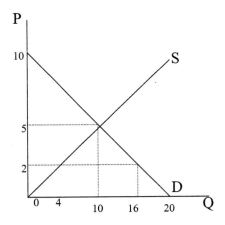

18. What is the costs of producing the 10 tacos?

a. 2

b. 13

c. 25

d. 50.

19. If the government set the price of tacos to be $2, how much does producer surplus change by?

a. 0

b. 2

c. 21

d. 25.

Use the production table below to answer the next three questions

| Dulac | | Detroit | |
Gingerbread	Muffins	Gingerbread	Muffins
20	10	700	60
40	9	775	45
60	8	850	30
80	7	925	15

20. What is an acceptable price for both parties to trade at?
    a. 1 muffin for 4 gingerbread
    b. 1 muffin for 10 gingerbread
    c. 1 muffin for 25 gingerbread
    d. 1 muffin for 50 gingerbread.

21. What will Detroit want to do?
    a. Trade gingerbread for muffins
    b. Trade muffins for gingerbread
    c. Produce 925 Gingerbread and 15 Muffins
    d. (a) and (c).

22. If Dulac produces 55 gingerbread and 8 muffins, then for maximum efficiency it should
    a. Increase production of gingerbread
    b. Increase production of muffins
    c. Trade gingerbread for muffins
    d. (a) and/or (b).

23. If the price of gravy increases, then it is probable that
    a. Technology increased and incomes increased
    b. Technology decreased and incomes increased
    c. Costs of production decreased and the cost of producing biscuits (the goods are complements) increased
    d. Costs of production increased and the cost of producing biscuits increased.

24. The price of a donut at Stan Mikita's was 25 cents, and they sold 200 a day. They ran a sale for a month selling donuts for 5 cents. Given the second law of demand, when Stan Mikita's raised the donut price back to 25 cents, how many donuts per day would they sell?
    a. fewer than 200
    b. 200
    c. more than 200
    d. Not enough information.

25. The first week of the sale mentioned above, Stan Mikita's sold 250 donuts. How many would you expect to be sold the second week of the sale, according to the second law of demand?
    a. fewer than 250, and the market would be in equilibrium
    b. 250, and the market would be in equilibrium
    c. more than 250, and the market would be in equilibrium
    d. 250, and there would be excess demand.

26. If the natural level of employment increases and the nominal wage increases, then
    a. Technology has increased
    b. The Fed has increased the money supply
    c. Population has increased
    d. All of the above.

27. If the natural level of <u>output</u> increases then
    a. Technology has increased
    b. Population has increased
    c. Cyclical component of output increased
    d. (a) and (b).

28. Which of the following will cause the real wage rate to increase in the long run?
    a. Technology has improved
    b. Aggregate demand has remained constant
    c. LRAS has shifted inward
    d. Aggregate demand has shifted to the right.

29. If aggregate demand has increased due to an increase in the money supply, in the short-run the cyclical component of output is
    a. unchanged
    b. zero because LRAS has shifted inward
    c. positive
    b. negative.

30. If the cyclical component of the employment level is positive,
    a. wages are rising faster than prices
    b. prices are rising faster than wages
    c. AD shifted inward
    d. It will cause SRAS to shift right.

The Bush Administration decreased both the personal income tax rate as well as business taxes. The next three questions relate to this policy.

31. Which of the following will definitely be a result of such a policy?
    a. the deficit will decline
    b. the deficit will rise
    c. the price level will increase
    d. output will increase.

32. It is difficult to predict the impact on the deficit/surplus because
    a. a fall in tax rates will cause tax revenue to rise and the impact on output will cause tax revenue to fall
    b. a fall in tax rates will cause tax revenue to fall and the impact on output will cause tax revenue to fall
    c. a fall in tax rates will cause tax revenue to rise and the impact on output will cause tax revenue to rise
    d. a fall in tax rates will cause tax revenue to fall and the impact on output will cause tax revenue to rise.

33. Suppose the deficit rises as result of this policy. The reason why this deficit may be a larger problem than the deficit during the 1969–00 period is that
    a. the number of people employed in the future will be a greater percentage of the total population

b. The government will always borrow enough money to finance the deficit

c. The number of retired people in the future will be a smaller percentage of the total population

(d) The number of retired people in the future will be a greater percentage of the total population.

Alan Greenspan, the Chairman of the Federal Reserve, has pursued a policy of predicting the position of the aggregate supply and demand demand curves and then using monetary policy to insure that the aggregate demand is at a place such that the inflation rate should be equal to zero. This relates to the following two questions.

34. Suppose that Greenspan predicts that the future aggregate demand curve will cause prices to rise more than is desired. This suggests that

   a. Greenspan should do nothing today

   b. Greenspan should increase the money supply today

   c. Greenspan should lower the federal funds rate today

   (d) Greenspan should engage in an open market sale of bonds today.

35. Suppose that Greenspan predicts that the future aggregate demand curve will result in the cyclical component of output to be zero. Greenspan should

   a. lower the federal funds rate today

   b. engage in an open market purchase of bonds

   c. engage in an open market sale of bonds

   (d) maintain the current status of monetary policy.

36. When the federal government is running a surplus, an increase in government expenditures will cause the aggregate demand curve to shift outward because

   a. the government has to borrow to finance this expenditure

   b. the government is injecting additional resources into the economy even though they have to borrow to do so

   c. Interest rates are rising

   (d) additional resources are injected in the economy.

37. An increase in business taxes should have which of the following impacts

   (a) shift the LRAS curve inward and cause prices to rise

   b. shift the SRAS curve outward and cause prices to fall

   c. shift the AD curve inward

   d. it should not have an effect on output.

38. A decrease in the personal income tax rate should

   a. cause the aggregate demand curve to shift inward

   b. cause the price level to decrease

   c. cause tax revenue to increase

   (d) cause the cyclical component of output to increase.

39. An increase in government expenditures that is financed by borrowing from the public will

   a. cause the aggregate demand curve to shift outward

   b. cause the aggregate demand curve to shift inward

c. cause the aggregate demand curve to remain unchanged

d. result in an unpredictable change in aggregate demand.

40. Cheesy Poofs and Cheetos are substitutes. An increase in the quantity of Cheesy Poofs demanded could mean that:

a. The price of Cheetos has increased

b. Quantity demanded of Cheetos has increased

c. Cheetos are a low quality good

d. The cost of producing Cheesy Poofs has decreased.

Final Exam A Key

1. A	2. B	3. C	4. B
5. D	6. D	7. B	8. B
9. C	10. C	11. B	12. D
13. C	14. B	15. A	16. A
17. D	18. C	19. C	20. B
21. B	22. D	23. B	24. B
25. C	26. A	27. D	28. A
29. C	30. B	31. D	32. D
33. D	34. D	35. D	36. D
37. A	38. D	39. D	40. D

Index